# DAVID & WINSTON

# DAVID & WINSTON

How the Friendship Between Churchill and
Lloyd George Changed the Course of History

## ROBERT LLOYD GEORGE

THE OVERLOOK PRESS
Woodstock & New York

This edition first published in the United States in 2008 by
The Overlook Press, Peter Mayer Publishers, Inc.
Woodstock & New York

WOODSTOCK:
One Overlook Drive
Woodstock, NY 12498
www.overlookpress.com
[for individual orders, bulk and special sales, contact our Woodstock office]

NEW YORK:
141 Wooster Street
New York, NY 10012

Cataloging-in-Publication Data is available from the Library of Congress

Manufactured in the United States of America
ISBN-13 978-1-58567-930-0
2 4 6 8 10 9 7 5 3 1

For my Father

# Contents

# Illustrations

1. David Lloyd George aged 16, 1879
2. Highgate: David Lloyd George's childhood home
3. Winston Churchill in the uniform of an officer of the 4th Hussars, 1895
4. Blenheim Palace, Churchill's birthplace
5. The backbencher, David Lloyd George, 1903
6. Parliamentary candidate Winston Churchill, 1900
7. Meeting of Colonial Prime Ministers, 1907
8. David Lloyd George and Winston Churchill at an air show, 1911
9. Lloyd George and Churchill at the Royal National Eisteddfod in Llangollen, 1908
10. Winston Churchill and Clementine Hozier on their engagement, 1908
11. Churchill's first day at the Admiralty, 1911
12. Budget Day, 1910
13. Lord Randolph Churchill, 1880
14. Herbert Henry Asquith as Chancellor of the Exchequer, 1905
15. First Sea Lord, Admiral John Fisher, 1905
16. Max Aitken, Lord Beaverbrook, 1930
17. The Lloyd Georges and the Churchills in Criccieth, 1910
18. Churchill, Lloyd George, the Asquiths and Sir Edward Grey in Scotland, 1913
19. Lloyd George and his brother William on Criccieth golf course, 1910

Picture credits: 1, 3, 4, 5, 6, 7, 10, 12, 13, 14, 15, 19, 20 and 28, Hulton Archive/Getty Images; 2, Gwynedd Archives; 9, The National Library of Wales; 11, 17, 18, 26, 27 and 30, Lloyd George Family Album; 16 and 25, National Portrait Gallery, London; 21, 22 and 31, House of Lords Record Office; 23 and 24, National Library of Wales; 29, Science and Society Picture Library; 32, Imperial War Museum; 33, Empics.

# Cartoons

*Preface and Acknowledgements*

THE LEGEND OF Winston Churchill is such a powerful one, and he has been so comprehensively written about, that it is very difficult to find a new angle on the great man's life. However, his friendship with David Lloyd George has never been fully covered in a single work and the argument of this book is that it constituted a vitally important influence on the young Churchill; and, indeed, he looked up to Lloyd George as a mentor throughout his life. Their friendship was unbroken for forty-four years, from the time of their first meeting in the House of Commons in February 1901 until Lloyd George's death in March 1945. They had many quarrels and disagreements, but their affection for each other never wavered.

In this book I have tried to relate the personal as well as the political aspects of this fascinating story. In addition to exploring their relationship with each other, and with their families and friends, I have included meetings and conversations which took place away from the political world of Westminster to suggest how the close friendship between the two men may have influenced events of great historic importance for Britain and for the wider world: the People's Budget of 1909; the declaration of war in August 1914; the 1921 treaty giving independence to Ireland; the Balfour Declaration of 1917, pledging Britain's support for a Jewish homeland in Palestine; the 'Norway' debate in the House of Commons in May 1940, in which Lloyd George decisively intervened to bring down Neville Chamberlain and elevate

Winston Churchill to the post of Prime Minister, at the moment of Britain's greatest peril. In relating these historical events in detail, it is hoped that a new light may be cast on Churchill and the influence that Lloyd George had on his life.

I am indebted to my father, Owen, 3rd Earl Lloyd George of Dwyfor, for his advice and encouragement during the writing of this book and for the use of many family letters and photographs. My cousin William George, who is Lloyd George's nephew, has taken many hours to correct, and comment on, my draft chapters and has given me valuable insight into his uncle from his own memory and experience. His daughter Anita gave helpful advice on quotations in Welsh. My cousin William, 3rd Viscount Tenby, was very helpful in researching the visitors' book at the Lloyd George family home at Churt in Surrey. Sadly, I did not have the opportunity to talk to the late John Grigg about his brilliant biography of my great-grandfather, to which I also owe so much.

Among others, I would like to thank the National Library of Wales and in particular John Graham Jones, head of archives; the House of Lords Record Office where the other Lloyd George papers are deposited, and especially Miss Katherine Bligh; and Churchill College, Cambridge. Thanks are also due to Mary, Lady Soames, with whom I had a most illuminating conversation about her father, Winston Churchill, and her memories of Lloyd George. The staff at Chartwell, Churchill's country house in Kent, have been helpful and supportive in enabling me to study the Chartwell visitors' book, and I have also drawn valuable material from the National Archives of Scotland, Edinburgh (Lothian Papers), the Imperial War Museum archives (Sir Henry Wilson's diaries) and the British Library. My cousin, Robin Carey-Evans, who lives in Sydney, Australia, also gave me a lot of support and encouragement. Some early archival research was done by Catherine Field and the picture research by Rebecca Snow.

My cousin Dr Margaret Macmillan, author of *Peacemakers* (2002), has read some of the chapters and made useful comments, as has Professor Avi Shlaim of St Anthony's College, Oxford. My oldest friend, Philip Snow, has helped greatly with his advice and suggestions about the shape of the book. I have also consulted the Lloyd George family genealogist, Harry Harrison. Jennifer Longford and her daughter Ruth Longford were very helpful and provided me with some letters and photographs of Lloyd George. James Arbuthnot MP kindly introduced me to the House of Commons and elucidated the meaning of the 'Bar'.

With thanks also to Hugo de Klee, Gillon Aitken, Roland Philipps, Kenneth Rose, Sir Martin Gilbert and Michael Meredith. I would especially like to thank my secretary, Kim Waterfield, who valiantly typed and retyped the many drafts of *David & Winston*. Finally, I would like to thank my beloved wife Donna and my children Ricky, Alice, Julia, Alexander, Nicholas, Robert, David, Sophia and Elizabeth, without whom I might have been able to finish the book a lot earlier, but whose love, support and encouragement has helped me to complete it.

# I

# 1863–1904: An Unlikely Friendship

'This book does not seek to rival the works of professional historians. It aims rather to present a personal view.'

Churchill's Preface to *A History of the English Speaking Peoples* (1956–8)

O N THE EVENING of 18 February 1901, the chamber of the House of Commons was crowded and the atmosphere expectant. The debate was to be on the South African war, in which Britain had been struggling to exert her authority over the Boers since 1899. Among the speakers whom the House eagerly awaited were the Liberal MP for Caernarvon Boroughs, David Lloyd George, and the newly elected Conservative Member for Oldham, Winston Churchill.

By then the thirty-eight-year-old David Lloyd George had been in Parliament for ten years and was already sufficiently well known, both nationally and at Westminster, to guarantee that the chamber would fill up quickly, once it was known that he would be speaking. He was feared and respected on both sides of the Commons as the voice and conscience of Welsh radicalism. But he had not generally spoken on issues other than those which directly concerned Wales and his constituents in Caernarvonshire. All this, however, had changed with the Boer War: the Liberal Party had become divided between those such as Rosebery, Asquith, Grey and Haldane, who supported the conflict, and John

Morley (Gladstone's disciple and biographer) and Lloyd George, who bitterly opposed it on the grounds that it was an unnecessary, expensive, imperialist campaign against a small nation. (Lloyd George made much of the fact that the total Boer population was less than that of Carmarthenshire.)

Lloyd George was risking his marginal seat in Parliament by his outspoken opposition to the Boer War. In 1900 he had very nearly not been reselected as the Liberal candidate for Caernarvon Boroughs because of his unpopular stand against it. Before the so-called 'Khaki Election' in October of that year, he had told his constituents: 'Five years ago the electors of the Caernarvon Boroughs handed me a strip of blue paper, the certificate of my election, to hand to the Speaker as their accredited representative. If I never again represent the Caernarvon Boroughs in the House of Commons, I shall at least have the satisfaction of handing them back that piece of blue paper with no stain of human blood upon it.' He was castigated nationally as 'pro-Boer' and his elder son Richard had to be taken out of school in London because he was unmercifully bullied for his father's political opinions. But in the longer term Lloyd George's stand on principle won him much respect, and support from nonconformists (a significant constituency), especially as the war wound down to its grim conclusion of burning Boer farms and herding the Dutch women and children into concentration camps.

Winston Churchill, by contrast, was almost twelve years younger than Lloyd George but had already come to national prominence: he had returned to England from South Africa six months earlier, after a triumphant escape as a prisoner of war in Pretoria, whereupon he was elected to Parliament as part of a Conservative landslide in the general election of October 1900. But he too had problems of political allegiance. Although he had fought and won the parliamentary seat of Oldham under the banner of the Conservative Party, Winston did not share the feudal creed of its leaders, Lord Salisbury and A. J. Balfour. Filial piety and a paternal concern for the working man led him instead to embrace the radical conservatism, or 'Tory Democracy', of his father, Lord Randolph Churchill.

Churchill had spent the next two months on a lecture tour, first in England and then in the United States and Canada, promoting his newly published book *London to Ladysmith via Pretoria* (1900) and earning himself the handsome sum of £10,000 (equivalent to almost £1 million today) to support his political career (MPs did not receive a salary until 1911). He therefore missed the State Opening of Parliament but was determined to make his maiden speech as soon as possible after his return.

Churchill's name appeared on the parliamentary list after that of Lloyd George on 18 February 1901. As the *Daily News* put it, the Commons keenly anticipated 'a duel between two young members in whom the House takes an interest'. Gladstone's former political deputy, Sir William Harcourt, told Lloyd George: 'I am going to stay in the House to enjoy the cockfight between you and young Churchill.' Lloyd George had written to his brother, William: 'I shall be speaking in the South African War debate before Winston Churchill. He is the new Tory bully. *Bydded* [So be it]. Quite prepared.'

Lloyd George had set down an amendment to criticise the King's Speech at the opening of Parliament, but announced on rising that he would not move his amendment after all. (He had probably been pressured by the Liberal leadership because they were generally supportive of the Government's policy on the war, and the Liberal imperialists considered his position unpatriotic.)

Lloyd George looked and sounded impressive. Always immaculately dressed, he looked much younger than his years. Though only five foot six-and-a-half inches tall, he had a powerful frame and a deep chest. He wore a magnificent moustache and his carefully tended wavy dark hair was rather longer than was the custom of the time. He had a large and distinctive head, a broad forehead and striking greyish-blue eyes which sparkled with humour one moment and flashed with anger the next. He had a commanding presence but the true magnetism of his personality only became apparent when he began to speak. His voice was, if anything, even more hypnotic than his piercing eyes: a pleasant light tenor with a musical cadence and a wide range of expressions accentuated by dramatic pauses learned in his youth when preaching in Welsh Baptist chapels, which enabled him to hold an audience in the palm of his hand. Because of this early experience of public speaking he was able to project his voice effectively to a large audience, and in the small chamber of the House of Commons he was easily heard before the age of the microphone (he never really became used to speaking on the radio).

In opening his broadside attack, the Member for Caernarvon Boroughs said that 'the Government have made every possible blunder they could make from any and every point of view' and that the British Army was being neglected and half starved. In response to the accusation that he was 'pro-Boer' he said that the Prime Minister, Lord Salisbury, had commented that whereas the Confederates in the American Civil War had held out for four years, the British had only been trying to subdue the Boers for sixteen months. And 30,000 Cuban guerillas had recently held out against 250,000 Spanish troops for ten years. In other words, a guerilla war could continue for a very long time. A solution lay in what Britain was prepared to offer as a fair and generous set-tlement to the Boers. '. . . whatever the blunder of going to war was, the still greater blunder was not to have offered terms when we captured Pretoria [in 1900].'

Lloyd George then turned to the conduct of the war and the policy pursued by Lord Roberts and his troops of burning farms and turning women and children loose in the wilderness. He quoted several Tory MPs who shared his view and spoke of an old Boer who had taken down the portrait of Queen Victoria from the wall of partially burned house and trampled on it, saying: 'I thought she was a good woman. If these are the things that are done in her name, she is not.' It was a simple, popular anecdote, typical of Lloyd George's speeches, which vividly brought home the point of his oratory.

He went on to quote a Reuters telegram from Pretoria, dated 15 January 1900, which contained the Army's threat that, unless the Boer commandos surrendered, their women and children would not be given full rations. At this telling point the Colonial Secretary, Joseph Chamberlain, walked out of the House (to Irish Members' cries of 'He flies the white flag'). Lloyd George redoubled his attack: 'It is difficult within the bounds of Parliamentary propriety to describe what one thinks about all this infamy which is perpetrated in the name of Great Britain in Africa.' The Army itself was in a terrible condition – '55,000 casualties, 30,000 men in hospitals' – and the remaining troops were described, even by Tory newspaper correspondents, as 'jaded, worn, broken'. Lloyd George had spoken rapidly; he suddenly announced that he would curtail his remarks so that a new Member of the House could be heard, and sat down.

Lloyd George was probably genuinely eager to hear the young Winston Churchill. He well remembered when he himself was twenty-one, in 1884, hearing Lord Randolph Churchill cheekily attacking the 'grand old man', William Gladstone, in a manner similar to the way in which he himself was now attacking the Tory leaders Salisbury and Balfour over the Boer War. It was possibly the only occasion on which Lloyd George saw Winston's father in action, or at least on his best form, but he undoubtedly related it to the young Churchill who, with eager and filial devotion, would write his father's biography in 1902–5. (Winston never tired of hearing Lloyd George and other, older, Westminster colleagues talk about his father, whom he revered.)

Young Winston, on the opposite bench, had been nervously following the twists and turns of his opponent's argument to find a way to 'hook on' his own carefully prepared speech. His friendly neighbour Thomas Gibson Bowles whispered a solution: 'You might say "instead of making his violent speech without moving his moderate amendment, he had better have moved his moderate amendment without making his violent speech".'

Like his Liberal opponent, Churchill was unexpectedly short in stature. About five foot six inches tall, he had a pugnacious expression, pale blue eyes and, as a young man, red hair. His head jutted forward in eagerness to enter into debate or battle. His oratory was of a completely different kind to that of Lloyd George; it consisted of sonorous, rhetorical, rolling orotund phrases, learned from his reading of Macaulay and Gibbon and painstakingly prepared and rehearsed until he knew his speeches by heart. He had trouble pronouncing the letter 's' and used to practise on the phrase 'The Spanish ships I cannot see, for they are not in sight'.

Churchill opened by defending Lloyd George's right to free speech and said that no national emergency short of the actual invasion of this country (remarkably prophetic of 1940) ought in any way to restrict the freedom of parliamentary discussion.

> I do not believe that the Boers would attach particular importance to the utterances of the hon. Member. No people in the world received so much verbal sympathy and so little practical support as the Boers. If I were a Boer fighting in the field – and if I were a Boer I hope I should be fighting in the field [at this point there was muttering on the Tory front bench; Chamberlain (back in the House now) said, 'That's the way to throw away good seats!'] – I would not allow myself to be taken in by any message of sympathy.

Churchill went on to defend the farm-burning by a rather tenuous argument: that the precedents set by the Germans during the Franco-Prussian War of 1870, and the Union generals in the American Civil War, justified the barbaric methods used in South Africa. Moving on to firmer ground, he remarked that he had travelled round much of South Africa during the previous ten months, so underlining the authority with which he spoke, even though it was his maiden speech. He returned to the original cause of the war: the extension of the franchise in giving the vote, and thus fair treatment, to the *Uitlanders* in considering what form of government would be most likely to restore the prosperity of the Transvaal. (The *Uitlanders*, 'foreigners' in Afrikaans, were mostly British businessmen, and included Cecil Rhodes, Barney Barnato and other mining magnates who had moved into the Transvaal since the discovery of gold and diamonds there in the 1880s.)

Churchill was against the idea of military rule since British officers were not equipped to impose it. 'I have often myself been very much ashamed to see respectable old Boer farmers – the Boer is a curious combination of the squire and the peasant . . . ordered about peremptorily by young subaltern officers.' He proposed a civil government under an administrator such as the High Commissioner, Sir Alfred Milner, which would bring back the British population and investment to the Transvaal. Churchill was in favour of a generous and magnanimous settlement to a brave and enduring foe. (Like Lloyd George, he was of the opinion that Britain should offer the fullest measure of autonomy to the Boers in order to encourage them to lay down their arms. And indeed a magnanimous settlement was what the two of them would later help achieve with the Transvaal constitution of 1910.)

In response to the criticism that the Boer War was a war of greed, Churchill said:

> If . . . certain capitalists spent money in bringing on this war in the hope that it would increase the value of their mining properties they now know that they made an uncommonly bad bargain . . . this war from beginning to end has only been a war of duty . . . actuated by . . . high and patriotic motives. . . . we have no cause to be ashamed of anything that has passed during the war.

He also referred to the participation of the Canadians and Australians in the war as strengthening the British Empire and concluded:

I cannot sit down without saying how very grateful I am for the kindness and patience with which the House has heard me, and which have been extended to me, I well know, not on my own account, but because of a certain splendid memory which many hon. Members still preserve [that of his father, Lord Randolph Churchill].

He was warmly congratulated on his maiden speech and, on leaving the House, was introduced to his opponent in 'the duel', David Lloyd George, at the Bar★ of the chamber. 'After compliments, he said "Judging from your sentiments, you are standing against the Light." I replied "You take a singularly detached view of the British Empire."' This perceptive comment anticipated Churchill's gradual shift towards a more progressive, reforming view of the world than his early military adventures had developed in him: the germ of Liberalism was already present, but it took his intense friendship with Lloyd George over the next few years to bring it to life – or to 'the Light'. 'Thus began', as Churchill was to remember in *My Early Life*, written in 1930, 'an association which has persisted through many vicissitudes.'

It is a strange historical paradox that one of these two MPs was forging a reputation by vociferously opposing the Boer War, while the other had become a household name due to his courageous actions in South Africa and subsequent escape from a Boer prison in Pretoria.

Both men had entered Parliament at about the same age, each with the same conviction of his own fitness to rule, but who would have predicted such a close friendship between two men from such diverse backgrounds?

David Lloyd George's father, William George, had been born

★ A white line drawn on the floor, at which MPs stand and bow to the Speaker or watch the debate.

in 1820 on a small farm in Pembrokeshire in south-west Wales. He was an imaginative and ambitious man, who longed to escape from what he saw as the tedium of country life and achieve a higher education. He became successively a pharmacist, a grammar-school teacher and a Unitarian preacher. He married twice in his twenties but both his wives died childless. Then, in 1859, he met and married Elizabeth ('Betsy') Lloyd, who was teaching in Pwllheli in north-west Wales. They lived for a time at nearby Llanystumdwy with Betsy's brother Richard, who was the village cobbler and employed two or three hands, but in 1861 William became restless and moved to Manchester to take a teaching job. Their first daughter, Mary, was born there in 1861; and in 1863, their first son – David Lloyd. Before the boy was one year old they returned to William George's native Pembrokeshire and there, in 1864, his father died suddenly, aged only forty-four (curiously enough, at the same age – within a year or two – as Winston Churchill's father, Lord Randolph).

David was only eighteen months old at the time of his father's death and his mother Betsy was expecting another baby (William). Afraid and alone, she sent a telegram to her brother, saying simply 'Come Richard', but it took two and a half days for him to reach them from North Wales. Richard Lloyd then took the children into his home and brought them up as his own.

William George had been a great reader and had yearned to be a writer and preacher of 'thoughts that breathe and words that burn'. His was a broad intellectual inheritance from which his son David benefited. As well as leaving £700 (perhaps £70,000 today) and a collection of books, he bequeathed to both his boys a burning ambition to be educated and to succeed.

It is important to the story of Lloyd George and the formation of his Liberal ideals to touch on the nonconformist element of his background. Nonconformists are Protestants who worship outside the 'conforming' Church of England and include Baptists, Methodists and Quakers. In the 1860s and 1870s the majority of

Welsh people belonged to one or other of these dissenting churches.

Richard Lloyd, the master shoemaker, had inherited from his father David the position of unpaid pastor and preacher in the Campbellite sect of the Baptists known as the Disciples of Christ, which had been started in the United States in the early 1800s. It was an austere sect which practised total immersion at the time of baptism and had a simple, unadorned chapel in Criccieth where Richard Lloyd would preach twice every Sunday.

Although 'Uncle Lloyd', as the boys called him, might be expected by the modern reader to have been a rather formidable and puritanical character, he was in fact a gentle, forgiving man of great compassion and piety, much loved and respected in the local community. He was entirely self-educated and deeply versed in the Bible. By the side of his shoemaker's bench he kept a note-book in which he would jot down thoughts and Bible quotations; it was a habit inherited by his nephew David (many of Lloyd George's own jottings in his notebooks and diaries can be seen in the National Library of Wales today).

Although David was not conventionally religious, and in fact confessed to his uncle soon after his baptism at the age of twelve that he had lost his faith in God, his thinking and his idealism were largely informed in his childhood and youth by Uncle Lloyd's example; this, and his own reading (Victor Hugo's *Les Misérables*, he later said, taught him more about poverty and the human condition than anything else: 'that decided me to do what I could to alleviate the distress and suffering of the poor'). In 1865 Uncle Lloyd had put up over the fireplace in Highgate, the little stone cottage where the family lived in Llanystumdwy, a framed portrait of Abraham Lincoln, the US President who had defeated the Confederacy and freed the slaves. David revered Lincoln and regarded him as an example of the 'cottage-bred' (or log-cabin to White House) man who had educated himself and, through his legal training, rose to the Presidency.

In 1868 an election was held in Caernarvon Boroughs, following which the Tory landlord and MP Hugh Ellis-Nanney turned out his tenants who had voted Liberal, an event which made a deep impression on the young Lloyd George. Ever after, he had a deep hatred of oppression and injustice.

Lucy Masterman, the wife of Lloyd George's Parliamentary Private Secretary and fellow MP Charles Masterman, later described a visit to his childhood home:

> The day after we arrived Lloyd George took Charlie for a walk and began remembering his childhood. We saw the cottage where he had been brought up – a tiny little place where his father's library had been stowed away on the top of a four-poster bed, from which he used to pull it down on wet days. 'I would not have my childhood again,' was his comment . . . He was a lonely creature. He used to wander about the woods, of which he knew every tree, imagining himself a great sailor or some other form of heroic person, or defending Wales against the English, or one of the knights of chivalry. At the age of eleven he woke up one night and as he lay awake he realised with a sudden flash that he did not believe one word of all the religion that was being taught him in church or chapel, that he regarded it all as fiction. It had not been produced by any special reading but by the sudden breaking of something in his brain. Revealed this to his uncle at 14. Old man not angry, commented he would come back to it all again. And so I have, LG said, in a way. 'From that time on,' he said, 'I was in a Hell. I saw no way out!' His deliverance came him – as to so many more – through Carlyle and *Sartor Resartus*, when he was about 17. He quoted with particular admiration the sentence: 'Let us take these outworn vestments to bind the sore and bleeding wounds of humanity.' [This was LG's mission – Churchill did not share his motivation.]

Uncle Lloyd encouraged David to learn the art of public speaking at an early age and he gave his first sermon when he was sixteen. The tradition of Welsh nonconformist preaching undoubtedly played a large part in Lloyd George's style and reputation as a spellbinding orator. In later years he would go and listen to visiting preachers in the London chapels and comment on their performance almost as a theatre critic might do today. He also liked the musical side of Welsh chapels and loved singing hymns.

> An early Easter [27 March 1921], Lloyd George, joined by his friends Lord Riddell, Robert Horne and others, made up a jolly house party at Sir Philip Sassoon's home in Lympne . . . Singing sessions at Lympne with many colleagues were a habit. The most interesting Chorus Minister was Churchill. He dwelt on old Music Hall songs with enthusiasm. But he was not quite successful in carrying a melody . . . Reading, who had served before the mast in his boyhood, sang sea shanties in a gentle, timid voice with much success . . . But the leading performer whose efforts were respected – if not admired in secret – was the Prime Minister himself. And his choice was 'Glorious Welsh Hymns'.

Churchill describes taking the Russian statesman Boris Savinkov to see Lloyd George at Chequers and having to wait for an hour or two while the Prime Minister listened to Welsh hymn-singing by a visiting choir from the Principality.

Uncle Lloyd became more than a father to David and William; he was their mentor and guide, to the extent that they both passed their law exams with honours and were qualified as solicitors. This is a more remarkable achievement than it seems today if one considers their humble background and the limited availability of books and teaching materials in Wales at that time.

With the help of his uncle, David had started work as an office boy at the age of fifteen with the solicitors' firm of Breese, Jones & Casson in the nearby town of Portmadoc. In this, he was emulating his hero Abraham Lincoln and also the American statesman Henry Clay, both of whom had started in this humble capacity and gone on to be political leaders.

David took to the law and was able to take his solicitor's exams in 1881 when he was eighteen; this was the occasion of his first visit to London. His diary entry makes interesting reading:

12 NOVEMBER

Went to the Houses of Parliament. Very much disappointed with them, grand buildings outside, but inside they are crabbed, small and suffocating, especially the House of Commons. I will not say but that I eyed the Assembly in a spirit similar to that which William the Conqueror eyed England on his visit to Edward the Confessor, as the region of his future domain. Oh vanity!

For an obscure Welsh youth to aspire to membership of the House of Commons was indeed aiming high. But like Winston Churchill, Lloyd George always set himself the loftiest of ambitions and goals.

By 1884 Lloyd George was back in London to take his final legal examination. While waiting for the results he again visited the Commons – this time to observe a debate – and it was on this occasion that he witnessed Lord Randolph Churchill's speech attacking William Gladstone.

By the following year, 1885 – when Lloyd George was just twenty-two – he had decided to strike out on his own and establish, with minimal financial resources, a legal practice in competition with Breese, Jones & Casson. For the first few years the young firm struggled to make ends meet and was greatly helped by David's younger brother William joining the practice. In honour of his uncle, David was always known as David Lloyd George, while his brother William was simply William George.

David squired several of the local ladies, including an opera singer, before he met the sensible and down-to-earth Maggie Owen. But there was a good deal of opposition to the match in both households. The Owens were a prosperous landowning family who lived in the hills above Criccieth and were members of the Methodist Church. Uncle Richard Lloyd was of course a Baptist minister and in the 1880s, even in such a small community, this meant a social divide. David, with typical ingenuity, resorted to the stratagem of befriending the Owens' maid, to whom he passed notes to Maggie, and he would also leave notes in the dry-stone wall on the edge of the Owens' sheep pastures.

In later years it was claimed that Margaret Owen had no inkling that her husband-to-be would become a Member of Parliament and live in London for much of his life. She preferred North Wales, often leaving her husband alone in a cold flat in the city, and indeed always returned there for the birth of her children. But it is clear from their early correspondence, in which he writes, 'I would thrust everything, even love, under the wheels of this jug-gernaut – ambition', that he was honest about his political ambi-tions. They were married in 1888 and by the time Lloyd George unexpectedly took his seat in the House of Commons two years later, they already had two children, Richard, born in 1889, and Olwen, in 1890.

Lloyd George began his legal career by taking minor cases such as defending poachers, and gradually established his name in Caernarvonshire. In 1888 he successfully defended the right of a nonconformist quarryman to be buried in the churchyard against the objection of the Anglican vicar who had locked the gate. This – the so-called Llanfrothen Burial Case – made him a household name, at least in North Wales. He was soon elected an alderman in Caernarvon (he was known as the 'Boy Alderman') and when the sitting Member for Caernarvon Boroughs died suddenly in 1889, Lloyd George was adopted as the Liberal Party candidate at the age of twenty-six. In 1890 he won the ensuing by-election by the narrow margin of eighteen votes and took his seat in Parliament. (He was to hold this seat for an unbroken fifty-five years, until his death in 1945 – still a record for parliamentary longevity. Churchill, by comparison, was to represent no fewer than five different con-stituencies during his equally long career as an MP.)

The early years in Parliament were hard for Lloyd George because he depended on his brother William's support to finance his career. Indeed, the family firm of solicitors Lloyd George & George was to finance David's parliamentary career for the next fifteen years. Meanwhile he gradually built up his detailed knowledge of parliamentary procedure and, in the 1890s, became acknowledged as one of the liveliest speakers and foremost debaters both in the House and nationally.

Winston Churchill's origins could scarcely have been more different. In 1816, a rich young bachelor named Ambrose Hall was hunting in a remote virgin forest in the western part of Massachusetts and, getting lost, knocked on a log-cabin door. The door was opened by a sixteen-year-old girl, Clarissa, the daughter of David Wilcox, a frontiersman, and his Iroquois wife. Clarissa was 'brown and lithe', she was beautiful, and Ambrose Hall returned a month later and married her. Their two daughters, Catherine and Clara, endowed with a quarter Indian blood, were famous as the most beautiful girls in the town of Palmyra in upstate New York; and the two sisters married the two Jerome brothers, Lawrence and Leonard, of Huguenot stock.

Leonard Jerome, born in 1818, was a buccaneering entrepreneur typical of mid-nineteenth-century New York. He was a lawyer and a newspaper proprietor, part-owner of the *New York Times*. He had a passion for opera singers (he built an opera house in New York) and racehorses (he founded two prominent racecourses – Belmont and Jerome Park). He was also a traveller, and briefly US Consul in Trieste. In 1868 he took a house in Paris, from which the Jerome ladies, mother and three daughters, escaped to England during the Franco-Prussian War of 1870. There, on the Isle of Wight in 1873, Lord Randolph Churchill met Jennie Jerome and after a year of waiting (while Lord Randolph was duly elected to the family constituency of Woodstock) they were married at the British Embassy in Paris on 15 April 1874. Winston was born seven and a half months later.

This American background was to be an important element in

Winston Churchill's makeup; when he gave a speech to Congress in December 1941 he famously remarked that had his father been American he 'would have got there on his own'. But it is to Blenheim and the Marlborough tradition that we must look for his greatest influences. The two biographies which he completed during his long life were those of his father, Lord Randolph Churchill, and his ancestor John Churchill, the first Duke of Marlborough. Growing up and spending much of the school holidays at Blenheim Palace in Oxfordshire, as a boy Churchill would have been deeply conscious of the military and political tradition to which he belonged. His own namesake, Sir Winston Churchill, had been a free-booting Cavalier in the English Civil War; he died in the 1680s, having survived a long period of penury owing to his loyalty to the Crown (thus giving substance to the family motto *Fiel per Desdichado* – Loyal but Unlucky).

Sir Winston's son, John Churchill, made his way at the court of Charles II and through a rapid preferment became one of the most successful generals in European history, leading the alliance of British, Dutch and German armies against the might of Louis XIV, with successive victories at Blenheim, Ramillies, Oudenaarde and Malplaquet. In gratitude (and perhaps also because his wife Sarah was her most trusted confidante), Queen Anne conferred the dukedom of Marlborough on John Churchill and with it the extensive, formerly royal estate of Woodstock Manor, as well as a large sum of money with which to build Blenheim Palace. The Churchills were, however, always somewhat profligate and twice married American heiresses (Consuelo Vanderbilt, Winston's aunt, was the other one) to restore the family fortunes.

One of Winston's favourite games was playing with his large collection of lead soldiers, which he would organise in battle formation on the floor of the family playroom. His father, Lord Randolph, observing this passionate interest of his son, concluded that because the boy was not gifted academically – as his school reports maintained – he had better go into the Army. It is now recognised that Churchill was probably dyslexic; his disappointing school record compared with his great intellectual successes in later life (he was awarded the Nobel Prize for Literature) would seem to confirm this. After a fairly undistinguished career at Harrow, he succeeded on his third attempt at gaining entrance to the Royal Military Academy, Sandhurst, and achieved his coveted ambition of being commissioned into the cavalry just before his father died in 1895.

Although he never had much money, Churchill lived, even as a young man, in considerable style – in marked contrast to the circumstances of an impoverished Welsh solicitor. Among other things he kept a string of polo ponies while stationed in India. He mixed with his fellow cavalry officers and members of the aristocracy. Unlike Lloyd George, he had access to the society in which Lord and Lady Randolph moved with ease and, through his father, to the leading political figures of the day. In 1895, for example, he was able to meet both Asquith and Balfour at Lord Rothschild's house in Tring.

Churchill's relationship with his parents was typical of upperclass Victorian children. His childhood was largely spent in the nursery and away at boarding school, and he rarely saw his parents. He later said that he adored his mama, but from afar, 'like the Evening Star'. His only real emotional support as a boy came from his nanny, Mrs Everest, whom he called 'woomany' or 'Woom'. It is perhaps not entirely fanciful to suggest that through Mrs Everest, Winston gained some imaginative perception of the life of the lower classes; and that through his work with Lloyd George on old-age pensions, he was able to realise his youthful desire to help the 'Mrs Everests' of the Edwardian world. (She had received no pension from Lord Randolph and Winston had attended her funeral alone, with his younger brother Jack.)

His father, Lord Randolph, was a brilliant and complex man whose career rose and fell like a meteor in the space of two or three years. His campaign in 1884–5 against the Liberal Prime

Minister Gladstone's policy of Home Rule for Ireland – 'Ulster will fight and Ulster will be right' was Lord Randolph's slogan and 'I will play the Orange card and I hope it will prove an ace' his strategy – was hugely influential in bringing the Tories back to office the following year. The Conservative Prime Minister, Lord Salisbury, rewarded Lord Randolph by making him Chancellor of the Exchequer in 1886. Within six months Lord Randolph had resigned over a trifling matter of army expenditure and his political career was never to recover.

Unfortunately, as a young man Lord Randolph may have contracted syphilis and by the early 1890s this was beginning to affect his health, and in particular his mental faculties. He continued to make political speeches, both in the Commons and around the country, but – to the acute embarrassment of his family – his powers of concentration and oratory were failing increasingly. This also made him very autocratic and bad-tempered towards his family and especially towards his bumptious and high-spirited elder son Winston.

Winston was rather pleased with himself for having succeeded in scraping into Sandhurst. While on a walking holiday in Switzerland in 1894 he received a letter from his father, saying, 'I am rather surprised at your tone of exultation over your inclusion in the Sandhurst list. There are two ways of winning an examination, one creditable the other the reverse. You have unfortunately chosen the latter method, and appear to be much pleased with your success.' Winston was bitterly disappointed by his father's lack of praise, or appreciation of his hard-won success, and it was perhaps at this time, and when his father died the following year, that he acquired his resolute determination to prove Lord Randolph wrong in his low opinion of him.

Many years later, in 1947, Winston wrote a short story called 'A Dream' in which his father, whose portrait he is painting, appears to him in person. Lord Randolph is anxious to know what has happened to the world in the last half-century and

Winston describes the two world wars, but his father believes him to have become a society painter and wonders why he did not take a more active public role in all these great events. Winston has no chance to correct this impression before the vision fades.

No relationship in Churchill's life was more important than that with his father. When he died at the premature age of forty-six, Winston was only twenty. He wrote: 'All my dreams of comradeship with him, of entering Parliament at his side and in his support, were ended. There remained for me only to pursue his aims and vindicate his memory.' He went into politics to vindicate Lord Randolph's reputation and to 'raise the tattered flag from the stricken battlefield' which his father had let fall. Soon after taking his seat in the House of Commons he started work on his first major book, the two-volume biography of his father that was published in 1905. All his life he was searching for a father figure – a mentor – and this played a large part in his relationship with Lloyd George during the first ten years of their friendship. The older politician understood this need in Churchill because he was an intuitive and imaginative man himself. Following a Cabinet debate in 1908 in which Winston, taking up Lord Randolph's lost cause of curtailing military spending, opposed the then First Lord of the Admiralty, Reginald McKenna, Lloyd George wrote: 'I am a Celt, and you will forgive me for saying that I saw your father looking on with approbation as you raked McKenna's squadron . . .'

Churchill's main interest as a young man was in seeking military adventures and covering himself with glory. Soon after being commissioned into the 4th Hussars, he manoeuvred himself an invitation to observe the Spanish Army's attempts to contain the rebels in Cuba. This was his first taste of front-line action, and he loved it. In the following year, 1896, he left for India to serve with the Hussars in Bangalore. It was there that he found the leisure to do so much of the reading which was to shape his political thinking and philosophy (and his literary style, moulded on Gibbon and Macaulay). Like Lloyd George, Churchill was largely a self-educated man, despite being an Old Harrovian. Neither went to university. Both were, to a great extent, outsiders and mavericks in the Edwardian political establishment.

In 1897 Churchill found another scene of action when he managed to attach himself to the Malakand Field Force on their expedition to Afghanistan to quell rebellious Pathan tribesmen on the North-West Frontier. From this exciting adventure he was able to work up his first book, *The Story of the Malakand Field Force* (published in 1898). Next, it was the Sudan war, in which Churchill, despite the opposition of Lord Kitchener, managed to inveigle himself a position as a journalist attached to the 21st Lancers. In the Sudan, Churchill participated in the last cavalry charge in British military history – against the Dervishes. In after-years he used to say that this was the most exciting experience of his life. About this Sudanese adventure Churchill wrote the two-volume *The River War* (1899), which was very critical of Kitchener's actions after Omdurman.

Then, in October 1899, Churchill took ship for South Africa, eager once again to be at the battle front. Within days of arriving in South Africa, he was stationed in Natal as a war correspondent attached to the British Army. One of the novel forms of warfare which was then being tried out was the concept of an armoured train, which was essentially a steam engine pulling iron-clad carriages with narrow spaces for firing guns. Churchill had volunteered for an early-morning reconnaissance mission and while this was in progress the Boers blew up the railway line and derailed the engine, before mounting a lightning attack by armed horsemen. After the commanding officer was killed Churchill, despite his non-combatant status, showed his natural gift for leadership. He took command of the small detachment of men aboard, and led them to the front of the train to try and get the engine back on the rails and reverse it towards the British camp. Several witnesses later said that he showed extraordinary courage and coolness under fire.

However, he soon found himself isolated and facing an armed Boer commando on horseback, by whom he was captured; it later transpired that the horseman who had the honour of his capture was probably the young Louis Botha, whom he was to meet again eight years later as Colonial Secretary. (Louis Botha became Prime Minister of South Africa in 1907 and the first President of South Africa three years later.)

Churchill was taken to Pretoria where he was put with the other British officers in the Model School reformatory prison. It was, by later standards, lightly guarded and within days of his imprisonment Churchill and his friends were busy making plans for their escape. In traditional Victorian *Boy's Own* style, they got together maps, provisions and civilian clothing. The plan was for three of them to scale the wall of the latrines at midnight while the guard was otherwise occupied. Churchill went first and waited for his comrades. They never appeared. A whispered conversation took place over the wall and Churchill decided to go on alone. He had little money, no map and only the stars to guide him. Walking north, he managed to strike the main railway line running east to Mozambique. In the early hours of the morning, a goods train came trundling along at about 15–20 miles per hour. Churchill clambered aboard and gratefully sank into a van carrying sacks of coal.

When he awoke several hours later, the train had stopped outside a station in the Eastern Transvaal. Gingerly he disembarked and spent the day hiding in the woods, being observed by a hungry vulture. The heat was intense. By nightfall he was hungry, thirsty and desperate. By extraordinary good fortune, he stumbled on a house near the railway at Balmoral to the east of Pretoria, which was occupied by the British manager of the Transvaal and Delagoa Bay Collieries. Once again Churchill's lucky star had saved him. The colliery manager, John Howard, agreed to hide him at the bottom of the mine until they could effect his safe escape over the South African border into

Portuguese territory. He was given food and a sustaining drink and hidden in the bottom of the mine for forty-eight hours. Within three days he arrived back in Durban where he was acclaimed as a national hero for his daring escape and made an impromptu speech to the crowd assembled on the pier to greet him. In England the music halls took up the refrain:

> 'He's the latest and the greatest
> correspondent of the day.'

Conservative Party leaders must have thought that, seen as a war hero by the electorate, Churchill would be a useful Tory asset. But from the time of his maiden speech in 1901 Winston marked himself out as an independent thinker, willing, as his father Lord Randolph had been, to attack the leaders of his own party. Some said this was to gain notoriety but Churchill claimed that it was to maintain his own political philosophy. He made nine speeches to his constituents in his first year as an MP. In May 1901 he had taken up his father's lost cause by quixotically crusading for economies in the Army. The cast of characters was the same: Lord Salisbury was still Prime Minister, as he had been in 1886 when Lord Randolph resigned, and the Secretary of State for War was St John Brodrick. From attacking the army estimates to attacking his own leaders was but a short step for Churchill and soon, like his father's 'Fourth Party', he would form a party within a party, the 'Hughligans' (named after Churchill's best friend, Lord Hugh Cecil).

After their introduction in February 1901, Churchill and Lloyd George, the two young members from opposing parties, met, in the course of their daily attendance at the House of Commons, in the friendly, gregarious way of the parliamentary 'club'. As Lloyd George would proudly write to his family in Wales: 'Men of opposite parties meet on most friendly and amiable terms, a condition of things which very few countries can compete in.'

However, these two men gradually found more and more political common ground. Lloyd George told his constituents in Caernarvon in 1902: 'Last week there was a very interesting speech by a brilliant young Tory member, Mr Winston Churchill. There is no greater admirer of his talent, I assure you, than the individual now addressing you – and many a chat we have had about the situation. We do not always agree, but we do not black each other's eyes.'

In December 1901, Lloyd George went to speak against the Boer War at Birmingham Town Hall. The city was of course the stronghold of Joseph Chamberlain and almost entirely Tory. Over 100,000 jingoistic supporters of the South African war surrounded the hall, with – as the Welshman later wrote – 'intent to kill me'. The angry mob broke every window in the building and rushed the speaker's platform inside the hall, armed with sticks, bricks, hammers and knives. Lloyd George was only able to make his escape out of the back door by putting on a policeman's helmet and uniform.

Fortunately, at this stage in his career he was not widely recognised, although he may have been rather short in stature to qualify as a policeman. Joseph Chamberlain appeared to take pleasure in the rioting of his followers and openly regretted that Lloyd George had made his escape. Two others were killed and forty people injured.

Not only did Lloyd George risk his life by his outspoken opposition to the war, he also ruined his solicitors' practice during these years because of his unpopular stand. When he became a government minister in 1905, and was thus for the first time eligible to receive a salary, he was still £400 overdrawn at the bank.

Perhaps the most significant result of the Boer War was the perception of British military weakness that it engendered, particularly in Germany. It had required an army of almost half a million British troops, had claimed 22,000 lives and cost £223 million for the British Empire to subdue Boer guerillas who never numbered more than 70,000. Churchill later commented that 1899 had led to 1914. Even as early as 1902 he warned of a 'dragging, draining, dangerous war'. Rudyard Kipling wrote in his poem 'The Islanders':

> . . . then was your shame revealed,
> At the hands of a little people, few but apt in the field.

The glaring incompetence of the British Command was a shock to the home audience and it had not been rectified when the First World War broke out twelve years later. The same generals, Kitchener, French, Haig and Robertson, were to be in charge, and were to show the same disregard for casualties as in the South African conflict. Kitchener actually wrote, 'I look more to the numbers I kill or capture than anything else' and commented to Brodrick: 'The real criterion of the war is my weekly bag.'

Churchill's reaction to the Birmingham Town Hall riot was more statesmanlike than Chamberlain's; he wrote to the leader of the Birmingham Conservatives Association to express his disgust, saying, 'I hope the Conservative Party have kept their hands clean'. He told his correspondent that Birmingham would be blamed for the treatment of Lloyd George while he was there, adding, 'Personally, I think Lloyd George a vulgar, chattering little cad, but he will have gained a hundred thousand sympathisers in England by the late proceedings.'

This tone of aristocratic disdain did not last long and the friendship between the two men ripened. Churchill was always willing to see the good points in his opponents – he was warm-hearted, magnanimous and good-humoured. One of the things Lloyd George liked best about him was his puckish sense of humour. (In the 1920s, however, the Duke of Westminster hosted a dinner party in London at which he had hired a magician to perform. During the course of the evening Churchill's braces were removed by the magician. He was enraged and demanded an apology. It is safe to say that if this had happened to Lloyd

George, he would have roared with laughter. He always enjoyed a good joke at his own expense.)

At any rate the two MPs obviously enjoyed each other's company: by the summer of 1903, they were already close enough friends for David to write home to his family in Criccieth, 'I am spending Sunday at Blenheim with Winston.' And they often found themselves thinking along the same political lines. Several months before Churchill changed parties in 1904, Lloyd George received a New Year greeting from a fellow Liberal MP: 'How do you like your new stable companion Winston Churchill? You will make a perfect matched pair, but I should be devilish sorry to try and drive you.'

The political issue which had brought Lloyd George and Churchill this close together was that of free trade. In May 1903 Joseph Chamberlain, the new Prime Minister Arthur Balfour's Colonial Secretary, had called for a new system of imperial tariffs. Britain had traditionally been a nation that believed in, and prospered from, free trade and low tariffs. But as the competition from goods manufactured in the United States and Germany increased, and as the price of agricultural products such as corn and wheat fell drastically in the last quarter of the nineteenth century owing to the enormous increase in production from the North American prairies, so Britain's farmers suffered. The Conservative Party was divided between those who believed in free trade and others, such as Joseph Chamberlain, who espoused a form of protectionism that would increase tariffs for American imports but allow the produce of the Empire, particularly Canada and New Zealand, to enter Britain free of duties. By embracing protectionism for the first time since Sir Robert Peel had repealed the Corn Laws in 1846, Chamberlain effectively split the Tory Party.

Both Lloyd George and Churchill instinctively believed in free trade because protectionism favoured the rich and the few – the manufacturers and the farmers. Free trade helped all consumers, especially the poor, for whom the price of bread was a basic concern. The average labourer's wage in Victorian times was 13s. 6d. a week (representing an annual salary of £4,000 today). The price of a loaf of bread was 2½d.*

On 28 May 1903 Lloyd George attacked the Government in the House of Commons, asking whether Chamberlain's protectionist views were endorsed by Balfour and his party. Balfour replied that fiscal opinions were not a test of party loyalty. Churchill rose to his feet and asked why the Government policy had changed; 'Never was the wealth of the country greater, or the trade returns higher' and there was 'no popular demand for this departure'. Within a few weeks of Chamberlain's speech Churchill had, together with almost sixty Conservative MPs, founded the Free Food League to protest against Chamberlain's new policy, which Balfour was apparently endorsing.

Was the issue of free trade alone enough to push Churchill to leave the Tory Party? He was busy writing the biography of his father and in the course of so doing discovered many issues and policies on which Lord Randolph too had differed from the Conservative leaders in the 1880s in taking his stand for 'Tory democracy'. Winston found himself increasingly alienated from Balfour and the Tory leaders, and attracted to leading Liberal statesmen and thinkers such as Asquith, Morley, Grey and Lloyd George. Liberalism seemed to represent not only the future but also, in a curious way, a continuity with the ideas for which his father had fought twenty years earlier.

Lloyd George too was speaking out against protectionism. In early 1904, for instance, at Bradford, he said:

> You have to go back fifty years to the time when the bread of the people was taxed; eighty years to the time when slavery was rampant in the Empire [referring to Chinese indentured labourers in South Africa]; . . . over four hundred years to the time when the priesthood had a monopoly of the instruction of the people;

*Department of Employment and Productivity, 1981.

and over three thousand years to the time when a great Empire was governed by a man called Joseph ... But there is this difference – the ancient Joseph in his dreams made provision for an abundance of corn for the people. The modern Joseph [Chamberlain] is dreaming about a scarcity of corn.

It is typical of Lloyd George's genius that he had quickly seen in Chamberlain's protectionist programme an opportunity for an alternative, positive programme. He had talked this over with Churchill when they lunched together on 31 December 1903. As Churchill wrote to Lord Hugh Cecil soon afterwards:

LG spoke to me at length about a positive programme. He said unless we have something to promise as against Mr Chamberlain's promises where are we with the working men? He wants to promise three things which are arranged to deal with three different classes, namely, fixity of tenure to tenant farmers subject to payment of rent and good husbandry: taxation of site values to reduce the rates in the towns: and of course something in the nature of Shackleton's Trade Disputes Bill for the Trade Unionists. Of course with regard to brewers, he would write 'no compensation out of public funds'. I was very careful not to commit myself on any of these points and I chaffed him as being as big a plunderer as Joe [Chamberlain]. But *entre nous* I cannot pretend to have been shocked. Altogether it was a very pleasant and instructive talk and after all LG represents three things:– Wales, English Radicalism and Nonconformists, and they are not three things which politicians can overlook.

Churchill had already written to Cecil in October 1903 in unequivocal terms: 'I am an English Liberal. I hate the Tory party, their men, their words & their methods.' Cecil, because of family loyalty (Lord Salisbury was his father), would never leave the Conservative Party, and would lose his seat in 1906 because he too was in favour of free trade. But Churchill saw which way the wind was blowing – the Liberals were winning seat after seat in by-elections in 1903–4. He was drawing closer to Lloyd George:

they had frequent conversations at the House of Commons and started to have lunch and dinner together on a regular basis. As John Grigg, Lloyd George's last great biographer put it, 'Churchill soon fell under Lloyd George's spell and for the rest of his life never ceased to regard the Welshman as his master.' Lloyd George warmed to Churchill's adventurous agnostic spirit, as Churchill warmed to his. And it was probably Lloyd George who arranged for Churchill to meet with the Liberal chief whip, Herbert Gladstone (son of William Gladstone), in order to enquire about the possibility of a Liberal seat.

In one of the final dramas of the young Churchill's life as a Tory MP, on 29 March 1904, Balfour spoke in the Commons; he was followed by Lloyd George, who attacked the Prime Minister for 'clutching at power'. As Lloyd George wound up and Churchill rose to speak, Balfour walked out of the Chamber. 'Mr Winston Churchill said he was very sorry the Prime Minister had left the House as he had desired to ask him one or two questions.' At this, first the ministers on the Conservative front bench, and then the Tory backbenchers, rose and followed Balfour out. Resuming his speech, Churchill said he had tried, without success, to discover what the Prime Minister's policy was on free trade. He announced that he had passed formally from the position of an independent supporter to that of a declared opponent of the present Government.

Though he was cheered on the Liberal benches, the Tory boycott clearly shook Churchill and accelerated his move to cross the floor to the Liberals. He was followed by his cousin Ivor Guest and his friend Jack Seely, who both became prominent Liberals.

On 22 April Churchill spoke again, on the Trades Disputes Bill, and had the misfortune to a break down in the middle of his speech, losing the thread of his argument. There were fewer Tory jeers than might have been expected because it was feared that he might be following in the tragic footsteps of his father, who had suffered from mental decline before the eyes of the House.

Towards the end of April 1904 Churchill agreed to run as a Liberal candidate in North-West Manchester, where free trade was a strongly held belief. Finally, on 31 May 1904, he crossed the floor in such a way as to give his new relationship with Lloyd George dramatic emphasis.

> He [Churchill] entered the Chamber of the House of Commons, stood for a moment at the Bar, looked briefly at both the Government and Opposition benches and strode swiftly up the aisle. He bowed to the Speaker and turned sharply to his right to the Liberal benches. He sat down next to Lloyd George in a seat that his father had occupied when in opposition – indeed, the same seat on which Lord Randolph had stood waving his handkerchief to cheer the downfall of Gladstone in 1885.

As Churchill himself later put it, speaking of Lloyd George: 'Naturally such a man greatly influenced me. When I crossed the floor of the House and left the Conservative Party in 1904, it was by his side I took my seat.'

Churchill had become a Liberal. More precisely, he was a Lloyd George Liberal. When speaking of his relationship with Lloyd George, Churchill consistently referred to himself as the older man's 'lieutenant'. He never spoke of anyone else in the same way during his long career. Throughout his two decades as a Liberal he followed Lloyd George's lead in social reform, even though he was not the party leader, and again during the wartime Coalition, whereas he showed no inclination to do likewise with Stanley Baldwin, and still less with Neville Chamberlain, the nominal leaders of the Conservative Party.

Neither Lloyd George nor Churchill was instinctively a party man, and as their political careers developed in the twentieth century, it became clear that they both hankered after a coalition government. Lloyd George remained faithful to the Liberal Party for most of his life, despite presiding over the Coalition Government of 1916–22. Churchill's rejection of the Conservative Party in 1904 was a wholesale rejection of his own Tory inheritance. Lord Randolph had criticised the party and its leaders, but had never forsaken it. His son was doing this for him, at no little personal cost – it was a wrench to break with all that glittering hierarchy, and what did he have to look forward to? Clearly there was some understanding between him and the Liberals and in particular with Lloyd George, the leader of the radical wing of the party.

## "THE SHELVING OF 'C.-B.'"

"It's all very well to dissemble your love, but why do you kick me upstairs?"

"C.-B." (very much awake): "Boo—oo—I don't want to go to bed; I ain't sleepy."

[Concurrently with the suggestion that Sir H. Campbell-Bannerman should find a safe anchorage in the House of Lords, Mr. Lloyd-George and Mr. Winston Churchill have elaborated a new Radical Programme.]

Within a week, on 6 June, Churchill and Lloyd George were the opening speakers at the Cobden Centenary Debate when they addressed over 10,000 people under the great glass roof of Alexandra Palace. In the public eye and in newspaper reports they were already seen as a pair of radicals working together. In fact, the *Pall Mall Gazette* presciently published a cartoon in 1904 showing them holding their joint 'New Radical Program' and urging the Liberal leader, Henry Campbell-Bannerman, to retire to the House of Lords. It seems probable that in addition to finding a safe seat in Manchester for the new Liberal convert, Lloyd George had used his good offices to assure him that, if the Liberals took power, Churchill would attain some ministerial appointment. Considering that Churchill was not yet thirty years old when he crossed the floor, this was a testament to his ability and to the fact that he was already perceived in political circles as a man with a great future. We know that by this time he had a bust of Napoleon on his desk and that his ambition was to be Prime Minister by the time he was forty. Lloyd George, on the other hand, was now forty-one and had been in Parliament for fifteen years. There was no doubt that Churchill would be included in any new Liberal government and would play a prominent role.

In fact, for almost the next twenty years Lloyd George and Churchill would work together, effectively formulating the policies which would direct the British Empire in peace and war.

# 2

# 1904–11: The 'Heavenly Twins'

'Friendship is the noblest relationship that can exist between
two human beings.'

Sandor Marai, *Embers*, 1942

ONCE THEY WERE formally of the same party, Lloyd George and
Churchill quickly came to be seen in political circles as a pair,
'the heavenly twins' of political and social reform. It was an alliance
that would, over the next twenty years, have profound consequences
not only for the Liberal Party but for the country as a whole.

From the beginning Churchill looked up to the older man, and
sought his counsel and advice. He wanted to demonstrate his
commitment to the Liberal Party by moving towards its more
radical wing, which was led by Lloyd George. At this stage
Churchill was still, in many ways, the overgrown schoolboy – a
genius, certainly, but impetuous, impressionable, grasping the
ideas of Liberalism with all the passion of a convert to a new religion, anxious to prove his sincerity and commitment before the
older acolytes of the faith.

His switch of allegiance from the Tories to the Liberals would
mark a deep divide in Churchill's social as well as political life. He
had to resign from the Carlton Club in St James's, to which senior
Conservative Party members normally belonged; and – somewhat surprisingly, considering it was a sporting rather than a political club – he was blackballed by the Hurlingham Club, the first

time such a thing had happened to a polo player. Instead he became a member of the National Liberal Club, which was close to the House of Commons and provided a convenient watering hole at which to meet his new political colleagues.

"SUPPORTERS" RAMPANT.
AN HERALDIC INVERSION.

In the summer of 1903, as a singular mark of friendship, Churchill had taken Lloyd George to visit Blenheim Palace, his birthplace and ancestral home. It was also a rare outing for Lloyd George because he did not typically like grand country houses or aristocratic society. The experiment was repeated only once – in 1908, when Lloyd George had become Chancellor – and on this occasion there appears to have been some slighting remark by the Duke of Marlborough which persuaded him never to return. By contrast, in these early years when they had formed a common front to promote free trade and to attack, at every opportunity, the protectionist policies of Joseph Chamberlain, Churchill accompanied Lloyd George on many of his speaking engagements, both in London and in North Wales.

It is perhaps unnecessary to dwell on the social distinctions which bedevilled so much of British life at this time. In the case of two such men of genius as Lloyd George and Churchill, there was no special consciousness of background or class. As Lloyd George's devoted secretary Frances Stevenson divined:

> The plain fact was [LG] had not much time for friendship . . . There was an aloof and withdrawn quality, an essential secretiveness which forbade access to any abiding intimacy.
>
> But again in his relations with Churchill there was a difference. It was 'Winston' and 'David' almost from the first. I think Mr Churchill was the only one of LG's friends who called him 'David'. From the earliest political days these two were strangely and prophetically drawn together. Each divined in the other, the quality of genius, which separated them from the ordinary run of men, and drew them together – the village boy and the Duke's grandson. Class distinctions meant nothing to either of them.

The Liberal Party in 1905–6 was still very much a party of gentlemen, its membership including many Whig landowners as well as 'provincial attorneys' (as its founding father Edmund Burke called them) like Lloyd George. In an era when many fortunes were being made in commerce and manufacturing, the new millionaires gravitated naturally towards the Liberal Party. Although it would increasingly become the party of social progress and reform in 1909, it was by no means unsympathetic to business interests.

The year 1905 saw Arthur Balfour, the Conservative Prime Minister, hanging on to power, despite losing several by-elections, and trying to conceal the growing divide within his party on the free-trade issue. Both Churchill and Lloyd George were among the most vociferous opponents of Balfour in the House of Commons. Churchill in particular attacked him in such violent language that Balfour retorted: 'As for the junior member for Oldham, his speech was certainly not remarkable for good

## THE MYSTERY EXPLAINED.

THE PRIME MINISTER (to Messrs. Lloyd-George and Churchill): "I'm afraid, gentlemen, that in this persistent mud-throwing you only waste your time!"

MESSRS. LLOYD-GEORGE and CHURCHILL: "Not a bit of it, we're qualifying for 'high positions' in the next Liberal Government."

["The man who may hope most to be appointed to a high position (in the Government) is not the man who has given proof of the qualities of administration; it is the man who can make the most active political campaign, *who can make the most speeches*, and who can apply the most stinging epigrams to the tender places of a decadent Government."—LORD ROSEBERY at the Liberal League Meeting.]

taste . . . It is not on the whole desirable to come down to this house with invective which is both prepared and violent.' There would seem to have been a good deal of truth in the cartoon which appeared in the *Pall Mall Gazette* on 18 April 1905, showing Churchill and Lloyd George with mud in their hands, being addressed by Balfour: 'I'm afraid, gentlemen, that in this persistent mud throwing you only waste your time.' The mud-slingers reply, 'Not a bit of it, we're qualifying for "high positions" in the next Liberal Government.' Another cartoon, 'Too Old at Sixty', also makes clear that Lloyd George and Churchill were seen in the political world as the two young firebrands on the left wing of the Liberal Party, ready to move on old diehards like Campbell-Bannerman, Morley and Harcourt.

TOO OLD AT SIXTY.

LLOYD-G.: " I say, Winston, what *are* we going to do with these poor old Duffers when we get into power ? "
WINSTON C.: " We've made them take a back seat already, and they'll have to learn to like it."

Balfour finally resigned the premiership on 4 December 1905 and the Liberal leader Henry Campbell-Bannerman rose to the challenge and formed a government. The ensuing general election, of January 1906, resulted in a landslide victory for the Liberals who gained a majority of 220 seats over the Tories. They won every seat in Wales and 80 per cent of the seats in Scotland. Balfour himself lost his seat. According to Lloyd George it was, by British standards, 'a quiet but certain revolution, as revolutions come in a constitutional country, without overthrowing order, without doing an injustice to anybody, but redressing those injustices from which people suffer'.

The 1906 vote had above all been a vote for free trade, and during Campbell-Bannerman's premiership (which lasted until 1908) the Liberal Government stayed true to its Whig roots and did not embark on any radical reforms. The size of its majority nevertheless paved the way for the Liberals to propose a much more radical programme of social reform during the following four years.

Lloyd George was appointed President of the Board of Trade in the new Government, and quickly proved himself a pragmatic, competent and effective minister who was able to deal with business questions as well as being a brilliant radical orator. Churchill meanwhile (after only two years as a Liberal and still only thirty-two) was offered the post of Financial Secretary to the Treasury. Instead he chose to be Under-Secretary at the Colonial Office, partly because his immediate superior, the Colonial Secretary, Lord Elgin, sat in the House of Lords, which would allow Churchill a more prominent role in Commons debates, and also because he would be handling the constitutional settlement with South Africa, on which he held strong views. Because he had fought in the Boer War, and respected his former opponents, Smuts, Botha and the other leaders, Churchill wished above all to show magnanimity in the settlement that was made by the British to create a new union of South Africa, incorporating the provinces of Transvaal and the Orange Free State. The first photograph of Churchill and Lloyd George together was taken at the Colonial Prime Ministers' meeting in London in the summer of 1907. The two young ministers stand out as twentieth-century figures – the coming men – in contrast to the bearded and rather portly Victorian gentlemen from the colonies. In both of them there is a sense of latent power.

★

Churchill had first accompanied Lloyd George to his Caernarvon constituency in 1904 to make a speech on the free-trade issue as a newly converted Liberal MP; it was there that he put himself on good terms with the people by describing his friend as 'the best fighting general in the Liberal Army'. When Lloyd George took the young Winston to meet his family at their London home in Routh Road, Wandsworth, in about 1905, his elder son Dick's first impression of Churchill was that he was a 'lordly young man'. Churchill, however, quickly endeared himself to the family, especially Lloyd George's wife Margaret, and became one of their favourite guests.

The Welsh national Eisteddfod at Llangollen in North Wales in the summer of 1908 might have seemed an unlikely event to attract the young Churchill. But he was always eager to learn and to enter into the spirit of any occasion. Suitably dressed in a bowler hat and long coat, he was taken on a tour of the proceedings (which were conducted entirely in Welsh) by his host Lloyd George and his five-year-old daughter Megan. It was on this occasion that Winston met A. G. Edwards, the Bishop of St Asaph, who was to officiate at his forthcoming marriage to Clementine Hozier.

Churchill's friendship with Lloyd George at this stage remained something of a junior–senior relationship (he did not in fact yet address him as 'David' in letters). When they were out walking at Llangollen, with Lloyd George's friend D. R. Daniel, Churchill burst out: 'You are much stronger than I am. I have noticed that you go about things quietly and calmly, you do not excite yourself, but what you wish happens as you desire it. I am too excitable, I tear about, and make too much noise.'

These visits to Wales with his friend David are not covered by any of Churchill's biographers and he does not seem to have written much about them in letters to his family and friends. But they surely constituted an important chapter in his expanding horizons and his growing knowledge of, and sympathy for, the many different elements composing British society in the early 1900s.

During these years when Churchill travelled widely around England, Wales and Scotland, he must have felt like a diver descending into unknown social depths. For the first time he had the opportunity of meeting country people, those from the industrial working classes and even the poorest inhabitants of the great industrial cities. On a visit to Manchester in 1908, he commented to his private secretary, Eddie Marsh, 'Fancy living in one of these streets, never seeing anything beautiful, never seeing anything brilliant, never eating anything savoury' (Churchill loved his food).

As a young bachelor soon to marry, however, he certainly enjoyed the opportunity to spend time with Lloyd George's young family. Their Criccieth home had a comfortable middle-class atmosphere even though the language spoken was Welsh. Undoubtedly politics was the principal topic of conversation between the two men but their friendship clearly went far beyond this, as they spent many happy family occasions together.

Violet Bonham Carter, the daughter of Asquith and herself in love with Winston, was in an excellent position to observe the growing friendship between Lloyd George and Churchill. She later referred to it as

> the closest, and in some ways the most incongruous alliance . . .
> the most curious and surprising feature of their partnership was
> that while it exercised no influence whatsoever on Lloyd George,
> politically or otherwise, it directed, shaped and coloured Winston
> Churchill's mental attitude and his political course during the next
> few years. Lloyd George was throughout the dominant partner.
> His was the only personal leadership I have ever known Winston
> to accept unquestioningly in his whole political career. He was
> fascinated by a mind more swift and agile than his own, by its fer-
> tility and resource, by its uncanny intuition and gymnastic nim-
> bleness and by a political sophistication which he lacked.

The two men were constantly in each other's company. Violet Bonham Carter said to Churchill one day, 'You've been talking to Lloyd George . . . he's "come off" on you.' Winston indignantly replied that Lloyd George was 'the greatest political genius of the day' and that he admired and revered him.

In the first two years of the new Liberal administration, 1905–8, radical legislation came about slowly. Campbell-Bannerman (whose slogan was 'Peace, retrenchment and reform') was a more traditional Liberal than Asquith would later prove to be. Nevertheless Lloyd George soon brought forward a major piece of legislation to amend the law relating to merchant shipping. His unconventional approach in inviting the shipowners to the Board of Trade, and asking their advice, had much to do with its successful outcome. As Hudson Kearley (later Lord Devonport), his Parliamentary Private Secretary, commented, 'By getting on the right side of the owners Lloyd George was able to do a good turn for the men . . .'

In addition, in his Census of Production Act, Lloyd George enlisted the help of commercial attachés in British embassies abroad in an effort to provide the country with accurate and up-to-date commercial intelligence and economic data. In 1907 he amended patent law, again taking advice from the experts, and introduced a Companies Amendment Act to ensure fuller information for shareholders and creditors. His main job, however, in the latter part of that year was in resolving the railwaymen's dispute. Once again his approach was first to consult the intransigent chairmen of the railway companies.

In November of this year tragedy struck Lloyd George's family. His eldest daughter Mair, who was seventeen years old, died suddenly of appendicitis. In 1913 Lloyd George would write to his brother William, who had lost his own son Dafydd two years previously:

> When the blow fell, it seemed so wantonly cruel. Fate seemed to me to have inflicted torture without any purpose. I had just settled a great railway strike which had threatened untold misery and it all seemed to me to be a piece of blind fury. I know now what it was for. It gave me a keener appreciation of the suffering of others. It

deepened my sympathy. Little Mair's death has been the inspiration of all my work to relieve human misery during recent years . . .

Another maxim I found comfort in was given to me by Winston – 'never press the spear to your breast', which means don't brood unnecessarily and dwell incessantly on the details of the catastrophe and travel over its burning surface again and again.

Winston was on safari in Uganda at the time of Mair's death, and only arrived back in London on 18 January 1908, after spending four months touring British colonies in Africa. He too was to lose a daughter, Marigold, at the age of three in 1921; in consequence the youngest daughters of both men to some extent replaced the lost ones: Megan Lloyd George, who became her father's favourite and was a radical orator in her own right, and Mary (Lady Soames), who has written movingly about her mother and edited her parents' correspondence.

The role of the Board of Trade was to oversee trade, industry, transport, labour relations and industrial disputes. At this early date, the laissez-faire approach of nineteenth-century British government meant that it was a relatively quiet backwater when Lloyd George took control. Within two years he had shaken up the formerly peaceful lives of the civil servants employed there. For another thing, the number of strikes went up sharply in these years; consequently he was called upon to mediate not only in the railway strike, but also in the coalminers' and dockworkers' strikes. In such matters he proved himself much more accomplished than his successor at the Board of Trade, Churchill. Lloyd George was brilliant at understanding the causes of a dispute. He would put himself in another man's shoes, empathising with the grievances and concerns of both workers and employers. He made his listeners feel that everything they said mattered, for he really wanted answers to the questions he asked. Whereas he thought best when in conversation with other people, Churchill did his best thinking when he was alone. (The novelist C. P.

Snow described Churchill's mind as having the 'brooding, vatic quality' of prophetic vision.)

Churchill, on the other hand, was to make himself notorious in labour circles for his heavy-handed approach to solving disputes.

**LLOYD THE LUBRICATOR.**

THERE 'S A SWEET LITTLE CHERUB THAT FLOATS UP ALOFT
TO WATCH O'ER THE LIFE OF JOHN BULL.

[With *Mr. Punch's* compliments to Mr. LLOYD-GEORGE on his successful intervention in the late Railway Dispute.]

During a strike at the Welsh coalmine of Tonypandy in 1910, he was publicly seen as having sent in the troops; again, when shipping deliveries were halted in 1911, his first reaction as Home Secretary was to bring in the Navy. Whereas Lloyd George was a solicitor, trained to analyse and weigh up the rights and wrongs of a dispute, Churchill's military training was the key to his reactions. Temperamentally, too, the two men had this difference: Lloyd George was a listener, Churchill predominantly a talker. As the former's personal secretary, A. J. Sylvester, later recorded:

> LG said he always remembered Winston saying that he (LG) understood politics better than he did, because he had been brought up a soldier. 'My mind', said LG, 'goes back to the time when Winston was Home Secretary. I was called in by Asquith to settle a railway strike. I settled it. Afterwards I went to the Home Office to see Winston. He was very angry with the result. There he stood before a huge map showing police stations all over the country, and all the available forces ready to take action wherever necessary. His mind was on a fight. Charles Masterman . . . was sitting there drinking whiskey and making fun of him.

Churchill was later to write about Lloyd George's genius being most visible and effective in Cabinet discussion, but these talents proved equally useful at the Board of Trade:

> No one can have worked as closely as I have with Mr Lloyd George without being both impressed and influenced by him. The reputation which he has long enjoyed as a parliamentary and platform speaker has often been an exaggerated one. Extra-ordinary as have been his successes in public, it is in conclaves of eight or nine, or four or five, or in personal discussion man to man, that his persuasive arts reach their fullest excellence. At his best he could almost talk a bird out of a tree. An intense compre-hension of the more amiable weaknesses of human nature: a pure gift of getting on the right side of a man from the beginning of a talk: a complete avoidance of anything in the nature of chop-logic reasoning: a sure, deft touch in dealing with realities: the sudden presenting of positions hitherto unexpected, but apparently con-ciliatory and attractive – all these are models and methods in which he is a natural adept. I have seen him turn a Cabinet round in less than ten minutes, and yet when the process was complete,

no one could remember any particular argument to which to attribute their change of view.

He has realized with intense comprehension the truth of the adage 'A man convinced against his will, is of the same opinion still'. He never in the days when I knew him best thought of giving *himself* satisfaction by what he said. He had no partiality for fine phrases, he thought only and constantly of the effect produced upon other persons.

Never was the friendship more intense, the political alliance closer, between David and Winston, than during the years 1908–10. And the fact that they were both feared and hated, attacked and reviled with vitriolic force by their political opponents, inevitably brought them closer.

During these years the two politicians enacted a torrent of radical legislation which changed the face of Britain. It made, in effect, the transition from a traditional, paternalist, laissez-faire, Gladstonian government of the nineteenth century into a modern, twentieth-century, social-planning, interventionist and eventually centralised government. This was a process which the two world wars would enormously accelerate. The People's Budget, which included old-age pensions, national insurance, unemployment and sickness benefits, and introduced labour exchanges, was to be the centrepiece of this whole architecture of reform.

Unemployment had been growing rapidly with the slowing-down of trade after the 1907 financial crisis\* and, in March 1908, Churchill rightly identified the problem of labour as the 'new and untrodden field in British politics', very much echoing the Liberal thinking and speeches of his mentor. Churchill argued that the Liberal Party – unless it was to disappear in favour of the infant

---

\*This originated with the San Francisco earthquake of 1906: 15 per cent of Britain's gold reserves were paid out to meet US insurance claims, and the bank rate jumped to 7 per cent, causing a slump in both shares and bonds.

Labour Party (which was indeed to happen after 1922) – had to respond to the needs of the new working classes.

As Lloyd George put it in a speech in Swansea in October:

The new Liberalism . . . devotes part of its endeavour also to the removing of the immediate causes of discontent. It is true that man cannot live by bread alone. It is equally true that a man cannot live without bread . . . It is a recognition of that elemental fact that has promoted legislation like the Old Age Pensions Act but it is just the beginning of things. We are still confronted with the more gigantic task of dealing with the rest – the sick, the infirm, the unemployed, the widows and the orphans. No country can lay any real claim to civilization that allows them to starve . . .

I have had some excruciating letters . . . from people whose cases I have investigated – honest workmen thrown out of work, tramping the streets from town to town . . . begging for work as they would for charity, and at the end of the day trudging home tired, disheartened and empty handed, to be greeted by faces, and some of them little faces, haggard and pinched with starvation and anxiety. The day will come, and it is not far distant, that this country will shudder at its toleration of that state of things when it was rolling in wealth.

The vision was Lloyd George's; he was the prophet of social reform, of the need for change. No one caught the torch of reform more eagerly than the young Churchill, who himself would devise the plan for labour exchanges.

In the spring of 1908, Lloyd George prepared the Port of London Act, which established the Port of London Authority. He had carefully researched the ground by visiting Hamburg and Antwerp, and had of course consulted the owners of the dock companies who were compulsorily bought out of their property holdings along the banks of the River Thames. This important bill was introduced in the House of Commons in the summer of 1908 by Winston Churchill, who had by then succeeded Lloyd

George at the Board of Trade. Lloyd George told Masterman that he had asked Churchill to redraft some parts of the bill. 'Oh, that's detail,' Churchill said scornfully; 'I'm not going to do detail.'

In April 1908, Asquith had taken over as Prime Minister from Campbell-Bannerman, who had resigned for reasons of health. One of his most significant appointments was that of Lloyd George as Chancellor of the Exchequer. As for Churchill's promotion, it had been astonishing enough that he had become a junior Cabinet minister in the previous Liberal Government within eighteen months of his conversion. He was still climbing fast.

Churchill's elevation to the Board of Trade necessitated a by-election because in those days a minister had to be formally re-elected before he could take office. Perhaps because of his change of party, and also having changed his stance on Ireland, he lost his first by-election in North-West Manchester but was later adopted by Dundee, where he was comfortably returned as a Liberal.

On becoming President of the Board of Trade, Churchill complained that 'Lloyd George has taken all the plums!' of social reform. But a careful analysis of their work together shows that while Churchill was indeed the follower and disciple, he worked hard on the practicalities of social legislation. For instance, although – to Churchill's extreme annoyance – Lloyd George received most of the credit for the Unemployment Insurance Bill, it had originally been Churchill's idea.

He saw the functions of the Board of Trade in military terms. These, he wrote,

> seem to me to bear the closest resemblance to those of the Intelligence Department of the Army. The Intelligence Department does not govern military policy, it does not command the troops, it does not organise the commissariat, or purchase the supplies, or execute the field works, or select the Staff Officers, or pay the bill. It studies war from every possible point of view; it accumulates, sifts and examines the numbers and dispositions of the enemy; it computes the resources needed to overcome him. Now,

applying this example to the unemployment problem, it seems to me that the Board of Trade ought, each year, to endeavour to forecast, from all the information at its disposal, the relative degree of unemployment which will be reached . . . we should reproduce for the defence of this country against poverty and unemployment, the sort of machinery that we have in existence in the Committee of Imperial Defence to protect us against foreign aggression. There should be formed a Committee of National Organisation analogous in many respects to the Committee of Imperial Defence.

While President of the Board of Trade, Churchill intervened to resolve the engineering strike of November 1908. He was not a natural conciliator, being more prone to rapid action and to speech-making than to listening, and had much to learn from the 'Master', Lloyd George, who had successfully brought together the two sides in a number of industrial disputes.

Clearly, in 1908–10, Lloyd George's crusading spirit and Liberal reforms were having a deep influence on Churchill's thinking. After the resolution of the engineering strike Churchill wrote to his friend:

Can nothing be done to place a few Admiralty orders on the north-east coast and the Clyde in anticipation of the inevitable programme for next year; if not big ships, surely a few cruisers may be begun so as to carry the engineers and shipbuilders through the winter trade which promises to be exceptionally stringent. It does seem to me clumsy to let these people starve and have their homes broken up all winter and then some time in June and July when things are beginning to revive to crack on with a lot of new construction and have everybody working overtime. These ought to be the sort of situations which you and I are capable of handling.

From Lloyd George, Churchill was also learning the language of radicalism. It was Lloyd George's native tongue, not his own, and despite his efforts he spoke it with 'a difference'. This difference may not have been detected by his audiences but it was recognised by those who knew both the teacher and the pupil.

Lloyd George's former private secretary, Charles Masterman, wrote to his wife Lucy in 1908: 'Winston is full of the poor, whom he has just discovered. He thinks he is called by providence – to do something for them.' This was after Churchill's reading of Seebohm Rowntree's study of poverty in York, and his subsequent work at the Board of Trade to establish labour exchanges. As he told the Edwardian poet and traveller Wilfred Scawen Blunt: 'I would give my life to see [the poor] placed on a right footing in regard to their lives and means of living. That is what I am paid for, and I would really give my life.'

For Lloyd George, born and brought up in a small Welsh village by his uncle, the village cobbler, there was no need to discover the poor. To him, poverty was not a political concept but a stark fact which had entered into his being, bringing with it an instinctive hatred of the rich. Squires, landowners and even parsons were his hereditary enemies. As C. P. Snow put it in his collection of biographical portraits, *Variety of Men*:

> [Lloyd George] . . . saw England and the English class structure as a foreigner sees it. He never liked it, any more than his friend Beaverbrook, another foreigner, liked it. He chose never to be inside. He became one of the kings of this world: but there lurked within him the resentment of his upbringing, of a poor people outside the fringe, of a despised culture, of the Chapel against the Established Church . . . For years, right up to 1914, he was the only powerful politician with a voice that went deep into the population . . . he was the effective spokesman of the country's left . . . He had been a great tribune, but he was also a great minister.

In August 1908, Winston proposed to Clementine Hozier after taking her for a long walk in the rain to the summer pavilion at Blenheim, and she accepted. The marriage was arranged for a month later, 12 September, at St Margaret's, Westminster. Evidently the young bridegroom had not given much thought to the arrangements. Lord Hugh Cecil, writing to congratulate him, asked, 'Who is to be the best man?' Churchill replied, 'You will be.' Lloyd George also wrote to congratulate Churchill: 'Your luck has followed you into the most important transaction of your life.'

Writing on 29 August 1908 to thank Lloyd George for the wedding gift of a silver fruit basket, Churchill declared: 'It will always be preserved in my family as the gift of a remarkable man and as the symbol of a memorable political association . . . I shall remember the pleasant hours we have passed together in topics grave and gay, and the warm feelings of comradeship which unite us.' (Unfortunately, the silver basket is not in fact preserved in the Churchill family, and nobody knows its whereabouts.)

The fact that Churchill's stag dinner, held on 11 September, the night before his wedding, was attended by both Lloyd George and by A. G. Edwards, the Bishop of St Asaph, suggests that it was a decorous and well-behaved affair. Winston's son, Randolph, in his biography of his father, puzzles over the choice of this obscure Welsh divine to officiate at the wedding. Yet Edwards was an old and close friend of Lloyd George and the evidence suggests that it was he who chose the bishop on Churchill's behalf.

Lloyd George remembered with amusement that Churchill talked politics to him in the vestry, while waiting for his bride to arrive. He commented that he knew nobody else so obsessed with politics as Winston. It was a great bond between them, and to some extent their womenfolk had to put up with it. Winston was later to apologise to his wife Clemmie for his frequent absences from home, although he had made clear to her before their marriage that his 'political life' would have to take precedence over everything else. He was, however, to prove a loving husband and father over the next fifty-seven years.

Lloyd George was the only non-family friend invited to sign the register, and the only Cabinet colleague of Churchill's to attend his wedding (Asquith, Grey, Morley and the others were all away shooting in Scotland or otherwise enjoying the long summer recess). As the sole Minister of the Crown present at the reception, it was understandable that Lloyd George had to be 'marched round and round like the army in the pantomime', as one guest described it.

At the time of the wedding, Clemmie told F. E. Smith (later Lord Birkenhead) that '[Winston] was completely under Lloyd George's thumb'. Nevertheless she encouraged Churchill in his radical and Liberal sympathies and tried to influence him to lead a less extravagant lifestyle. Despite her efforts, Churchill remained incorrigibly aristocratic, with a love of champagne, cigars, gambling at the Monte Carlo casino, hunting and weekends at Blenheim Palace.

'My dear David', Churchill wrote in January 1909, 'This will be a critical year for both of us and also for the historic party we adorn.' The critical issue was the forthcoming Budget but there was also the question of the naval estimates over which, at this time, Churchill and Lloyd George were united in opposing the First Lord of the Admiralty, McKenna, in his desire to build four more Dreadnought battleships. Lloyd George would continue to put the financial needs of social reform before those of armament. Churchill's support for him over this issue is a sign of how radical he had now become.

The political alliance that was taking shape in the private recesses of Westminster between Lloyd George and Churchill did not burst upon the public consciousness until the so-called People's Budget in April 1909, when it became clear that Winston Churchill was indeed Lloyd George's principal disciple. There is no doubt that the People's Budget was a joint effort.

On Budget Day, 29 April, the Chancellor of the Exchequer and the President of the Board of Trade – both wearing pinstripe trousers, waistcoats, gold watches and chains, and top hats – walked together towards the House of Commons, carrying the despatch boxes. The Chancellor was observed to walk 'lightly and with twinkling eyes', while the President of the Board of Trade was 'grave with the weight of his colleague's responsibility'. The night before, Churchill had written: 'Tomorrow is the day of wrath!'

Lloyd George described the 1909 Budget as a 'war budget,' designed to raise money 'to wage implacable warfare against poverty'. Income tax was raised to 6 per cent; death duties to 15 per cent. He proposed several new taxes, including (red rag to a bull) taxes on land. Halfway through the Budget speech, which at four and a half hours was the longest ever, Lloyd George began to lose his voice. Churchill took him out for a short pause – and perhaps the 'usual restoratives'– after which he resumed his speech.

The People's Budget was historic because it changed the purpose of British government: its objective would be to redistribute the national wealth. As Lloyd George had said in 1906: 'There is plenty of wealth in this country to provide for all, and to spare. What is wanted is a fairer distribution.' Traditionally, the Liberal Party had stood for the promotion of individual freedom and laissez-faire economics; in other words, capitalism. The 1909 Budget was an enormous leap forward from Gladstone's Liberal philosophy, which had meant freedom from government intervention: governing best when governing least.

Despite a lack of enthusiasm among the rest of the Liberal Cabinet, Lloyd George and Churchill were determined to create the foundations of a British welfare state. Together they were first to fight against the Establishment between 1909 and 1911. It was to bind them closely for the rest of their careers because of the hatred which it engendered among peers and established property owners. Lord Rosebery, for example, who had been Liberal Prime Minister in 1894, described the 1909 Budget as 'the end of all, the negation of faith, of family, of property, of Monarchy, of Empire'.

During the long months of debates about the People's Budget there were a total of 554 divisions on different aspects of the bill. Lloyd George and Churchill would spend their mornings together, planning parliamentary strategy. Churchill was not always present in the Commons in the evenings because he was presiding over mass meetings of the Budget League, an organisation created to build up popular support for their cause. On one occasion, however, a story circulated at Westminster that Churchill had been seen attending a late-night division in the

LEGISLATION BY PYJAMA.

THERE ARE OTHERS BESIDES THE LANDOWNERS OF THE COUNTRY WHO ARE MADE TO "SIT UP" BY THE BUDGET.
(Mr. Winston Churchill was supposed to have been discovered on the Treasury Bench in pink pyjamas.)

House in his pyjamas. There is also an amusing Beerbohm cartoon of him, with his hands on the shoulders of his cousin the Duke of Marlborough, saying: 'There, there! There is nothing in the Budget which will prevent an honest working man from living in reasonable comfort in his own little home!'

Some historians maintain that Lloyd George and Churchill planned and hoped to provoke the House of Lords into rejecting the Budget Bill. Indeed, nearly thirty years later Lloyd George told Winston's son Randolph that he had deliberately included the land taxes to provoke the House of Lords.

Certainly the campaign against the House of Lords was a concerted one between Churchill and Lloyd George. Their rhetoric was similar; their tactics were conceived together; they had the

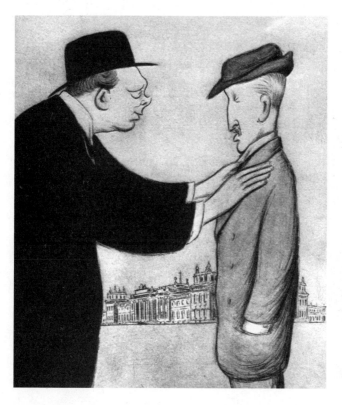

same objectives and favoured the same means of achieving them. Churchill told Asquith that their idea was to 'clink the coronets in their scabbards'. When, at the Free Trade Hall in Manchester in 1907 he had attacked the House of Lords as 'the fortress of negation and reaction' he had confidently expected that this fortress would fall and that the House of Commons 'will be master'. In 1908 he had declared: 'We shall send them up such a Budget in

June as shall terrify them, they have started the class war, they had better be careful.' Speaking in Birmingham the following year, Churchill said that the conflict would be 'upon the plain simple issue of aristocratic rule against representative government'.

The reaction to the People's Budget, not only of the House of Lords, but among the English upper classes in general, and many of Churchill's friends, relatives and closest acquaintances, was one of outrage; it provoked strong feelings against the two radical ministers who were dubbed, 'Cleon and Alcibiades' – the demagogue shoemaker and the renegade aristocrat. In some ways, the fiercest resentment was against the renegade aristocrat Churchill, who was perceived as a traitor to his class. And inevitably the social exclusion which followed the political divisions in these great years of reform, 1909–11, had an impact on the lives of the newly-married Churchills.

To the Lloyd Georges, social exclusion made little difference as they did not dine out in society and kept to their own small circle of friends. Winston and Clemmie, on the other hand, would still spend weekends at Blenheim. In the summer of 1911, Lloyd George had made an important and radical speech on his land reform and land-tax policies at Swindon. Clementine Churchill, staying at Blenheim with her sister-in-law Goonie (married to Winston's brother Jack), drew attention to the newspaper reports of Lloyd George's speech over breakfast, to the exasperation of the Duke of Marlborough. Later she sat down in the Blenheim library to write a letter of congratulation and support to the Welsh Chancellor but was discovered by the Duke. Seeing that she was writing on Blenheim paper (the letter is in the Lloyd George archives), 'Sunny' Marlborough announced, 'You cannot write to that man on my notepaper in my house!' Clementine rose without a word, packed her bags and took the first train back to London, despite the Duke's efforts to apologise. To Winston's great embarrassment, this caused a rift within the Churchill family for a year or two. It illustrates the way in which society was divided by the Liberal Government's radical policies and how the Churchills' strong support for Lloyd George cost them a good deal of social acceptance.

During the next two years, Lloyd George progressively took the case for social and political reform around the country, beginning in the East End of London with his famous Limehouse speech on 30 July 1909: 'It is rather hard that an old workman should have to find his way to the gates of the tomb bleeding and footsore, through the brambles and thorns of poverty. We cut a new path for him, an easier one, a pleasanter one, through fields of waving corn . . .'

He spoke at length about the 'unearned increment' of value gained by landlords such as the Dukes of Westminster or Northumberland, or the coalmine owners.

> Have you been down a coal mine? I went down one the other day. We sank down into a pit half a mile deep . . . The earth seemed to be straining . . . You could see the pit props bent and twisted . . . Sometimes they give way . . . Often a spark ignites . . . and the breath of life is scorched out of hundreds of breasts by the consuming flame . . . yet when the Prime Minister and I knock at the doors of these great landlords, and say to them: 'Here, you know these poor fellows who have been digging up royalties at the risk of their lives, some of them are old . . . they are broken, they can earn no more. Won't you give them something towards keeping them out of the workhouse?' they scowl at us. We say 'Only a halfpenny, just a copper.' They retort 'You thieves!' . . . If this is an indication of the view taken by these great landlords of their responsibility to the people who, at the risk of life, create their wealth, then I say their day of reckoning is at hand.

The Limehouse speech had wide repercussions; it was regarded as no less than revolutionary for the Chancellor himself to speak to working men in this vein, and the King was most upset, telling him that it represented 'a menace to prosperity and a socialistic spirit, which is peculiarly inappropriate and unsettling in a holder of your office'.

But on 9 October, in Newcastle, Lloyd George continued in the same vein: 'Who made ten thousand people owners of the soil, and the rest of us, trespassers in the land of our birth?'

Churchill could sound like a socialist too, as when arguing that landowners should have the option of paying death duties in the form of land:

> The more I think about it, the more it appeals to my sense of justice and to my notions of policy . . . its possession [land] by private people [is] undesirable . . .
>
> It may be in the public interest, and certainly it is in the public mood, that great estates should be broken up; but it cannot be in anybody's interest that they should merely be encumbered. The reduction, paring off, or division of large landed properties may easily be attended with an increase of population and prosperity in the district affected. But to have great landed estates strictly entailed, drifting about in a sort of waterlogged condition, only kept afloat by grinding economies and starvation of development, must be attended in this country, as in Ireland, with severe evils to the rural population . . . we must, I take it, view with favour all transferences of land to the State. We shall require, as the years go by, a continued supply of land, spread about all over the country . . . All comes back to the land; and in proportion as the State is the owner of the land, so in the passage of years, all will come back to the State.

In fact, Churchill and Lloyd George intuitively saw the real danger of socialism in the global situation of that time, when economic classes were so divided. In other European countries, revolution would indeed sweep away monarchs and landlords within the next ten years. But thanks to the reforming programme of the pre-war Liberal Government, Britain evolved peacefully towards a more egalitarian society. It is arguable that the peaceful revolution of the People's Budget prevented a much more bloody revolution, such as overtook Russia, Germany and Austria in the closing years of the First World War and soon afterwards. The paradox is that, in attacking the aristocracy and the House of Lords, these two radical statesmen enabled the old order to survive by changing. A century later, Britain still has a monarchy and an aristocracy, and a free democracy in which talent and wealth can flourish, while the poorest have the protection of a welfare state. The reforms passed in 1910–11 built a 'safety net', as Lloyd George had put it, under the working classes of Britain, helping to protect them from the worst effects of poverty, hunger, sickness, unemployment and old age.

Although in later life Churchill appeared as the archetypal Tory, he made clear in his eulogy at Lloyd George's memorial service in 1945 (see Epilogue) that no other British statesman had done so much for working people as had Lloyd George as Chancellor of the Exchequer. He (Churchill) had been 'his lieutenant and disciple in those bygone days' and had fully supported the strategy of laying the foundations of the future Welfare State . . . 'the pillars of [Lloyd George's] life's toil [will prove] upstanding, massive and indestructible.' And on these foundations was indeed to be built the broad superstructure of the welfare state, including the National Health Service, by Attlee's government between 1945 and 1951. (All of which, ironically, was to be bitterly opposed by Churchill in his Conservative old age.)

Sidney and Beatrice Webb, founders of the socialist Fabian Society, had invited Churchill to dinner in 1908 and were struck by how serious he had become about political and social reform. (He had been flirting with socialist ideas since 1907, particularly in his writings as Colonial Secretary in *My African Journey* [1908] and also in his book of speeches, *Liberalism and the Social Problem*, which is little read nowadays.) In 1909 Churchill declared:

I want things done. I want dreams, but dreams that are realizable. I want aspiration and discontent leading to a real paradise and a real earth in which men can live here and now, and fulfil the destiny of the human race. I want to make life better and kinder and safer – now at this moment. Suffering is too close to me. Misery is too near and insistent. Injustice is too obvious and glaring. Danger is too present.

Yet Lloyd George was always the radical leader, with the real credentials as the people's champion. From Churchill, as the grandson of a duke, Lloyd George's Limehouse speech of 1909 would have sounded somewhat incongruous: 'Oh these dukes – how they harass us . . . A fully fledged duke costs as much to keep up as two dreadnoughts [battleships] . . . Plough up the grouse moors, they are needed to grow food for the people . . . We shall squeeze them [the Lords] with taxes until the pips squeak.'

Within the Liberal Party, and the Liberal Cabinet, Churchill and Lloyd George stood alone in their reforming zeal. But Asquith, the Prime Minister, solidly supported them. On one occasion in 1909, when Lloyd George had expounded on his plan for land taxes, Asquith asked each Cabinet minister to give their view. Except for Churchill, they were, to a man – Grey, Morley, Harcourt, Crewe, McKenna . . . – opposed to the radical measures. Asquith summed up calmly by saying, 'Well, I think the general sense of the Cabinet is in favour [of the Chancellor].' As Lloyd George had told his friend D. R. Daniel in May 1909, 'I should say that I have Winston Churchill with me in the Cabinet, and above all the Prime Minister has backed me up through thick and thin with splendid loyalty. I have the deepest respect for him and he has real sympathy for the ordinary and the poor.' In the cartoon 'Getting into Deep Water', Papa Asquith tries to restrain his two young terrors from driving the Cabinet into the rising waters of political reform. Some of the speeches by Lloyd George and Churchill rather startled the old-fashioned Liberals.

The question as to whether Lloyd George and Churchill deliberately included the land taxes to trap the Lords into rejecting the People's Budget has been much debated. Wilfred Scawen Blunt recorded in his diary: 'Winston . . . began by saying that his hope and prayer was that [the Lords] would throw out the Bill, as it would save the Government from certain defeat if the Elections were put off.' But John Grigg, in his masterful biography of Lloyd

George, concludes that, although this may have been a distinct possibility, Lloyd George at any rate was a 'doer' who was, above all, anxious to get the key aspect of the People's Budget – national insurance – on to the statute book. The threat which Asquith

**GETTING INTO DEEP WATER.**

Master Winston (*to* Master Lloyd). "LAY INTO HIM, DAVID."
Papa Asquith. "STEADY ON, YOU YOUNG TERRORS; YOU 'RE MAKING IT VERY UNCOMFORTABLE FOR US IN HERE."

presented to the new king, George V, in 1910, that his Government would create five hundred Liberal peers to ensure the passage of the People's Budget through the Lords, was in the end sufficient to carry the vote.

When the Lords did indeed reject the Budget on 30 November 1909, a general election became inevitable. As Lloyd George may have foreseen, the outcome of the January 1910 election was by

### THE CHANCE OF A LIFETIME.

Our Mr. Asquith. "FIVE HUNDRED CORONETS, DIRT-CHEAP! THIS LINE OF GOODS OUGHT TO MAKE BUSINESS A BIT BRISKER, WHAT?"
Our Mr. Lloyd George. "NOT HALF; BOUND TO GO LIKE HOT CAKES."

no means assured for the Liberal Party, whose majority in fact dwindled from over 100 to 2. Only with the support of the Irish Nationalists, and therefore the promise of Home Rule, was Asquith able to form a new administration.

★

In the early years of the Liberal Government, from 1905 to 1910, the question of Home Rule for the Irish had loomed in the background; it did not become an acute issue until the Liberals lost their overall majority in 1910 and were therefore dependent on the eighty-two Irish Nationalist seats to form a governing majority. In this year Wilfrid Scawen Blunt recorded in his diary that he 'did not think Asquith or Grey or Haldane was really in earnest about Home Rule, though Churchill and Lloyd George were'.

Lloyd George and Churchill had reached this proposed solution to the Irish problem from opposite camps. Lloyd George's first public speech on the subject had been made in North Wales in 1886 when he introduced the Irish Fenian leader Michael Davitt to a crowded public meeting at Blaenau Ffestiniog. He sympathised with Irish aspirations to Home Rule and even seemed to lend his support to some of the more violent measures proposed by the Irish radicals.

Churchill, by contrast, had been born and bred a Unionist. In his first speech, delivered to a Conservative Association in Bath in 1897, Churchill had said, 'The Liberal Party is bound around the neck with the millstone of Home Rule.' Even after he had crossed the floor in 1904 Churchill wrote to his Manchester Liberal Association: 'I remain of the opinion that the creation of a separate Parliament for Ireland would be dangerous and impracticable.' But within a few months he had begun to change his tune. It can be no accident that the first hint of this was on his joint appearance with Lloyd George at Caernarvon Boroughs in October 1904, when he spoke of an extension of self-government being appropriate for the Irish.

Lloyd George's influence on Churchill was at its height during these early years. Not only did he persuade the younger man to take a more generous view of the need for social reform for the poorer working classes in Britain; he also no doubt persuaded him to take a broader view of the Irish problem. This, Churchill found easier by comparing possible solutions to the generous constitutional settlement which the Liberals were able to effect in South Africa.

Once Churchill was in the Cabinet he became more focused on the great political issues of the day, including the question of Home Rule. In April 1908 he wrote to Asquith that he had adopted Lloyd George's phrase, 'A free hand next time'; in other words, he favoured Home Rule after the next election because the Liberal Government might very well have to depend on Irish votes for its survival. His letter read:

> My opinion on the Irish question has ripened during the last two years, when I have lived in the inner counsels of Liberalism. I have become convinced that a national settlement of the Irish difficulty on broad and generous lines is indispensable to any harmonious conception of Liberalism – the object lesson is South Africa.

By early 1908 Churchill was appealing for Irish votes in his North-West Manchester constituency. In this, he enlisted the support of John Redmond, leader of the Irish Nationalist Party. Churchill told Redmond that it was 'the ambition of [his] life to bring about a Home Rule bill as chief secretary of Ireland'.

Another of the most controversial issues to affect the lives of both Churchill and Lloyd George in these years of their partnership was women's suffrage. During the second half of the nineteenth century the male franchise had expanded steadily to all households by 1884; this coincided with Lord Randolph Churchill's call for 'Tory democracy', and Gladstone's radical programme and final embodiment as 'the people's William'. It was not long before women too sought the vote, arguing that a wholly male Parliament had failed to achieve the many social changes that were needed. Women were able to play their part in local government, in which they had had the vote since 1894, and on school boards and local education committees, where they were very active. To the suffragists it seemed absurd that women were allowed to participate in all these political activities – and to act as canvassers and campaigners during elections – yet still were excluded from the national franchise.

Churchill and Lloyd George had radically different attitudes towards women and these coloured their approach to demands for suffrage. Churchill's may be characterised as Victorian: perhaps because of his parents' unconventional private lives, he reacted by becoming, if not prudish, at least reserved with young women. He showed a healthy romantic interest in music-hall actresses, and later in Pamela Plowden, among other young ladies, but did not enter into a full relationship until, at the age of thirty-four, he married Clementine Hozier. Lloyd George, on the other hand, had an active sex life in Criccieth and later in London. This reflected the difference between the 'natural' approach of growing up in the Welsh countryside and the artificial environment of an all-male public school and the Army.

Churchill's attitude to women was one of old-fashioned chivalry – see, for example, the character of Lucile in his novel *Savrola* (1900), whose virtue and public character the hero (Churchill in disguise) protects. In the eyes of the young Winston, woman was on a pedestal.

During his military service in India, Churchill commented on the parliamentary debate on women's suffrage, which he studied in the *Annual Register*. '. . . I shall unswervingly oppose this ridiculous movement [to give women the vote] . . . Once you give votes to the vast numbers of women who form the majority of the community, all power passes to their hands.' It was a reactionary sentiment fully in accord with those of his fellow cavalry officers in the Raj.

Even a decade later, in 1906, after he had joined the Liberal Party and begun to absorb and express fairly radical opinions about reform, Churchill still responded to his constituents in Manchester (a staunchly Liberal area) on the matter: 'I am not going to be *hen-pecked* [thus coining the word] on a question of such grave importance . . .' And instead of dealing with the demands of the suffragettes who disrupted his political meetings, he avoided the question by saying, 'We must observe courtesy and chivalry to the weaker sex . . .'

When a reference was made at a dinner party to the action of certain suffragettes in chaining themselves to railings and swearing to stay there until they got the vote, Churchill's reply was: 'I might as well chain myself to St Thomas's Hospital and say I would not move till I had had a baby.'

Nevertheless, it is noticeable that after his marriage to Clementine, his view of women began to change. He became more liberal and more worldly. His colleagues in the Liberal Cabinet, however, continued to tease him that his carefully prepared speeches were often interrupted by 'What about votes for women, Mr Churchill?'

Lloyd George, on the other hand, was known to support the 'suffragist' movement and had, early in life, taken a progressive view of female capabilities. He said in 1913 that seeing a production of Ibsen's *A Doll's House* in 1889 had a much greater influence on his views than hearing a speech by one of the early suffragettes, Lydia Becker. While he noted that Becker was rather sarcastic, Ibsen's portrayal of the dilemmas and injustices faced by married women had a marked impact on him: 'Ibsen was a great man. He converted me to women's suffrage. He had wonderful foresight and intuition.'

Lloyd George's knowledge of women was therefore far wider and deeper than Churchill's. He had been married in 1888, and by 1902 was the father of five children. Twice during his early career in Parliament he had been threatened by divorce cases: although he was exonerated, we may surmise that there was 'no smoke without fire'; he certainly took a great interest in the opposite sex and enjoyed their company. Later, Frances Stevenson – who in 1913 had become Lloyd George's mistress – would introduce him to novels of H. G. Wells, particularly such works as *Ann Veronica* (1909), which portrayed the liberated 'New Woman' in Edwardian society.

Lloyd George provided an example of his respect for women and their opinions when he was at supper with the Mastermans in 1910. Before the meal, he and Charles Masterman had discussed in detail Lloyd George's fourteen-point memorandum for a coalition – a highly confidential and politically explosive document. Masterman's wife, Lucy, recorded in her diary: 'As we sat down he said, "I'd like to know what you think of it, Mrs Masterman," and handed it to me.' Being a highly intelligent and politically acute young woman – not to mention, Gladstone's granddaughter – she was of course delighted to be consulted.

With these different attitudes, then, the two friends found themselves at some variance on the issue of votes for women.

The suffragette Emmeline Pankhurst had founded the Women's Social and Political Union (WSPU) in 1903. Its weekly newspaper would have a circulation of 160,000 readers at its peak and attracted major advertisers such as Express Dairy, Dunlop and the large London department stores, which dressed their windows in WSPU colours. More extreme demonstrations did not take place until the Liberals assumed power in 1905, when advocates of votes for women were encouraged by the inclusion in Campbell-Bannerman's Cabinet of four ministers who were said to be strong supporters of the cause: Grey, Haldane, Birrell and Lloyd George. As *The Times* reported on 7 December:

> For the first time a Prime Minister had declared it to be an open question, not merely for his party but for his Cabinet as well; and it was that declaration which enabled him [Lloyd George] without imputation of disloyalty to his chief or his colleagues, to stand there and advocate women's suffrage, and it was that declaration which would enable him and several of his colleagues to vote in the House of Commons for the inclusion of women's enfranchisement in the Government's Reform Bill to be submitted to the present Parliament.

But Asquith was against giving women the vote. One of the problems for the Liberals was that, if they granted a franchise that was limited to women of property (as had happened to men in the later nineteenth century), such women were likely to vote Conservative. On the other hand, it was almost unthinkable – and revolutionary – to give 6 million women the vote overnight.

Both Lloyd George and Churchill attracted close attention from suffragettes between the years 1906 and 1909. This further alienated Churchill from their cause: 'For the last five years you have disturbed me or tried to disturb me at every meeting I have addressed . . . if I have been returned [to Parliament] on three occasions, it has been in spite of every effort of the militant suffragettes to prevent me.' In this speech of 1911, Churchill seems to have missed the point: that, as the focus of publicity wherever they went, he and Lloyd George were obvious targets for Christabel Pankhurst and her followers.

The suffragettes took pleasure in ruining Churchill's meetings while he was campaigning for the People's Budget of 1909. When he spoke of the 'moral, spiritual, civic and scientific forces to be released' by the Budget, they demanded the release of their moral, spiritual, civic and scientific comrades from prison and, by way of argument, threw coke at him. When he went to Newcastle to inspect the shipyards, he was approached no fewer than fifteen times on the first day by enthusiastic suffragettes. On the second day they waylaid him at his hotel, at a reception in his honour, on the quay, in the launch that took him to a ship, in the ship herself, and at the railway station when he returned to London. Because of this he had to travel with two detectives; even his daughter Diana, born in 1909, had to be guarded in her pram in case the suffragettes tried to kidnap her. (Diana was a particularly beautiful child on whom Churchill doted, as he did on all his children. Lloyd George once remarked to him, 'Like her mother, I suppose?' Churchill's response was: 'No, she is exactly like me.' During the suffragette attacks Lloyd George is quoted as saying that the only way to get Churchill to react would be 'if they cut Diana's throat'.)

Following the general election of 1910, Asquith appointed Churchill to the Home Office. As Home Secretary he incurred even more suffragist hostility, for he was then responsible for both police and prisons. Even though the suffragettes benefited from the more humane measures of prison reform which Churchill pressed through – allowing those in prison to wear their own clothes, have their hair cut, obtain food from outside, receive books and socialise with other prisoners – this attempted alleviation of their self-imposed martyrdom only infuriated them the more.

Nor was it exclusively female suffragettes who were to target the two politicians. Hugh Franklin of the Men's Political Union achieved notoriety by attempting to whip the new Home Secretary on the train to London. (Churchill allegedly took the dog whip and pocketed it.) In December 1911 Lloyd George also came under attack: 'On Saturday Lloyd George was violently assaulted by a male suffragist . . .', *The Times* reported, 'because they thought he was a little devil who had a knack of getting things through, and that if stimulated he would secure the vote'. A cartoon in *Punch* showed Churchill promising his radical associate, dressed as a poacher, that he will protect him if he can. Male suffragists undermined Churchill's scheme of refusing to admit women to meetings unless their ticket was signed by a member of the Liberal Party by allowing in women who they knew intended to cause a disturbance.

It did not help Churchill to avoid the suffragettes' close attention that his position on the vote for women was apparently so changeable. According to Christabel Pankhurst's sister, Sylvia, at a meeting in the Free Trade Hall in Manchester on 4 February 1907 he had stated that he would not vote for a bill to enfranchise women on the same terms as men. During the Manchester by-election of April the following year, however, Churchill is quoted as saying: 'Trust me, ladies, I am your friend, and will be your friend in the Cabinet. I will do my best, as and when occasion offers, because I do think sincerely that the women have always had a logical case, and they have now got behind them a great popular demand amongst women.'

"WHEN CONSTABULARY DUTY'S TO BE DONE."

Mr. Lloyd George (to the new Home Secretary). "I SUPPOSE YOU'RE GOING TO SETTLE DOWN NOW?"
Mr. Winston Churchill. "YES; BUT I SHAN'T FORGET YOU. IF YOU FIND YOURSELF IN TROUBLE I'LL SEE
IF I CAN'T GET YOU A REPRIEVE, FOR THE SAKE OF OLD TIMES!"

Campaigning in Dundee, after his defeat at Manchester, he went a stage further and said: 'The next Parliament, I think, ought to see the gratification of the women's claim: I do not exclude the possibility of the suffrage being dealt with in this Parliament.'

In spite of these affirmations, on 12 October 1910 Lucy Masterman reported in her diary:

Winston and Charlie had a very curious morning over the Conciliation Bill. He is, in a rather tepid manner, a suffragist (his wife is very keen) and he came down to the Home Office intending to vote for the Bill. Charlie, whose sympathy with the suffragettes is rather on the wane, did not want him to, nor did Lloyd George. So Charlie began to put to him the points against Shackleton's Bill – its undemocratic nature, and especially particular points, such as that 'fallen women' would have the vote but not the mother of a family, and other rhetorical points. Winston began to see the opportunity for a speech on these lines, and as he paced up and down the room, began to roll off long phrases. By the end of the morning he was convinced that he had always been hostile to the Bill and that he had already thought of all these points himself. (The result was a speech of such violence and bitterness that Lady Lytton wept in the gallery and Lord Lytton cut him in public. Charlie thinks that his *mind* had up till then been in favour of the suffrage but that his *instinct* was always against it. He snatched at Charlie's arguments against this particular Bill as a wild animal snatches at its food. At the end the instinct had completely triumphed over the mind.)

The Conciliation Bill was designed to conciliate the suffragist movement by giving a limited number of women the vote, according to their property holdings and marital status. While it did not meet women's demands for the vote on the same footing as men, most women were prepared to support it and a truce was called on militancy so as not to alienate potential support. However, the bill foundered.

On 18 November 1910, protesting against the casting of the Conciliation Bill into the political wilderness, small bands of women started moving from WSPU headquarters towards Parliament Square, carrying banners with legends such as 'Where there's a Bill there's a Way' and 'Women's "Will" Beats Asquith's "Won't"'. In Parliament Square the police were under instruction to keep the women away from the House of Commons and not to arrest them, except under provocation. In these simple tactics may be detected the hand of Churchill, the Home Secretary, whose once loud support for women's suffrage had dwindled until the WSPU were inclined to count him among the subtlest of their enemies.

Soon afterwards the enraged Pankhursts led a deputation – or an army – to Downing Street. There they encountered an unprepared and paltry police presence and set upon both Asquith and the Irish Secretary, Augustine Birrell. When the street was finally, and with difficulty, cleared, who should make his appearance but the Home Secretary. Only one suffragette remained, leaning against the wall in utter exhaustion. Churchill, as usual, was unable to resist the dramatic gesture and, beckoning to a policeman, instructed him to drive 'that woman' away, even though he knew her to be Mrs Cobden-Sanderson, an intimate friend of his wife's family and his hostess on several occasions. The story went round London and reflected badly on the Liberal Government.

It was Churchill more than any other politician who, in 1910, killed the first Conciliation Bill by pointing out its 'undemocratic' nature; in fact, he argued in debate in the Commons that it was more than undemocratic, it was anti-democratic:

It gives an entirely unfair representation of property as against person. I have only to turn to what we have heard quoted frequently in the debate – namely Mr [Charles] Booth's figures in regard to London [Life and Labour of the People in London, 1903] . . . Of the 180,000 women voters it is calculated that 90,000 are working women, earning their living. What about the other half? . . . The basic principle of the Bill is to deny votes to mothers and wives – that is to say, to deny votes to those who are upon the whole the best of their sex. We are asked by this Bill to defend the proposition that a spinster of means living on the interest of man-made capital is to have a vote, and the working man's wife is to be denied a vote even if she is a wage-earner and a wife. This is the new democracy.

Lloyd George too had been exercised by the political consequences of the Conciliation Bill, which gave only a limited franchise – to propertied women. On 11 August 1911, during a visit to Lloyd George's home in Criccieth, Charles Masterman reported that:

> He was very much disturbed about the Conciliation Bill, of which he highly disapproved although he is a universal suffragist. 'I don't want to get tangled up in it,' is his view. We had promised a week (or more) for its full discussion. Again and again he cursed that promise. He could not see how we could get out of it, yet he regarded it as fatal (if passed) or if the Lords appealed against it.

Lloyd George, as the Chancellor of an anti-suffragist Prime Minister, found himself in an awkward position. When he spoke at Liberal meetings in favour of women's suffrage, he was subjected to the usual interruptions from suffragettes who wanted to know, not whether he was in favour in principle of giving women the vote, but when his government intended to do so. On the other hand, the Chancellor was one of the most influential factors in the failure of the first Conciliation Bill. He objected to it as being insufficiently broad and incapable of amendment. He voted for a new definition in 1911 (Churchill abstained) but when the bill was reintroduced in 1912 he greatly offended its supporters by claiming that it had been 'torpedoed' by the Government's Reform Bill. It was hardly surprising that offence was taken: suffragists who had laboured for half a century to get the vote, had finally been given a pledge of support by the Liberal leaders – and then disappointed.

The zeal shown by Lloyd George and Churchill in frustrating the Conciliation Bill casts suspicion on their attitude towards votes for women. Surely a pilot scheme on such a controversial issue ought to have been favoured by all who believed in the principle? Sylvia Pankhurst seems to have made an accurate assessment when she said: 'Churchill, a weathercock towards this cause, as to many others, was probably an opponent at heart . . . Lloyd George was attempting to win laurels as the heroic champion of women's suffrage without jeopardising his place in a cabinet headed by an anti-suffragist Prime Minister.'

After the failure of the Conciliation Bill, the stakes were raised on both sides. Lloyd George remarked: 'The Liberal Party ought to make up its mind as a whole that it will either have an extended franchise which would put working men's wives on to the Register, as well as spinsters and widows, or that it will have no female franchise at all.' Meanwhile, women's pressure groups, in particular the Women's Liberal Federation (WLF), warned that the Liberal Party risked alienating their support if a Reform Bill were to be enacted without giving the vote to women. Such an outcome would be seriously embarrassing to both sides, and both pro- and anti-suffrage campaigners increased their efforts for a final push. As Grey and Lloyd George addressed suffragist rallies (Lloyd George declaring optimistically to the WLF, 'Our success next year, I think, is assured. I do not see what there is to prevent it'), their high-profile role had the effect of driving other Liberal ministers, notably McKenna and Harcourt, to attend an anti-suffragist rally at the Royal Albert Hall.

Asquith was put into what his wife called a 'hopeless and even ridiculous' situation, seemingly unable to avert the schism of his Cabinet. In the event, the entire enterprise was wrecked by the Speaker of the House unexpectedly declaring that because the Reform Bill was purely a registration bill it would be impossible to alter its character by including women's suffrage – a manoeuvre for which most blamed the Prime Minister. Morale among Liberal women was at rock bottom: 'There is nothing to hope for from the Liberal Party even when Home Rule and Welsh Disestablishment are out of the way,' wrote the prominent suffragist Catherine Marshall. 'I am becoming rather discredited as a false prophet because I have so often predicted better things of Mr Lloyd George than he has performed.'

In fact, Lloyd George remained the strongest proponent of women's suffrage, despite the fact that, in 1913, the suffragettes exploded a bomb at the back of his house at Walton Health in Surrey (fortunately he was away at the time). Asquith was against female suffrage and Churchill at best was lukewarm on the issue. Eventually it was to be the contribution of women to the 1914–18 war effort, especially in the production of shells and armaments under the auspices of Lloyd George's Ministry of Munitions, that made it inevitable that the vote be granted to women. Fittingly, it was under his premiership that the 1918 Representation of the People Act was passed which gave a vote to women over thirty who were either householders or graduates.

# 3

## 1910–14: In the Shadow of the Great War

'*Y Gwir yn Erbyn y Byd* (The Truth Against the World)'
Proclamation made at the annual Eisteddfod,
adapted by Lloyd George as his family motto

IN RESPONSE TO the House of Lords rejection of the People's Budget in November 1909, Asquith had reportedly asked the King to agree to the immediate creation of five hundred Liberal peers. This was to ensure the passage of the Budget through the Upper House.

Both Lloyd George and Churchill despised the House of Lords and were quite prepared to promote Asquith's plan to swamp the votes of the Tory peers. (Interestingly, Lloyd George would become an earl in old age. Churchill, having been briefly, as a young boy, heir to the dukedom of Marlborough, refused the offer of George VI in 1946 to become Duke of London. He refused it again in 1955 and died as 'plain' Sir Winston.)

On the subject of the House of Lords, Charles Masterman noted that 'At some point Lloyd George and Churchill were thinking in vague terms about coalition governments and reform of the House of Lords that would be acceptable to both parties. Their friendship was still close, although now Lloyd George was less of a father-figure and more of an equal.' At a weekend in Folkestone in February [1910], Churchill, over-tired and suffering from a chill, worried about having 'every mortal disease

74

under Heaven'. After absorbing some whisky, some champagne and some port, he took a more cheerful view of life.

> They are extremely funny together, with their different weaknesses and different childishnesses. At one point Winston said, 'I am all for the social order.' George, who had had a glass of champagne, which excites him without in the least confusing him, sat up in his chair and said, 'No! I'm against it. Listen. There were six hundred men turned off by the G. W. [Great Western railway] works last week. Those men had to go out into the street to starve. There is not a man in that works who does not live in terror of the day when his turn will come to go. Well, I'm against a social order that admits of that kind of thing.' 'Yeth, yeth,' said Winston hurriedly, subdued for a moment, and then rather mournfully: 'I suppose that was what lost us Cricklade.' 'Yes, and Swindon,' said George. Churchill cocked his nose in the way he does when he knows he is going to be impertinent. 'That's just what I say,' he answered, 'you are not against the social order, but against those parts of it that get in your way,' and George crumpled up with amusement.

Three days after Asquith's showdown with the King about the Labour peers in 1910, Lloyd George and Churchill were playing golf on the Walton Heath links when they ran into Joseph Lawrence, the Conservative MP for Monmouth Boroughs. Their conversation on the golf course typified the light-hearted spirit in which the Edwardians approached an election:

L. GEORGE: Hello, Lawrence why aren't you electioneering?
LAWRENCE: I am waiting for you.
L. GEORGE: What's the betting?
LAWRENCE: Two to one on us!
L. GEORGE: I'll take you.
LAWRENCE: In Sovereigns?
L. GEORGE: All right!
LAWRENCE: Agreed.
WINSTON: Will you lay me the same odds?

LAWRENCE:  Yes – in Sovereigns.

WINSTON:  Right!

Lloyd George had started playing golf in Wales in the early 1900s and became an enthusiastic player with a handicap of about fifteen. Much as the aristocratic politicians of the nineteenth century spent their country weekends hunting, shooting and fishing, Lloyd George was perhaps typical of the new middle class in the Edwardian era in taking up golf as his principal form of recreation. In the years before the First World War, golf often provided the opportunity for a weekend rendezvous with his fellow Liberal MPs and Cabinet ministers. Walton Heath, about half an hour's drive from Westminster in those days, was the most popular golf course among politicians; it was in the countryside and provided a welcome retreat from the daily pressure of political life. (On the day of a big Budget debate in the Commons the Prime Minister, Asquith, was surprised to meet his Chancellor of the Exchequer in Downing Street, dressed for golf. But Lloyd George reassured him, 'Don't worry, I'll be back in time for the debate.')

Lloyd George was introduced to the Walton Heath golf club in December 1907 by its proprietor, the solicitor and newspaper owner George Riddell, who became a close friend and confidant. He in turn brought his friend Winston Churchill in as a member in 1910. Other members of the club included Balfour and Bonar Law on the Conservative side, and Rufus Isaacs, Masterman, McKenna, Lord Crewe, Alexander Murray and the Chief Whip Percy Illingworth on the Liberal side.

Churchill, who was never as enthusiastic a player as Lloyd George, was inclined to regard golf as a background to political gossip and debate. He would often remain in the clubhouse, rehearsing his speeches for the House of Commons. But he recognised the therapeutic value of the game, writing to his wife in 1911: 'My darling one, I shall be back between 11 and 12 and I thought it would do us both good to play a little golf at Walton

Heath.' Although he claimed to have a handicap of eighteen he was not a very good player, describing golf as 'like chasing a quinine pill around a pasture' or 'a game whose aim it is to hit a very small ball into an even smaller hole, with weapons singularly ill-designed for the purpose'.

The unexpected death of King Edward VII in May 1910 threw the political world into turmoil. When he died, the King had still given no commitment on the question of the House of Lords.

The new King, George V, who was inexperienced in political matters, therefore found himself faced with a constitutional crisis which led ultimately to the Parliament Act of 1911. J. L. Garvin, editor of the *Observer*, made the suggestion that there should be 'a truce' between the two parties for a period of six months. His suggestion was adopted, and during the truce period a constitutional conference was convened with four leaders from each party: Asquith, Lloyd George, Crewe and Birrell from the Government and Balfour, Lansdowne, Austen Chamberlain and Lord Cawdor from the Opposition. They reached no agreement on the issue of the House of Lords and so, on 17 August, Lloyd George drew up a memorandum that would pave the way for a coalition government; in it, he covered housing, drink, insurance, unemployment, the poor law, education, defence, local government, trade, farming, imperial problems and foreign policy. Churchill was probably the most important supporter of Lloyd George's initiative. Asquith's view, as always, was 'wait and see', and so the six-month party truce petered out without resolution.

Lloyd George and Churchill had spent much of the summer of 1910 (the year of Halley's comet) discussing the idea of a coalition with the Conservatives. Both men had good friends on the other side of the House. Churchill had formed a close friendship with F. E. Smith, perhaps the most gifted barrister, orator and wit of his generation. And despite having crossed the floor, he had retained his friendship with other Conservatives, men such as Hugh Cecil, Lord Curzon and Sir Edward Carson. Lloyd George had become friendly with Andrew Bonar Law, the son of an Ulster Presbyterian Minister who represented a Glasgow constituency and had unexpectedly been elevated to the leadership of the Tories when Balfour stepped down in 1911.

At the end of September Winston and Clementine visited the Lloyd George family at their new home, Brynawelon, the 'House of the Breezes', on top of the hill in Criccieth. Shortly before their arrival, on 25 September, Lloyd George had written to Churchill:

> I am delighted to find that Mrs Winston Churchill and yourself will be able to spend a few days with us here. I think I can guarantee you an enjoyable time, weather permitting.
>
> I hope you will bring your golf clubs with you. We can arrange an excellent 'foursome'. My big boy, [Richard was twenty-one], who has just finished his Cambridge career, plays much better golf than either you or I used to play at Walton Heath, and he and Mrs Winston Churchill, with a couple of biscs [shots handicap], will more than hold their own against us. The motor-runs around here are very fine; and if you care for sea-fishing, there is plenty of it in the Bay. But I hope we shall be able to squeeze in some serious talk about the future.
>
> I have never known a time when things were as uncertain as they seem to be now: our real danger is that the Government will drift along without any clear definite policy or purpose. I am perfectly certain that our more important associates have no plan of operations in their minds . . .

During the Churchills' stay Lloyd George took them golfing, boating and picnicking in the mountains but it seems inevitable that the two statesmen also continued to discuss in some detail the idea of a coalition. Winston and Clemmie then went deer-stalking in Scotland, from where Winston wrote a warm letter of thanks:

6th October 1910 (from Scotland)

My dear David,

We enjoyed our visit to your beautiful country and house very much indeed. My wife and I will always remember your kindness and hospitality; and Wales in sunshine, shadow and sunset did the honours by sea and land not less agreeably. I hope we may some day be asked again.

. . . if we stood together we ought to be strong enough either to impart a progressive character to policy, or by withdrawal to terminate an administration which had failed in its purpose. Let us dine on Tuesday and talk to Grey about it all.

The year 1911 was, in the words of his biographer John Grigg, Lloyd George's *annus mirabilis* – a year of heavy legislation during which he dominated the House of Commons. In particular he steered the Finance Bill through the House and when it came to the moment of decision regarding the People's Budget, the Cabinet accepted the 'Lloyd George/Winston view of tactics, the wisest and the boldest'.

Churchill, who had now been promoted to the Home Office, was anxious as always to hog the limelight. He was to make himself somewhat notorious by his conduct during the Sidney Street siege of 3 January 1911. A gang of anarchists, holed up in a house in Stepney that was surrounded by police, had killed two constables and wounded a third. For the first time, the Home Secretary authorised the issue of revolvers to the police and, in line with his usual military approach to crises, Churchill also instructed twenty Scots Guards armed with rifles and the Royal Horse Artillery with cannon to break the siege. Churchill, unable to resist the front line, was photographed in his top hat behind the police sharpshooters. The siege was brought to an end when the house caught fire and the anarchists, who turned out to be from Latvia, were burned to death inside. Churchill, when questioned at the inquest about his actions, accepted responsibility for not having allowed the fire brigade to intervene. His opinion of the anarchists was similar to his later opinion of the Bolsheviks, whom he despised. When he got back to the Home Office, Charles Masterman burst into his room and asked, 'What the hell have you been doing now, Winston?' Churchill replied, '*Now* Charlie. Don't be croth. It was such fun!'

On the other hand, as Home Secretary Churchill made some important reforms in the treatment of prisoners, in particular with regard to the practice of solitary confinement which the writer John Galsworthy had highlighted in his prison drama *Justice* (1910). Churchill himself, having been a prisoner of war for a few weeks in Pretoria during the Boer War, could sympathise with the plight of those held in similar circumstances.

For two years, Churchill and Lloyd George had been engrossed in the People's Budget and the ambitious programme of social reform that was associated with it. Among the most admired models for national insurance and old-age pensions was the German scheme, originally established by Bismarck. This had led Lloyd George to visit Berlin and Hamburg, where he met the German Vice-Chancellor for the Interior, Theobald von Bettmann Hollweg. In 1908 Churchill had been invited to observe military manoeuvres with the Kaiser, Wilhelm II, and had been equally impressed by what he saw. Neither of them took seriously the threat of German naval and military expansion – and its impact on British interests – until they were confronted with the Agadir crisis of 1911. Events, however, were soon to awaken them from their complacency.

On 1 July, Berlin announced that the Kaiser had dispatched his gunboat *Panther* to Agadir, on the coast of Morocco, to monitor and protect German interests. Since Morocco was, in all but name, a French Protectorate, this constituted a direct challenge to the existing 'balance of power' in Europe. Britain – because of her *Entente Cordiale* with France of 1904 – was also drawn into the dispute.

Agadir was essentially a repeat of the Kaiser's attempt in 1905, while ashore at Tangier, to claim that he was the Sultan of

Morocco's protector; but, like that previous German sally, the Kaiser's grandiose imperial ambitions and impetuosity had the opposite effect to what he intended. The whole of Europe was now alerted to his aspirations and their naval significance.

On 4 July the Foreign Secretary, Sir Edward Grey, informed the German ambassador Count Metternich that the British Government could not overlook events in Morocco. There was no apparent reaction from Berlin.

Churchill recounted in the first volume of *The World Crisis* (his history of the First World War) that during early July he had numerous conversations with Lloyd George, who gave him the impression of wavering between the radical pacifists and the Liberal imperialists. Since his stand against the Boer War in 1899–1901 he had been widely seen as a pacifist and a 'little Englander'. In fact, despite his nonconformist origins, Lloyd George was deeply interested in military history and strategy, and by no means an opponent of the British Empire, to which he was later responsible for making significant additions in the Middle East and Africa. We may be sure, however, of Churchill's position, and in which direction he urged his friend to move. He does not betray their private discussions in his account of Agadir:

> On the morning of July 21, when I visited [Lloyd George] before the Cabinet, I found a different man. His mind was made up. He saw quite clearly the course to take. He knew what to do, and how and when to do it. The tenor of his statement to me was that we were drifting into war. He was to address the Bankers at their Annual Dinner [at the Mansion House] that evening, and . . . intended to make it clear that if Germany meant war, she would find Britain against her.

Lloyd George showed the draft of his Mansion House speech to Churchill and to Asquith and Grey. 'I said that of course they would be very much relieved; and they were, and so was I. The accession of Mr Lloyd George in Foreign Policy to the opposite wing of the Government was decisive.'

What Lloyd George said at the Mansion House was:

> . . . if a situation were to be forced upon us in which peace could only be preserved by the surrender of the great and beneficent position Britain has won by centuries of heroism and achievement, by allowing Britain to be treated, where her interests were vitally affected, as if she were of no account in the Cabinet of Nations, then I say emphatically that peace at that price would be a humiliation intolerable for a great country like ours to endure.

Although the City bankers may not have grasped its full significance, it did not need a trained diplomat to translate this message to the Chancellery in Berlin. Lloyd George's speech was a thunderclap to the German Government. They were furious with Metternich, the German Ambassador, who would be swiftly recalled to Berlin. How, after ten years' residence in London, could he not have anticipated Lloyd George's reaction? But in fact, as Churchill wrote, 'Until a few hours before, his colleagues did not know. I did not know. No one knew. Until his mind was definitely made up, he did not know himself . . .'

Four days later, Churchill and Lloyd George were walking by the fountains outside Buckingham Palace when a messenger approached them, urgently requesting that they go at once to see Sir Edward Grey. Lloyd George turned to Winston and said, 'That's my speech. The Germans may demand my resignation as they did Delcassé's [the French Foreign Minister].' Churchill replied, 'That will make you the most popular man in England.' (According to C. P. Snow, 'For many years in Conservative circles Lloyd George was the most hated man in England [because of the new taxes in the People's Budget].'

Grey's first words to them were: 'I have just received a communication from the German Ambassador so stiff that the Fleet might be attacked at any moment. I have sent for McKenna [First Lord of the Admiralty] to warn him!'

Churchill's account of this incident endorses the view of Bob

Boothby, his Parliamentary Private Secretary, who once observed: 'Although Keynes rightly described *The World Crisis* as one of the most powerful tractates against war ever written, War was [Churchill's] element and Power his objective':

> They sound so very cautious and correct, those deadly words. Soft, quiet voices purring, courteous, grave, exactly-measured phrases in large peaceful rooms. But with less warning, cannons had opened fire and nations had been struck down by this same Germany. So now the Admiralty wireless whispers through the ether to the tall masts of ships, and captains pace their decks absorbed in thought. It is nothing. It is less than nothing. It is too foolish, too fantastic to be thought of in the twentieth century. Or is it fire and murder leaping out of the darkness at our throats, torpedoes ripping bellies of half-awakened ships, a sunrise on a vanished national supremacy, and an island well-guarded hitherto, at last defenceless? No, it is nothing . . . Civilisation has climbed above such perils. The independence of nations in trade and traffic, the sense of public law, the Hague Convention, Liberal principles, the Labour party, high finance, Christian charity, common sense have rendered such nightmares impossible.

The German diplomats soon changed tack and became more accommodating. They had been surprised by Britain's belligerent stance and firm support for France and were clearly not ready for war at this stage. In consequence, however, the Germans accelerated their ship-building programme and naval build-up.

A week later, Churchill attended a garden party at 10 Downing Street. Here, by chance, he talked to the Chief Commissioner of Police, Sir Edward Henry, from whom he learned that the Home Office was responsible for the security of the magazines near London where the reserves of naval cordite were stored. Churchill's imagination was fired by a vision of German saboteurs blowing up this strategic stockpile; he hurriedly left the garden party, telephoned the Admiralty and then called the War Office with instructions to dispatch troops to guard the cordite reserves.

Churchill had made the discovery that there was a network of German agents operating in Britain. He assumed that, in the event of war, Britain, France and Russia would form an alliance against Germany and Austria, and that decisive military operations would be between France and Germany. On 13 August he dictated a memorandum to the Committee of Imperial Defence, embodying his his vision of how the first months of a European War would develop:

'The German army is at least equal in quality to the French, and mobilizes 2,200,000 against 1,700,000. The French must therefore seek for a situation of more equality. This can be found either before the full strength of the Germans has been brought to bear or after the German army has become extended. The first might be reached between the ninth and thirteenth days; the latter about the fortieth'. . . . [Churchill] stressed that the German attack would break through the line of the Meuse on the twentieth day and that the French would then fall back on Paris and the south . . . 'All plans based upon the opposite assumption ask too much of fortune.'

He showed how the impetus of the German advance would be weakened as it progressed. 'By the greater losses incidental to the offensive; by the greater employment of soldiers necessitated by acting on exterior lines; by having to guard their communications through Belgium and France (especially from the sea flank); by having to invest Paris (requiring at least 500,000 men against 100,000) and to besiege or mask other places, especially along the sea-board; by the arrival of the British Army; by the growing pressure of Russia from the thirtieth day; and generally by the bad strategic situation to which their right-handed advance will commit them as it becomes pronounced.'

The result of this would mean that by the fortieth day Germany 'should be extended at full strain both internally and on her war fronts' and that this strain would become daily 'more severe and ultimately overwhelming . . . Such a policy demands heavy and hard sacrifices from France, who must, with great constancy, expose herself to invasion, to having her provinces occupied by the enemy, and to the investment of Paris, and whose armies may be committed to retrograde or defensive operations. Whether her rulers could contemplate or her soldiers endure this trial may depend upon the military support which Great Britain can give; and this must be known beforehand, so that we may know, before we decide, what they would be prepared to do.'

Churchill then outlined the measures Britain should take, including 107,000 men to be sent to France on the outbreak of war and 100,000 troops of the British Army in India who should be moved at once out of India, enabling them to reach Marseilles by the fortieth day.

'This fine army, almost entirely composed of professional soldiers, could be assembled around (say) Tours by the fortieth day, in rear of the French left (instead of being frittered into action piecemeal), and would then become a very important factor in events. The Russian army would also by then be engaged in full force on the eastern frontiers of Germany and Austria, and the power of the three allies should then be sufficient either to hold the Germans in a position of growing difficulty, or if desirable, to assume the offensive in concert . . .

'The steady augmentation of British military strength during the progress of the war would, however, put us in a position by the end of the twelfth month to secure or re-establish British interests outside Europe, even if, through the defeat or desertion of the allies, we were forced to continue the war alone. No lesser steps would seem adequate to the scale of events.'

This was one of the most prescient strategic documents that Churchill ever wrote. Its forecast of the military timetable of the German invasion of Belgium and France, three years later, proved right almost to the day.

On 23 August 1911 the Committee of Imperial Defence (which had been established by Balfour in 1903) met secretly under Asquith's chairmanship to discuss what action Britain should take if France were to be attacked by Germany. The all-day meeting opened with a brilliant exposé by General Sir Henry Wilson (later to be Lloyd George's Chief of the Imperial General Staff) of how a British Expeditionary Force could help the French to withstand a German invasion through Belgium. The Army had clearly done some forward thinking. It was obvious, however, that the Admiralty was seriously unprepared to transport troops across the English Channel, let alone for a European war.

Asquith realised that he needed to replace Reginald McKenna, the First Lord of the Admiralty, in order to reform the administration of the Navy. His first choice of successor was Richard Haldane, his oldest friend and legal colleague. However, the First Lord of the Admiralty would be better placed as a Member of the House of Commons and Haldane sat in the House of Lords. Lloyd George therefore strongly suggested to Asquith that Churchill was the right man for the job.

That September Churchill and his wife went to Scotland, staying first at Balmoral where he had long talks with King George V. The King was very worried by the 'electrifying disclosures' of Lloyd George on a recent visit – that it might be better to have a war with Germany immediately, even though the country was unprepared. After spending a few days at Balmoral the Churchills went on to stay with the Asquiths at Archerfield, near North Berwick. While Winston and Asquith were playing golf, the Prime Minister offered Churchill the post of First Lord of the Admiralty. As Asquith's daughter, Violet, recalled: she was just finishing tea when Winston came in, looking radiant. 'Will you come out for a walk with me – at once?' he asked. Did he want tea? she inquired. He replied, 'No, I don't want tea.' They were hardly out of the house when he continued, 'I don't want anything – anything in the world. Your father has just offered me the Admiralty.' Later he said, 'Look at the people I have had to deal with so far – judges and convicts! This is a big thing – the biggest thing that has ever come my way – the chance I should have chosen before all others. I shall pour into it everything I've got.' Churchill recalled their walk in *The World Crisis*. 'The fading light of evening disclosed in the far distance the silhouettes of two battleships steaming slowly out of the Firth of Forth. They seemed invested with a new significance to me.'

Lloyd George's hand in the appointment is confirmed by George Riddell: in October 1911, having completed a long afternoon of golf at Walton Heath, Riddell told Lloyd George that Churchill had divulged to him, in the changing rooms, the carefully guarded secret of his imminent move from the Home Office to the Admiralty (adding, 'You must tell no one'). Lloyd George replied, 'Yes, I know all about it because I travelled to Archerfield especially to see Asquith and ask him to appoint Winston to the Admiralty.'

The same month Churchill wrote to Lloyd George, addressing him as 'My dear David' and signing off, 'Always your friend W.' In it, he expressed optimism about the Admiralty which he was about to take over, saying, 'I am indebted to you for your influential aid', which confirms that he owed the job to Lloyd George's suggestion to Asquith. 'I am sure we shall square the circle together,' the letter continued. 'We shall both hold plenty of stock in each other's concerns. If the Germans get hold of you, you will hardly have time to sing "Land of My Fathers".' As ever, the light-hearted tone of their friendship – their sense of *fun* – was uppermost.

In the Lloyd George family album there is a wonderful photograph of Winston crossing Horse Guards Parade with his top hat and cane, reputedly on his first day at the Admiralty. He appears to be practically dancing with delight. For the next four years, Churchill's life revolved around the Navy and, until he became Prime Minister in 1940, he regarded this as the happiest and most productive time of his career. He spent almost eight months a year on the Admiralty yacht HMS *Enchantress*, and often took the Asquith family and others on Mediterranean cruises.

Until 1911, Churchill had not been completely his own man;

he had first been under the shadow of his father, Lord Randolph, and then under that of his mentor, Lloyd George. Once he became First Lord of the Admiralty, he shook off the two helms-

**UNDER HIS MASTER'S EYE.**

Scene—*Mediterranean, on board the Admiralty yacht " Enchantress."*

Mr. Winston Churchill. "ANY HOME NEWS?"

Mr. Asquith. "HOW CAN THERE BE WITH YOU HERE?"

men who had guided his career. At the age of thirty-seven he was married to an exceptionally beautiful and charming woman, and had achieved the high office for which he had so ardently prayed. His concerns were no longer with social reforms – with the poor, prisons, trade unions or labour exchanges. His whole life how became caught up with naval matters and his relationship with Lloyd George was bound to change. His friend chided him, 'You

THE TAXABLE ELEMENT.

First Lord. "THE SEA FOR ME!"
Chancellor of the Exchequer. "WELL, YOU CAN HAVE IT. GIVE ME THE LAND!"

have become a water creature. You think we all live in the sea, and all your thoughts are devoted to sea life, fishes, and other aquatic creatures. You forget that most of us live on land.'

★

During the next three years Churchill visited practically every ship in the Navy and every port, not only around the British coast, but also in the Mediterranean. He frequently attended firing practices on board battleships. There is a story of his cruising on the *Enchantress* down the Adriatic coast with the Asquiths. Violet remarked, 'How perfect!' 'Yes,' Churchill replied. 'Range perfect – visibility perfect – If we had got some six-inch guns on board, how easily we could bombard . . .' Violet also reported that Churchill showed some impatience with Asquith's absorption with the classical past: 'Those Greeks and Romans, they are so overrated. They only said everything *first*. I've said just as good things myself. But they got in before me.' It was an irreverence which he shared with Lloyd George, since both of them had missed out on Asquith's classical education. Churchill was, however, enthralled by the technology of naval warfare, although he couldn't then foresee its consequences in human terms.

As First Lord of the Admiralty, Churchill made some important naval reforms. As early as 21 October 1911 he was writing to the Chancellor of the Exchequer – more formally now ('My dear Chancellor . . . Yours sincerely Winston Churchill') – expounding his thesis for the timely consideration of contingency plans to ensure the country's food supply 'in the event of a general strike or war'; he recommended a National Guarantee against the loss of ships bringing cargoes of food, stated that earlier plans, such as they were, were either inadequate or too tentative, and urged Lloyd George to appoint a subcommittee of the Committee of Imperial Defence 'with a view to settling a scheme which should be ready for adoption only if the actual circumstances of a future war rendered this necessary . . .' In view of his later wartime responsibilities it is particularly interesting that within two weeks of taking over the Admiralty, Churchill was concerning himself with aspects of national security and the need to ensure food supplies for the people.

As well as improving conditions for sailors, he was responsible for one of the best long-term investments ever made by Whitehall: the Navy's conversion from coal to oil. This persuaded the Admiralty to enter into a twenty-year contract with the Anglo-Persian Oil Company (later BP) in which the Government acquired a controlling interest.

Admiralty matters also ushered a new personality into Churchill's life: Admiral Lord Fisher of Kilverstone. Mainly responsible for updating naval weaponry, introducing the torpedo, the Dreadnought battleship and new 6-inch guns, 'Jacky' Fisher had retired as First Sea Lord in 1909. When Churchill became First Lord of the Admiralty he re-called Fisher, who bombarded him with advice on appointments and armaments. With his help, Churchill put together a naval war staff to parallel the Army's Staff structure, promoting young admirals like Jellicoe and Beatty. Fisher rightly predicted that 'Armageddon' would start in 1914 and the new Naval Board agreed to prepare for war against Germany. Churchill planned a fast division of five oil-powered battleships with 15-inch guns, which could cruise at 25 knots.

Inevitably his naval enthusiasm would lead him to clash with the Chancellor of the Exchequer over the cost of battleships. In July 1912 he increased the naval estimates from £30 million to £45 million; they were to reach £55 million by the following year. At a Cabinet meeting that month Lloyd George passed Churchill a note which read: 'Bankruptcy stares me in the face.' He replied: 'Your only chance is to get 5 million pounds next year and put the blame on me – then you will be in clover again for the rest of the Parliament.' Most of the naval estimates passed easily through the House of Commons since by this time both parties were agreed on the reality of the German naval threat. But, as usual, Churchill was making enemies by his impetuous and energetic approach, which led to the dismissal or resignation of several admirals, and the First Lord of the Admiralty became distinctly unpopular. Lord Charles Beresford in particular, the arch-enemy of Lord Fisher, attacked the new First Lord in the House of Commons.

In the middle of the growing political debate about rebuilding the Navy, and the costs involved, which were the cause of continuing tension between Lloyd George and Churchill, erupted

DOGG'D.

WINSTON. "*SHIP'S* BISCUIT, I THINK."

the Marconi scandal. This was, by contrast, to reinforce and strengthen their great alliance and, for the first time, to cause Lloyd George to feel that he was indebted, personally and politically, to the younger man.

The Marconi episode sheds strong light on the friendship

between Lloyd George and Churchill, and especially on the latter's loyalty to his friends in times of crisis. Without Churchill's faithful and energetic support, and without the backing of Asquith, the Prime Minister, Lloyd George's political career would almost certainly have been finished in 1913. Instead he went on to succeed Asquith as Prime Minister three years later.

In March 1912, a contract had been signed between the British Government – represented by the Postmaster-General, Herbert Samuel – and the English Marconi Company, to set up a chain of wireless stations throughout the Empire (Marconi having demonstrated the efficiency of his invention by passing messages across the Atlantic in 1909). English Marconi shares rose from £2 in 1910 to £9 in April 1912. Meanwhile the American Marconi Company was set to issue new shares. Lloyd George's friend, the Attorney-General Rufus Isaacs, whose brother Godfrey was a director of both companies, suggested that he should buy some shares in advance of the listing. Their value doubled within days of the share issue. Today this would be classified as 'insider dealing' but in 1912 it was a relatively innocent undertaking (although perhaps less so for the Chancellor of the Exchequer and the Attorney-General). In addition, the Liberal Chief Whip, Lord Murray of Elibank, bought shares not only for himself but, more significantly, for Liberal Party funds.

The world was soon alerted to these dubious transactions by the *Eye-Witness*, a paper edited successively by Hilaire Belloc, G. K. Chesterton's brother Cecil and W. R. Lawson. In making accusations against the Isaacs brothers and Herbert Samuel, the *Eye-Witness* was motivated partly by anti-Semitism. When the Paris newspaper, *Le Matin*, repeated the accusations, Rufus Isaacs and Herbert Samuel issued a writ for libel.

Churchill did all he could to help Lloyd George over the Marconi crisis and, according to Winston's son Randolph, 'it was probably at that time their lifelong friendship was cemented'. First he persuaded his friends F. E. Smith, and Sir Edward Carson (who had prosecuted Oscar Wilde) to act for the defendants. The fact that the two were leading Conservative barristers to a large extent deterred the Tory Opposition from criticising the ministers. (Lloyd George and Isaacs denied to the House of Commons that they had bought shares in the English Marconi Company, but four months later, in evidence given in the French libel case, admitted to buying American Marconi shares.)

Next, Churchill persuaded Lord Northcliffe, the proprietor of *The Times*, not to play the matter up in the press. He then took over communications between Lloyd George and Asquith while the Prime Minister was appearing in the ensuing debate in the House of Commons Select Committee. Asquith had a hidden motive in defending his colleagues from the charges of impropriety: as leader of the Liberals he knew that party funds were also involved. Had this been more widely realised, it could have brought down the Government. Certainly Churchill later said that if the affair had been properly handled by the Opposition, they could have toppled the Liberals but 'some of them were too stupid and, frankly, some of them were too nice'.

After Lloyd George had defended his conduct before the Select Committee, Churchill patted him warmly on the back. He told Riddell that his heart had bled for Lloyd George and that he was delighted with the favourable outcome.

In 1912 Churchill and Lloyd George were widely hated by the 'forces of conservatism' for their championing of the People's Budget, and attacks on the rich and the House of Lords. The Marconi scandal was an opportunity to hit back at them. In fact, Churchill himself was also suspected of having bought Marconi shares, and was wrongly named by two editors of the *Financial News*. He furiously rebutted this 'grossly insulting' charge before the Select Committee and again at the National Liberal Club, saying: 'My right honourable friend the Chancellor of the Exchequer is more bitterly hated in certain powerful classes . . . and more relentlessly pursued than even Mr Gladstone was in the great days of 1886. I do not believe the Attorney-General would have been attacked in this way but that they wanted to strike at Mr Lloyd George.'

The Master of Elibank was also called to give evidence to the Select Committee but was conveniently absent on business in Colombia for Lord Cowdray. Later, audiences would shout 'Bo-go-ta! Bo-go-ta!' whenever his name was mentioned on a public platform.

As Murray wrote to Lloyd George about Churchill after the scandal was over:

> It was just like him. I have always regarded him as a true friend who will always stand by me in foul or in fair weather – and that speech for its warmth of feeling for his injured friends and its scathing attack on their frankness will show to many what we already knew, that in time of trouble, Winston is the first to spring to the side of his friends.

Of Churchill's loyalty to his friends there could be no doubt. The hero of his novel *Savrola* had revealingly reflected: 'A man loves his friend . . . he has stood by him perhaps at doubtful moments.' Lloyd George, who was not typically so loyal to his friends, learned some of that virtue from Winston, as he would later have an opportunity to demonstrate.

Describing Lloyd George's state of mind during the Marconi affair, his son Richard wrote: 'Father was in a state of frightening depression . . . During this time, the man who did most to help, sustain and champion Lloyd George was Winston Churchill.' Indeed Churchill had been so concerned about Lloyd George's mental condition during the Marconi scandal that, with typical generosity, he took Lloyd George, his wife, and daughter Megan on a two-day cruise on HMS *Enchantress* up to the Western Isles of Scotland. A series of photographs in the family albums (now in the National Library of Wales, Aberystwyth) of Lloyd George, Asquith and Churchill in his yachting cap, together with Margot

Asquith and Clementine Churchill, all apparently in good spirits, was probably taken on this expedition.

Lloyd George's career was saved, but his political prestige and influence was greatly weakened by the Marconi case and the doubt that it cast on his honour and integrity. He was unable, for example, to enact his cherished land reform, and embarked on no further political initiatives before the outbreak of war. Churchill, on the other hand, pressed on at full speed with his magnificent work of rebuilding the Navy.

It fell to Lloyd George, as Chancellor of the Exchequer, to restrain Churchill's naval spending. His battle with his friend over the naval estimates illuminates the temperament and character of both antagonists. For Churchill, the only goal was always to win his battle, but in his stubborn determination also lay a weakness. Although he could lead and inspire great loyalty and although he could obey orders from his superiors – thanks to his military career – he had never learned how to co-operate with equals and was not generally liked by his Cabinet colleagues. Lloyd George's approach to an argument was quite different: every issue needed to be weighed against the claims of others, no setback was ever final, no victory was ever complete, and no threat of resignation ever serious.

The two men's policies on Germany were therefore at odds. As Wilfrid Scawen Blunt recorded in 1912: 'It is clear, however, from [Winston's] talk that he is bitten with Grey's anti-German policy. He said of the Germans, "I never could learn their beastly language, nor will I till the Emperor William comes over here with his army."' Blunt speculated:

> One might be excused for thinking what is commonly said by the Tories, that Winston will one day return to the Tory fold. His old connection with the army and now with the navy has turned his mind back into an ultra Imperialist groove. This, I think, will be a stronger temptation for him than any mere intrigue of ambition. Talking yesterday about his career, he said, 'I have never joined in any intrigue, everything I have got I have worked for and have

96

been more hated than anybody.' He speaks highly of both Lloyd George and Edward Grey, both of whom stand probably in the way of his becoming Liberal Prime Minister, while he would certainly lead the Tory party were he one of them again.

In 1911, there was indeed a lot of discussion about who would eventually succeed Asquith as Prime Minister – but, rather than Grey, it was chiefly seen as a contest between Lloyd George and Churchill, as Max Beerbohm's cartoon gleefully portrayed.

Lloyd George's proposal, on the other hand, had been to persuade the Germans to moderate their programme of naval rearmament. With this objective, Haldane, the Secretary of State for War, had been sent to Germany in February 1912. However, despite a personal interview with Kaiser Wilhelm II, he had failed to persuade the Germans to reduce their naval capacity.

By now Italy and Austria were also building Dreadnoughts, a further threat to British supremacy at sea. The French moved their fleet from the Atlantic to the Mediterranean, creating a gap in Britain's defences which made the Admiralty very nervous. Churchill, meanwhile, proposed to the Canadian Prime Minister, Sir Robert Borden, that Canada should provide three Dreadnoughts for imperial defence. When this request was turned down by the Canadian Senate, Churchill was left with the difficult task of persuading the Cabinet to authorise over £50 million in the 1914–15 Budget, to build four new battleships. Lloyd George decided to support Churchill's proposals in return for Churchill's support for his own pet project of land reform. As he told Riddell:

> I have made a bargain with Winston. He has agreed to support my land policy with which he is not in sympathy and I have agreed to give him more money for the Navy. You may call this a bribe, but I have nothing to gain personally. I am only endeavouring to carry out my scheme of social reform which I believe is for the good of the people. I am not at all sure that the bargain will meet with the approval of some of the members of our party. Indeed I already see signs that it will not.

## THE SUCCESSION

Mr. Churchill: Come, suppose we toss for it, Davy?
Mr. Lloyd George: Ah, but, Winnie, would either of us as loser abide by the result?

There was indeed strong opposition from the radicals in the Liberal Cabinet and a petition with about a hundred signatures was lodged in the House of Commons, asking the Government to abandon plans for two of the battleships. This led Lloyd George to join the protest. Churchill was furious. 'I consider that you are going back on your word: trying to drive me out after we have settled, and you promised to support the estimates,' he wrote on 13 December 1913 in one of his characteristic Cabinet notes slipped across the table. Lloyd George replied:

> I agreed to the figure for this year and I have stood by it and *carried it*, much to the disappointment of my economical friends. But I told you distinctly I would press for the reduction of a new programme with a view to 1915 and I think quite respectfully you are unnecessarily stubborn. It is only a question of six months' postponement of laying down. That cannot endanger our safety.

'No. You said you would *support* the Estimates,' Churchill retorted.

Some interesting features of these discussions were Lloyd George's refutation of the bargain which had evidently been struck between Churchill and himself, as soon as he saw that others were preparing to fight Churchill; Asquith's equally unblushing agreement with Lloyd George as to the construction of some words which had passed between himself and Churchill; and his desertion of Churchill as soon as the Cabinet was seen to challenge him.

> Even though Churchill frequently staged tantrums in Cabinet meetings, his anger on this occasion was genuine. He knew that many of the younger men disliked him and clearly suspected that the opposition to the building programme was organised as a means of driving him from office. He could not believe that LG would join in such a cabal. In fact, LG had told Riddell in mid-November: 'Some of our people would like to see him go over to the Tories'. LG opposed this. Churchill was less dangerous within

the Cabinet. But an element of the old friendship may have been present still . . . In the end LG would save Churchill from resignation and, not for the last time, from political extinction.

'Lloyd George did a fatal thing for Winston,' observed Charles Masterman to Riddell on the same day, 'when he persuaded the PM to send him to the Admiralty, and since he has been there he has lost all touch with Liberalism and has become a man of one idea.'

Despite the ongoing argument between the two men about the naval estimates, the strands of friendship were not broken. 'I shall be no party to driving Winston out of the Cabinet,' Lloyd George told Riddell a month later as the revolt of the Liberal ministers was growing. 'I do not agree with some of my colleagues.' Riddell responded, 'He was very loyal to you over the Marconi business.' LG replied:

> Yes, I know and I shall never forget it. Of course I have been too easy during the past two years regarding the Naval Estimates. When he went to the Admiralty, I made a bargain with him about expenditure. He has not kept it, he has been extravagant, now the feeling against him is very strong. I think, however, he will amend his figures to meet the views of the party.

During the Christmas holidays of 1913 Churchill went boar-hunting in France while Lloyd George embarked on a trip into the desert in Algeria. Before leaving, the Chancellor gave an interview to the *Daily Chronicle*, which was published on 1 January 1914 and filled the front page of the newspaper. Lloyd George claimed that the Agadir incident of 1911 had served a useful purpose in reminding Britain and Germany of the perils involved in the atmosphere of suspicion created by the press and politicians. He asserted that huge expenditures on naval and military equipment were less important than formerly because relations with Germany were improving as a result of Sir Edward Grey's diplomacy. This was in line with Lloyd George's concern always to emphasise the need for social reform rather than to waste money on armaments. On this occasion he was going over the heads of the Cabinet to appeal to the public, as he had done at the time of the People's Budget in 1909. Unsurprisingly, therefore, his interview stirred up quite a row between Churchill and his fellow Cabinet ministers.

On 20 January Churchill and Lloyd George had a meeting with the Prime Minister. Churchill threatened to resign. Lloyd George urged him not to do so: 'What will you resign upon? Everything has been conceded to you. You have your four ships; your estimates are up to over £53 million. You are not satisfied. You want more. And you will go out of office on top of that and expect the country to support you.'

According to C. P. Scott, editor of the *Manchester Guardian*, Churchill was both confused and taken aback by this attack. Then Lloyd George himself threatened to resign and this led Asquith to declare that he would dissolve Parliament and call a general election. Neither minister wanted this outcome and so Asquith succeeded in postponing the problem, although Churchill won his victory over the 1914 Budget. Asquith wrote cheerfully to his wife: 'I think we shall get through our little troubles over the Navy without much more ado, LG squeezing in one direction and Winston in the other. Neither of them wants to go, and in an odd sort of way they are really fond of one another. Even small crises reveal people's qualities.'

On 27 January Lloyd George replied to a letter from Churchill:

Dear Winston,
I have striven hard for a friendly and honourable settlement without the slightest regard for the effect upon my personal position, but your letter has driven me to despair, and I must now decline further negotiations, leaving the issue to be decided by the Prime Minister and the Cabinet . . .
 I have laboured these last few days – not to favour you or to save myself – but to rescue Liberalism from the greatest tragedy which has yet befallen it. I have a deep and abiding attachment

for Liberal causes, and for the old Party, and the prospect of wrecking them afflicts me with deep distress. That is why I have been prepared to risk the confidence of my friends and to face the gibes and sneers from friend and foe alike with which I foresaw the publication of the figures would be greeted. I knew too well that every paper would gloat over my humiliation. That I did not mind if the ship and its precious cargo could be saved. You decreed otherwise, and the responsibility is yours and yours alone.

Churchill responded by return:

My dear David,
Only a line to thank you for the warmth and kindness of your letter. It is a comfort to me that if the worst happens, personal ill-will between us will not be added to the many other causes for regret.

The cooling friendship between Lloyd George and Churchill survived, although with less intensity on the Chancellor's part. When Churchill introduced the Naval estimates in March 1914, in a speech lasting over two hours, which was generally regarded as a masterpiece of lucid and cogent exposition, Lloyd George noted that "The applause of the House" had become "the very breath of his nostrils".

Churchill, by contrast, particularly during a convivial evening, could still speak in the most sentimental terms of his intimacy with Lloyd George. In early March 1914 he attended a dinner at the home of Lord Morley with the other members of the Liberal Cabinet, at which, as Asquith wrote to his friend Venetia Stanley, 'in a rather maudlin mood [Churchill] said to Lloyd George, "It's a wonderful thing our friendship. I don't suppose there has been a single day in the past ten years, when we have not had a half hour's conversation together." (To which Augustine Birrell, the acerbic Irish Secretary, rejoined, "You must be very bored with each other by now.")' Sentimental as Churchill could be, this was none the less an extraordinary testament to the closeness of the political companionship between the two men. Churchill was the only person, it has been noted, who addressed the Chancellor as 'David' although the whole world knew the First Lord of the Admiralty as 'Winston'.

In his memoirs Lloyd George does not mention the issue of the 1914–15 naval estimates; his own story of the compromise was typically simple and light-hearted, on the advice of his wife Maggie. He had invited Churchill for breakfast at Number 11 and, when he arrived, told him what she had said: 'You know, my dear, I never interfere in politics; but they say you are having an argument with that nice young Mr Churchill about building Dreadnoughts. Of course I don't understand these things but I should have thought it would be better to have too many than too few.'

Reflecting later on the Agadir incident in 1911, Churchill wrote: 'For the next seven years I was to think of nothing else. Liberal politics, the People's Budget, Free Trade, Peace, Retrenchment and Reform – all the war cries of our election struggles began to seem unreal in the presence of this near pre-occupation, only Ireland held place.'

The historian may note that neither Lloyd George nor Churchill made more than a single visit to Ireland during these years, although they spent many hours studying its problems. Churchill's visit was in February 1912 when he went to Belfast to give a speech. In this, he advocated Home Rule while safeguarding the interests of the Protestants of Ulster. However, because of Unionist sensitivities the venue had to be changed from the Ulster Hall, where his father had spoken in 1886, to a marquee at the Celtic Football Ground in the Catholic district.

In April 1912 the Home Rule Bill was passed in the House of Commons. But this made no provision for Ulster – four of whose six counties were solidly Protestant – and would be rejected by the House of Lords in 1914.

The Conservative Party was now led by the quiet Canadian-Scottish businessman Andrew Bonar Law and the leader of the Ulster parliamentary group, Sir Edward Carson. Both threatened to resort to insurrection and violence rather than submit to the rule of a Catholic parliament in Dublin ('Home Rule was Rome Rule' went their case).

Churchill told the House of Commons on 30 April:

> At one stroke of the wand [the Ulstermen] could sweep the Irish question out of the light and into history, and free the British realm from the canker which has poisoned its heart for generations. If they refuse, if they take to the boats, all we say is that they shall not obstruct the work of salvage and that we shall go forward at any rate to the end.

He accused Carson and Bonar Law of treasonable activity. At one point in the debate, the Ulster leader Ronald McNeill threw a book at Churchill and drew blood.

Feelings ran high about the Irish question. It was clear to Lloyd George that a compromise would be needed, and it was he who first proposed that the six Protestant counties of Ulster should be separately provided for – a compromise which was to take its final shape in the 1921 settlement.

Ireland was the obsessive issue of the British political world in the summer of 1914, but it was soon to be overtaken by a far greater world crisis.

# 4

## 1914–16: Comrades – or Opponents?

*Fiel per Desdichado* (Loyal but Unlucky)

Churchill family motto

THE LONG HOT British summer of 1914 was hardly ruffled by the news that came at the end of June: Archduke Franz Ferdinand, heir to the Austro-Hungarian Empire, had been assassinated in Sarajevo, together with his wife, by a Serbian nationalist. The significance of this event was that Serbia was allied with Russia against Austria and Germany. The killing of the heir to the throne of the Austro-Hungarian Empire was a direct challenge to the existing order and caused a series of alliances to be activated; and the consequent mobilisation of armies in Austria, Russia, Germany and France. England seemed, as usual, to stand to one side in these Continental disturbances. The normal social programme continued: Lord's, Ascot, Henley, Wimbledon. In early July the Churchill family left for the beach in Norfolk and the Lloyd George family went home to Criccieth in North Wales.

In the final months before the outbreak of war, the battle over the naval estimates continued to be one of the main preoccupations of the Liberal Cabinet. On 17 July 1914, the Chancellor told an audience of City bankers that, in foreign affairs, 'the sky has never been more perfectly blue.' Six days later he told the House of Commons that, since British–German relations had improved, his future budgets could reduce expenditure on armaments.

But while Lloyd George was still urging naval economy, the Royal Navy was fully mobilised for action, under the orders of the irrepressible First Lord of the Admiralty. All one thousand ships, including fifty-three battleships and other ships of different classes, were inspected by the King at Spithead in late July. As the European scene darkened, Churchill asked Asquith for permission to keep the Navy mobilised, instead of dispersing after the manoeuvres. The Prime Minister gave him a fixed look, then just nodded. As Churchill proudly noted in his memoirs, 'The Fleet was ready.'

The Cabinet's other main preoccupation was Ireland. During the first six months of 1914, it seemed possible that civil war would break out over the Ulster question. Half a million Orangemen had signed a solemn covenant pledging to use all means to defeat Home Rule. Faced with this uncompromising opposition, in July the King intervened, in the hope that the Tories might accept Home Rule if Ulster was left out (at least temporarily). He invited the leaders of both parties to meet at Balmoral in September to try and reach agreement. (They actually met at Buckingham Palace in July.) Negotiations for Home Rule were narrowed down to what Churchill called 'the muddy byways of Fermanagh and Tyrone'. On the afternoon of Friday 24 July, the Cabinet was about to break up, after a long and boring discussion about the parishes of these Ulster counties, when a messenger handed the Foreign Secretary, Sir Edward Grey, a 'most immediate' dispatch. He read it aloud. It was the text of an ultimatum to Serbia from the Austro-Hungarian Government. 'The parishes of Fermanagh and Tyrone faded back into the mists and squalls of Ireland, and a strange light began immediately, but by perceptible gradations, to fall and grow upon the map of Europe.'

The fleet might have been ready for war but was the Cabinet? There was as yet little popular support for war, in the press, the City, or the Liberal Party. Labour were against it. Capital was against it. The Chancellor of the Exchequer said that, faced with the awful prospect of war, and a disruption of trade and finance, 'money was a frightened and trembling thing'. Gold payments were suspended because of the run on the pound that was expected in the event of war. The markets closed. Lloyd George, as Chancellor of the Exchequer, was responsible for introducing the so-called 'Bradbury' notes – the first paper pound- and ten-shilling notes which were issued by the Bank of England in lieu of gold sovereigns. Thus, within a matter of days of the outbreak of the First World War, Britain's pre-eminent position in world-wide finance and the dominance of the pound sterling in the global monetary system would rapidly begin to change. Within twelve months, the United States would replace Britain as the principal creditor of the nations of the world and especially of the warring nations of Europe.

Would the Liberal Government declare war? Britain had, of course, had a military understanding with France since the Entente Cordiale of 1904. But there was no treaty binding Britain to defend Belgian neutrality. Only Grey and Churchill were really in favour of war. Asquith, Morley, John Burns and Lloyd George were against it. Lloyd George – a heavyweight Cabinet minister with broad Liberal Party backing – was the key. Without his support for war, the Cabinet would split; with his support there would be war, and only Morley and Burns would resign. So Churchill went to work on his friend to persuade him of the necessity for war. He sent round a military expert to show the Chancellor the dispositions and expectations of the British Expeditionary Force (BEF). Lloyd George was unimpressed.

By the beginning of August the popular fever – the jingoistic mood – was rising in temperature, just as it had done at the time of Ladysmith in 1899 and Mafeking in 1900. Lloyd George was very reluctant to agree to British intervention in the conflict between Germany and France, writing to his wife Maggie: 'I am filled with horror at the prospect [of war]. I am even more hor-rified that I should ever appear to have a share in it but I must bear my share of the ghastly burden though it scorches my flesh to do so.'

By contrast, there had been a fascinating glimpse of Churchill's bellicose nature when, on 28 July, it seemed for a moment that war might be averted. He exclaimed moodily to Asquith that it looked after all as if they were in for 'a bloody peace'. Involved in, and excited by, the preparations going on day and night at the Admiralty, he wrote to Clemmie that he was 'geared-up and happy' at the military preparations, 'which have a hideous fascination for me. Is it not horrible to be built like that?'

On 1 August Churchill seemed to have enlisted the support of Lloyd George, as well as that of a number of more junior ministers. A set of Cabinet notes survives in the Lloyd George Papers which gives a taste of the arguments used by Churchill to bring the Chancellor of the Exchequer round to his point of view:

I AUGUST 1914

WSC [looking across the table at LG, scribbling]: I am deeply attached to you and have followed your instinct and guidance for nearly 10 years [but if you don't agree to war] all the rest of our lives we shall be opposed . . .

LG: Would you *commit* yourself in public *now* (Monday) to war if Belgium is invaded whether Belgium asks for protection or not?

WSC: No.

LG: If patience prevails and you do not press too hard tonight, we might come together.

WSC: Please God — it is our whole future — comrades or opponents. The march of events will be dominating.

LG: What is your policy?

WSC: At the present moment I would act in such a way as to impress Germany with our intention to preserve the neutrality of Belgium. So much is still unknown as to the definite purpose of Germany that I would not go beyond this. Moreover, public opinion might veer round at any moment if Belgium is invaded, and we must be ready to meet this opinion.

WSC:  I am most profoundly anxious that our long co-operation may not be severed. Remember your part at Agadir. I implore you to come and bring your mighty aid to the discharge of our duty. Afterwards, by participating in the peace, we can regulate the settlement and prevent a renewal of 1870 conditions.

[A reference to the aftermath of the Franco-Prussian War, which had caused bitterness in France over the loss of Alsace and Lorraine. The Treaty of Versailles would result in a similar bitterness in Germany and eventually lead to the rise of Hitler.]

2 AUGUST

WSC:  Together we can carry a wide social policy, all *on the conference basis*. Naval War will be cheap – not more than 25 million a year. You alone can take the measures which will ensure food being kept abundant and cheap to the people.

3 AUGUST

WSC:  The Welsh miners who had gone on their holidays after denouncing the war are returning in full force tomorrow – having apparently satisfied themselves of the justice of the war – and will cut all the coal we need. This relieves a dangerous situation. I want you to send them a strong Welsh message about small nations etc.

LG:  He is summing up much too unfavourably to our own friends.

WSC:  Yes.

LG:  Ready to defend ourselves. Whilst others are fighting our business is confined to the starving women and children including our own. What will be the effect on Italy, Belgium and Holland.

WSC:  *Please* study the question before you make up your mind. There are all sorts of vital and precise facts – which you *cannot* have at your fingers' ends.

WSC: I am so glad you are turning your mind to the *vital* question of safeguarding the credit and food supply of this country.

Such a prolonged interchange by ministers at Cabinet meetings is a rarity. These notes which passed between Churchill and Lloyd George were mostly torn up by the latter. The pieces were then gathered together and preserved, thanks to his dedicated private secretary, Frances Stevenson. They show how Churchill was wrestling with the conscience of Lloyd George, who appears to have given in reluctantly to the pressure from his friend.

During the weekend of 1/2 August, while the ultimata flew back and forth between the chancelleries, the Cabinet met almost continuously. The intense discussions about whether to declare war, which had at first deeply divided Churchill and Lloyd George – who were already at odds over the naval estimates – eventually brought them much closer together.

A major change had clearly taken place within the cabinet. That change centred on Lloyd George. According to Asquith, on the morning of 2 August, Lloyd George was still against any kind of British intervention in any event . . . Throughout that long Sunday he had contemplated retiring to North Wales if Britain went to war. It appears that until 3 August he intended to resign from the Cabinet upon any British declaration of war . . . In fact, Lloyd George was first firmly against war, and then equally firmly for war. That his change of mind was not without its inner pain was evident from his anguished reaction to the cheers of a London crowd on 3 August. 'This is not my crowd. I never want to be cheered by a war crowd.'

On the evening of 3 August, Asquith, Grey, Haldane, McKenna, Lloyd George and the other Liberal Cabinet ministers sat gloomy and silent around the table in the Cabinet Room, until the solemn chimes of Big Ben announced eleven o'clock and the expiry of the ultimatum which had given the German

Government twelve hours to withdraw its troops from Belgian soil. Britain was at war. Grey looked out of the window at the lights being extinguished in Horse Guards Parade and, echoing William Pitt in 1806 ('Roll up that map; it will not be wanted these ten years'), he said 'The lamps are going out all over Europe; we shall not see them lit again in our lifetime.'

Frances Stevenson recounts in her diary that 'Upon this grave assembly burst Churchill, a cigar in his mouth, radiant, smiling with satisfaction. "Well!" he exclaimed. "The deed is done!" The dream of his life had come to pass. Little he recked of the terrors of war and the price that must be paid. His chance had come!'

So the First World War began – in a fever of patriotism, enthusiasm and excitement. Young men from all over Britain rushed to volunteer. The general feeling was that the war would be over by Christmas.

In the first few months of the conflict, both Churchill and Lloyd George were frantically busy. The Chancellor had to calm the financial markets; the Treasury had to pay for an enormous increase in military expenditure, both in men and *matériel*. Meanwhile Churchill positioned the North Sea Fleet in an aggressive manner to counter any German attacks. He was alert and watchful in the defence of Britain, but soon his over-active imagination was attracted by the growing conflict in which the British Expeditionary Force had become engaged in Flanders. Not content merely to direct the Navy, Churchill was also becoming interested in the overall strategy of the war, especially from the military angle.

On 21 August the British and German armies fought for the first time since the eighteenth century near Mons; next morning Churchill learned that Namur had fallen and the BEF was in retreat. Shaken by this reverse, he felt an intense need to see his old comrade-in-arms, Lloyd George, to be buoyed up by his sense of purpose, so he walked across Horse Guards Parade to the

Treasury. Lloyd George was in a meeting, but immediately came out to see Churchill; he was resolutely confident and patriotic, as he had been in his 'Agadir' speech three years earlier. He no longer had any doubts about the rightness of Britain's participation in the European war.

Further evidence of this came on 19 September at the Queen's Hall in London, when Lloyd George appealed for patriotism, volunteers and sacrifice in words that were very close in spirit to the speeches Churchill would make in 1940. Many turned up to hear the 'pro-Boer' and 'Limehouse' orator turned patriot. He spoke about how Britain had striven to keep the peace of Europe over the previous ten years and now Germany, 'the roadhog of Europe', had cast the shadow of war across the Continent. His emotional peroration ended as quietly as he had begun:

> I know a valley in North Wales, between the mountains and the sea. It is a beautiful valley, snug, comfortable, sheltered by the mountains from all the bitter blasts. But it is very enervating, and I remember how the boys were in the habit of climbing the hill above the village to have a glimpse of the great mountains in the distance, and to be stimulated and freshened by the breezes which came from the hill-tops, and by the great spectacle of their grandeur.
>
> *We* have been living in a sheltered valley for generations. We have been too comfortable and too indulgent – many, perhaps, too selfish – and the stern hand of Fate has scourged us to an elevation where we can see the everlasting things that matter for a nation – the high peaks we had forgotten, of Honour, Duty, Patriotism, and, clad in glittering white, the great pinnacle of Sacrifice, pointing like a rugged finger to Heaven.
>
> We shall descend into the valleys again; but as long as the men and women of this generation last, they will carry in their hearts the image of those great mountain peaks whose foundations are not shaken, though Europe rock and sway in convulsions of a great war.

Lloyd George's Queen's Hall speech belied the common impression that he was in some way a pacifist and opposed to the war, as he had been to the South African war in 1900. Rather, it showed him to be wholly committed to winning, supporting conscription and increasing the output of munitions. Now that he had dedicated himself to the energetic prosecution of the war, no calls for peace or compromise were to divert him from his path and his patriotism was to carry him through the next four years.

In fact, though brought up as a nonconformist, Lloyd George was never a pacifist. In November 1914 he would tell a nonconformist audience that he recognised that, to those who followed biblical tenets, war was not justifiable under any circumstances, but that he himself could not quite attain that altitude of idealism in this world. And in 1940 he would refuse to meet 'one of those pacifist types, that I have never been, nor am likely to become, until I reach the infinite tranquillity of the Elysian Fields'.

The correspondence between Lloyd George and Churchill in these early months of the war is of a highly personal and affectionate nature. One can measure this by the fact that Churchill still addresses his friend as 'My dear David' whereas later he was to write 'Dear Lloyd George', 'Dear Chancellor' or 'Dear Prime Minister'.

In September 1914 they turned their joint attention to the question of soldiers' pensions, Churchill writing:

My dear David,
Please look at this.
   The 5/– pension is a scandal. No soldier's wife shd be dependent on charity. Your large outlook shd be turned on this.

Churchill had set up his Naval Division in August 1914 and it was soon known as 'Churchill's private army'. Formed from the naval reserves who could not go to sea, it included many of his young friends such as the poets Rupert Brooke and Julian Grenfell, Asquith's younger son 'Oc' (Arthur), his mother's ex-husband George Cornwallis-West and other Churchill friends and relatives.

The opportunity to exercise military power had been a secret ambition of Churchill, at least since 30 May 1909 when he had written to Clemmie from Camp Goring:

These military men vy often fail altogether to see the simple truths underlying the relationships of all armed forces, & how the levers of power can be used upon them. Do you know I would greatly like to have some practice in the handling of large forces. I have much confidence in my judgment on things, when I see clearly, but on nothing do I seem to *feel* the truth more than in tactical combinations. It is a vain and foolish thing to say – but *you* will not laugh at it. I am sure I have the root of the matter in me – but never I fear in this state of existence will it have a chance of flowering – in bright red blossom.

At the end of August the Naval Division was sent over to Ostend to help with the defence of Belgium. The German wing was turned at the Battle of the Marne in early September and Paris was saved. The next crisis came in the effort to hold Antwerp against the German onslaught. Churchill, determined as always to be in the front line, went to Antwerp and for four days masterminded the military operations to defend the city with his 'private army'.

In the excitement, on 5 October Churchill sent a telegram to Asquith offering to resign as First Lord if he could be given a suitable military rank (Major-General possibly) in order to command the troops in Antwerp. The Prime Minister did not take this suggestion too seriously. At that day's Cabinet meeting, when everyone asked when Churchill was coming home, Asquith read out his telegram and later wrote to his confidante Venetia Stanley that the message was greeted with 'Homeric laughter' by his colleagues.

Antwerp fell to the Germans on 8 October and Churchill returned to London. Lloyd George's initial reaction was to congratulate him on his courageous and 'brilliant effort to rescue Antwerp', which had delayed the German advance for one week. But he must have felt that Churchill, with his usual boyish enthusiasm for battle and lack of judgement, was getting things out of proportion because a week or two later he commented to *his* confidante, Frances Stevenson, that having been photographed at the front in various heroic poses in the midst of bursting shells, Churchill had made a fool of himself in Belgium and had also risked the lives of those in the Naval Division. Nevertheless he did not join in the initial criticisms of Churchill which were to be heard among his Cabinet colleagues and Tory opponents.

Churchill was heavily criticised for his highly publicised and risky adventures in the trenches around the port of Antwerp. As always, his lucky star endured and he suffered no wounds, but there were many casualties among the young and largely untrained battalion which he had raised. Asquith, who had at first merely referred to Churchill's behaviour as 'a zigzag streak of lightning in the brain', received a sobering first-hand account of the disorganised retreat of the Naval Division from his son Oc: 'nothing excuses Winston (who know all the facts) from sending in . . . a callow crowd of the rawest tiros, most of whom had never fired off a rifle . . .' The press were even more outspoken in criticising Churchill's role at Antwerp. Finally even his closest friends in the Cabinet, Asquith and Lloyd George, joined the critics. Although Antwerp was a sideshow in the history of the First World War, it was, in a sense, a prelude to the Dardanelles.

Much of the press criticism of Churchill was as unjustified as it was later with the Gallipoli expedition. As First Lord he did not have the authority to command and direct military operations in detail and therefore could not be blamed for their failure. Nevertheless, the key political consequence as far as Churchill's career was concerned was that now it was not just the Tories who mistrusted and disliked him, but also many of his Liberal colleagues. In particular, Asquith and Lloyd George, who until now had been his mentors, began to see the bellicose and impulsive side of his character and were less inclined to entrust him with high office and responsibilities thereafter.

Lloyd George, though always publicly supportive of his friend, was now privately critical. 'Winston's trouble,' he said, 'was personal ambition.' As Frances Stevenson wrote:

> LG was often mistrustful of Churchill's judgement. 'Winston often loses great opportunities because he is too self-centred', he was wont to say, and would quote a couplet which he had learnt in his youth:
>
> > 'When self the wavering balance shakes
> > 'Tis rarely right adjusted.'

In October 1914 Churchill wrote to Lloyd George to invite his eldest daughter Olwen, then twenty-one, to launch a cruiser from Pembroke in South Wales (adding that her sister ship had been launched by Miss Violet Asquith). He also added, 'I have not had a minute to congratulate you on your baptism of fire [Lloyd George had visited the trenches for the first time]. The taste forms if not cloyed by surfeit.' It was a typically Churchillian comment – Lloyd George, however, unlike his friend, never enjoyed military adventures.

On 5 November, Frances Stevenson confided to her diary:

> [LG] says . . . When [Churchill] returned from Antwerp after his failure he said to the Cabinet, 'Now that the administration of such serious & important affairs lies entirely in the hands of a few of us – since Parliament is not sitting – it behoves us to be quite frank with each other.' Everyone agreed, thinking that he was about to confess to his mistake. Instead, he went on to shift the whole of the responsibility for the disaster on to Kitchener, who happened to be absent from the Cabinet that day.

This provoked intense argument around the Cabinet table, some of which was caused by the inclusion of Lord Kitchener as Minister of War. The appointment had been made, at Churchill's suggestion, in the hours immediately following the declaration of war on 3 August since Kitchener was about to embark on a

Channel ferry to return to Egypt. Kitchener had had a brilliant military career in India, Egypt and South Africa but had no experience of political life or democratic discussion, such as characterised the Liberal Cabinet in 1914. Lloyd George famously compared Kitchener with 'one of those revolving lighthouses which radiate momentary gleams of revealing light far out into the surrounding gloom, and then suddenly relapse into complete darkness. There were no intermediate stages.' He had, above all, a very masterful and commanding manner and was, of course, represented to the nation in the famous poster 'Your Country Needs You!'. But, as the MP Victor Cazalet would write in his diary on 3 October 1927, to his Cabinet colleagues Kitchener could be very obtuse:

> Winston told a wonderful story of Kitchener at a Ministerial meeting early in the war of 1914. Kitchener was very obstinate and very reticent, never having had anyone question his authority for years. Lloyd George asked for the recruiting figures. But Kitchener refused to give any, while Asquith sat mute writing letters. The other Ministers bar Winston and Lloyd George accepted the situation. Then Lloyd George protested: they were Ministers, eager to win the War; they must know. Kitchener rose majestically and started towards the door. A tremendous crisis was probable, for Kitchener was a popular figure, and the Liberal Government had become unpopular. But Pease, who had been Whip for ten years in the House of Commons, rushed naturally to the door to stop Kitchener going out, and stood there with arms outstretched across the door, smiling. What could Kitchener do? Eventually he smiled and returned!

Kitchener opposed the formation of a Welsh Division, an idea of Lloyd George's to draw on the patriotism of the Welsh volunteers, as the Scots and the English already had their own regiments. There is a telling letter from Lloyd George in the Churchill Archives, written on 28 October 1914:

My dear Winston

I feel deeply grateful to you for the way you stood up for fair play to my little nationality this morning.

I am in despair over the stupidity of the War Office. You might imagine we were alien enemies who ought to be interned at Frimley until we had mastered the intricacies of the English language sufficiently to be able to converse on equal terms with an East End recruit.

I enclose copy of the order issued by the WO about the Welsh Army Corps. Under these conditions further recruiting is impossible.

Does K. [Kitchener] want men? If he does not let him say so then we will all be spared much worry & trouble.

Why cannot he give us 18 battalions out of the 30 new battalions already formed in Wales. We could send another division.

The Chancellor and the First Lord clearly formed a common cause in the early months of the war, as they had done during the great period of social reform in 1910. Both saw the need for strategic initiatives (for example in the East, against Turkey or through the Balkans) and for preparations at home for a total war involving massive reorganisation of munitions production which the War Office, under Kitchener, and the old-fashioned generals, vigorously opposed. Churchill had the advantage of knowing the military mind, having served in various campaigns and having managed the Navy for the previous three years. Lloyd George's quick grasp of events enabled him to make up for his lack of first-hand experience, but it was probably Churchill who taught him much about the military arts, just as Lloyd George had taught Churchill about the need for, and shape of, social reforms.

Two insights into Churchill from Margot Asquith's diary:

30 NOVEMBER 1914

Certainly not his judgement – he is constantly very wrong indeed (he was strikingly wrong when he opposed McKenna's naval

programme in 1909 and roughly speaking he is always wrong in
his judgement about people). It is of course his courage and
colour – his amazing mixture of industry and enterprise. He can
and does always – all ways put himself in the pool. He never
shirks, hedges, or *protects* himself – though he thinks of himself
perpetually. *He takes huge risks.* He is at his very best just now;
when others are shrivelled with grief – apprehensive, silent, iras-
cible and self-conscious morally; Winston is intrepid, valorous,
passionately keen and sympathetic, longing to be in the trenches
– dreaming of the war, big, buoyant, happy, even. It is very extraordinary, he is a born soldier.

10 JANUARY 1915
WINSTON: My God! This, this is living History. Everything we
are doing and saying is thrilling – it will by read by a thousand
generations, think of *that*!! Why I would not be out of this glori-
ous delicious war for anything the world could give me (eyes
glowing but with a slight anxiety lest the word 'delicious' should
jar on me). I say don't repeat that I said the word 'delicious' – you
know what I mean.

In the first five months of the war there had been over half a
million British casualties on the Western Front, and by Christmas
1914 the two opposing armies were at a complete standstill. In
January 1915 the War Cabinet met to consider how they could
respond to Russia's urgent call for action against Turkey to relieve
the pressure on the Eastern Front and reopen the way for the vital
grain traffic to and from the Black Sea. Both Lloyd George and
Churchill were in favour of an 'Eastern' strategy as opposed to
the 'Westerners', such as Kitchener, who thought the only
approach was to pour more and more troops into the trenches in
France.

Churchill was convinced that a naval attack through the
Dardanelles would be successful and that the Allies could quickly
capture Constantinople. Lloyd George was more hesitant, but
favoured an expedition through the Balkans to capture Salonika

and thereby bring Bulgaria in on the side of the Allies. It was the naval plan which won the support of Asquith and the War Cabinet and was swiftly put into action.

Undaunted by his escapades at Antwerp, Churchill's boyish thirst for military glory and adventure persisted. He had just passed his fortieth birthday; at the same age, his hero Napoleon had conquered the whole of Europe. In January 1915, referring to the planned Dardanelles expedition, he told Lloyd George, '*I shall be the biggest man in Europe, if this comes off.*' In fact, Gallipoli would dash his hopes of becoming Prime Minister for another twenty-five years.

On 18 March 1915 the Royal Navy very nearly succeeded in forcing the straits into the Sea of Marmara but retreated after three ships were sunk by mines. It later transpired, through Turkish records discovered after the war, that in fact there were very few Turkish ships or gun batteries to oppose a further Allied advance, and that with resolution and determination Churchill's plan would have succeeded. However, at this point there was a fatal hesitation of the admirals on the spot and in the War Cabinet in London. Eventually it was decided to send in a military expedition to land on the Gallipoli peninsula.

Frances Stevenson sheds light on the tension at the time:

APRIL 8TH 1915

The Dardanelles campaign, however, does not seem to be the success that was prophesied. Churchill very unwisely boasted at the beginning, when things were going well, that he had undertaken it against the advice of everyone else at the Admiralty – that it was 'entirely his own idea'. And then came the reverse . . . LG says Churchill is very worried about the whole affair, and looking very ill. He is very touchy too. Last Monday LG was discussing the Drink question with Churchill, and Samuel and Montague were also present. Churchill put on the grand air, and announced that he was not going to be influenced by the King, and refused to give up his liquor – he thought the whole thing was absurd. LG was annoyed, but went on to explain a point that had been brought up. The next minute Churchill interrupted again. 'I don't see –' he was beginning, but LG broke in sharply: 'You will see the point', he rapped out, 'when you begin to understand that conversation is not a monologue!'

Churchill went very red, but did not reply, and [LG] soon felt rather ashamed of having taken him up so sharply, especially in front of the other two. Later in the evening, LG wrote to apologise but received a note back from Churchill almost immediately.

My dear David,
It was *I* who was churlish & difficult.

It is kind indeed of you to write as you do.

I admire & value intensely the contribution of energy courage & resolve you are making to the progress of our affairs at their crisis. I share your anxieties, & am not at all removed in thought from your main policy.

Yours always,
Winston

The landing at Gallipoli in April 1915 was a disaster: 75,000 British and Allied troops lost their lives, all for the sake of capturing a small beachhead at Cape Helles and Anzac Cove. At this point the military crisis became a political crisis in London. Admiral Fisher, the First Sea Lord, resigned (thus seriously undermining Churchill's position) and the Liberal Government which had held power since 1906 collapsed, to be replaced by a coalition government with the Conservatives. One condition of the entry of Bonar Law, Curzon and Carson into the Cabinet was that Churchill should be excluded, and since he was held responsible for the Gallipoli disaster in the press and in political circles, his exclusion became a certainty.

Although Lloyd George fought to keep his friend in the War Cabinet, privately he conceded to George Riddell that he could not do so, not only because of Conservative opposition but also because Asquith had made Churchill the scapegoat for the failure of the Dardanelles expedition. Riddell recorded:

> LG said that Winston had acted badly inasmuch as he had not told the Cabinet that all the Naval Board were of the opinion that the Dardanelles operation should be combined sea and land attack.
>
> LG said he had fought to get Winston high office – the Colonies, the India Office, the Viceroyalty of India. His colleagues would not, however, agree to his having anything but a minor position. They would not listen to India, where things were in an unsettled state. LG said that McKenna had never said a word against Winston's appointment to any of the offices although he said nothing in his favour, which could be expected. He said that Winston had acted unwisely. He had written some foolish letters to the P.M., who had been angry and who had written Winston a sharp letter in reply. Amongst other things Winston had said 'no one but I can carry the Dardanelles operation to a successful conclusion' . . . When any man talks like that he is on the way to a lunatic asylum.
>
> . . . But since the war Winston has been intolerable, or rather he was during the first few months. If the P.M. was late [to Cabinet] he would not talk to anyone but Kitchener. The little dogs were not worth his notice. I am afraid he is angry with me just now. He came to me in quite a menacing way and said 'I can see you don't mind what is going to happen to me' or something to that effect. I replied, 'you are quite mistaken. We all have our ups and downs and must make the best of it.'

Frances Stevenson's version of events was slightly different but equally interesting:

19TH MAY 1915
LG told me last night that Churchill was taking his defeat very well. 'I feel like a wounded man,' he said to LG, 'I know I am hurt, but as yet I cannot tell how badly. Later on I shall know the extent to which I am damaged, but now I only feel shock.'

. . . Today, however, Churchill seems to be going to put up a fight. He brought up to show [LG] and Sir Edward Grey a long letter in justification of his policy against Fisher's, and announced his intention of publishing it. LG showed him that it would be a fatal thing to do. 'There is no public insinuation up to the present,' said LG to him, 'that the success of the Dardanelles operations is questioned. If you publish that, you will imply that it is.' Churchill saw that point of view, but later on completely losing his temper when he saw that LG and Grey took it for granted that he was going. 'You don't care', he said to LG, 'what becomes of me. You don't care whether I am trampled under foot by my enemies. You don't care for my personal reputation . . .' 'No', said LG, 'I don't care for my own at the present moment. The only thing I care about now is that we win this war.'

24TH MAY 1915

At the end of last week Churchill was making a big fight to stay at the Admiralty. First of all a letter came from Mrs Winston C. to the PM saying that Winston was the only man for the Admiralty & that if the PM listened to those who wished to turn Winston out, he would be showing great weakness. On Friday morning (15th May) a letter came from Winston himself to the PM, saying that no other man but himself would be able to cope with the naval situation during the war, that the things he had had to endure for the past 10 months were beyond imagination – he did not think it possible for a man to bear such anxiety – and that it would be a poor reward for him to be turned out after what he had done. There was no other man who could do as much. The PM became angry at these letters, & wrote him a stern note to say that he 'must make up his mind that he must go.' . . . Masterton-Smith, Winston's own private secretary, told the PM that on no account ought Churchill to be allowed to remain at the Admiralty – he was most dangerous there. It seems strange that Churchill should have been in politics all these years, & yet not have won the confidence of a single party in the country, or a single colleague in the Cabinet.

Churchill was forced to resign from his job at the Admiralty, and despite Lloyd George pestering Asquith with suggestions of alternative roles for him, in May 1915 the Prime Minister reduced him to the humiliating post of Chancellor of the Duchy of Lancaster. 'What is a Duchy and where is Lancaster?' he exclaimed.

Lloyd George said that, during the Boer War, he too had been made a martyr.

> I lost all my practice, people threw stones at my office windows in London. I was jeered at in restaurants. I told my wife to go back to Wales with the kids. She said she was prepared to live in a garret on 30 bob a week. She is a most courageous woman . . . That is the trouble with Winston, he has never been a martyr.

At the time of the final denouement of the Gallipoli crisis, Max Aitken, later Lord Beaverbrook, after dining with F. E. Smith and Churchill, spent the night at the Admiralty with the First Lord. Churchill had never understood the extent of the Tory hatred of him, nor of the growing feeling against him among his Liberal colleagues. He was single-minded and self-absorbed in his task of managing the Navy. During that night in May 1915, as the dawn came up, Aitken watched him with fascination and pity. A message was suddenly received at the Admiralty that the whole German fleet was coming out and was determined to attack the following day. Churchill had been waiting for this moment, as had the British fleet. It was an ironic twist of fate that it occurred while he was under notice to leave the Admiralty. Churchill went through twelve hours of torment – perhaps he would be recognised as the hero of the hour if there was a great naval battle and the British fleet destroyed the German Navy. Beaverbrook described the scene in his book *Politicians and the War.*

> Churchill was thus, on the Tuesday night I saw him at the Admiralty, a man suddenly thrown from power into impotence, and one felt rather as if one had been invited to 'come and look on fallen Antony'.

What a creature of strange moods he is – always at the top of the wheel of confidence or at the bottom of an intense depression.

Looking back on that long night we spent in the big silent Admiralty room till day broke, I cannot help reflecting on that extreme duality of mind which marked Churchill above all other men – the charm, the imaginative sympathy of his hours of defeat, the self confidence, the arrogance of his hours of power and prosperity. That night he was a lost soul, yet full of flashes of wit and humour.

But all those days of our acquaintance were his bad times, and then one could not resist the charm of his companionship or withhold from him the tribute of sympathy.

Perhaps the Dardanelles was Winston's catharsis, which humbled him and made him more aware of how others saw him. Subsequently his egotism and thirst for military glory began to be replaced by a more statesmanlike approach and a greater willingness to listen to others.

It is commonly believed nowadays that politicians have no other motive than ambition and self-advancement. It is interesting therefore to study the political situation in 1915, where we see for the first time in British history a coalition government, with a broad national mandate, being formed to prosecute a war. Furthermore, Lloyd George, who as Chancellor of the Exchequer stood as second-in-command to the Prime Minister, voluntarily relinquished his powerful job in charge of the nation's finances and went to an office in Whitehall Gardens, bare except for a table and two chairs, to establish the new Ministry of Munitions. This can only have been motivated by patriotism and his sense of what had to be done to supply the Army with the shells, machine guns and other supplies that it so urgently needed to fight the Germans in the trenches.

The fact was that the War Office under Kitchener was simply not facing up to the demands of the men at the front. Kitchener, when asked how many machine guns the Army needed, responded: two machine guns per battalion at the minimum, four at the maximum, and anything above this number was a luxury. Lloyd George's response was: 'Take Kitchener's maximum; square it; multiply that by two; and when you are in sight of that, double it again for Good Luck'; in other words, sixty-four machine guns per battalion.' By the end of the war the average per battalion exceeded eighty. As Churchill put it in his eulogy of Lloyd George in 1945:

> He was the first to discern the fearful shortages of ammunition and artillery and all the other appliances of war which would so soon affect, and in the case of Imperial Russia, mortally affect, the warring nations on both sides. He saw it before anyone . . . he hurled himself into the mobilisation of British industry. In 1915 he was building great war factories that could not come into operation for two years. There was the usual talk about the war being over in a few months, but he did not hesitate to plan on a vast scale for years ahead. It was my fortune to inherit the output of those factories in 1917 . . .

In many ways Lloyd George's work at the Ministry of Munitions was his finest hour, when he demonstrated to political and military leaders alike the energy and dedication which would carry him to the premiership a year later.

One of his innovations was to seek out and employ (usually without pay) leaders of industry such as Eric Geddes, general manager of North Eastern Railways, and Sir Joseph Maclay, whom he put in charge of shipping, construction and supplies. He had learned, during his years at the Board of Trade in 1906–8, that it was important to have both management and workforce on the same side in a national emergency – whether it be a strike situation or a war.

He did not, however, succeed with the Clydeside workers, whom he went to speak to at Christmas 1915. On this occasion he was greeted with the strains of 'The Red Flag' and was unable to deliver his speech, owing to the uproar.

He had also made a somewhat vain and ill-considered attempt to suppress drinking among the munitions workers. One result of this was that King George V 'took the pledge' not to drink alcohol until the end of the war. Lloyd George's fellow Cabinet ministers did not all follow suit (notably Asquith and Churchill), although there was a considerable improvement in the drinking habits in the country as a whole.

The difference between Churchill and Lloyd George in their approach to war is clearly illustrated by their response to events in 1914—15. Churchill, with the spirit of the young Hussar, was all for military adventures, acts of courage in pursuit of military glory, and for the striking strategic move, hence his exploits in Antwerp in October 1914 and the fiasco of the Dardanelles the following spring. Lloyd George on the other hand, who had no military background or training, looked at the prosecution of the war as a question of organisation. He was motivated by the need to save lives at the front, and to equip the British soldier with the weaponry he needed.

Though Churchill had done a magnificent job in reforming the Navy, the Army had not modernised at the same speed. Many of the politicians' difficulties with the generals stemmed from their old-fashioned mentality, which had been formed in the Victorian era and during the South African war of 1899—1902. The British generals were desperately slow to appreciate the way in which war had changed as a result of the new firepower of long-range shells and, more specifically, the machine gun, which had first been seen in action during the American Civil War fifty years earlier. Losses were so much greater than expected and yet even after the Battle of the Somme, when on 1 July 1916 there were 60,000 British casualties, General Haig refused to change his frontal-attack strategy.

Indecisive and obtuse, Kitchener was the epitome of this Victorian military mentality. Though to the general public he still appeared as the great warrior, and could not therefore easily be dismissed, the confidence of his Cabinet colleagues in his war leadership steadily sank. 'Too little, too late' was how Lloyd George characterised the War Ministry, especially in its slow response to the need to develop an 'Eastern' strategy in the Balkans and towards Constantinople.

Following the Gallipoli fiasco Kitchener had been reluctant to commit further troops to the Dardanelles. Finally Asquith sent him to Turkey to make a first-hand assessment of the situation, whereupon in November 1915 Kitchener recommended evacuation. This contributed to Churchill's decision to leave England to serve in the Army in France. On 20 December 1915, at the time of the Gallipoli evacuations, Lloyd George told the House of Commons:

> I wonder whether it will not be too late? Ah! two fatal words of this War! Too late in moving here! Too late in arriving there! Too late in coming to this decision! Too late in starting with enterprises! Too late in preparing! In this War the footsteps of the Allied forces have been dogged by the mocking spectre of 'Too Late'; and unless we quicken our movements damnation will fall on the sacred cause for which so much gallant blood has flowed!

In the end, any decision as to the future of the War Ministry was made by fate when, on 5 June 1916, the cruiser HMS *Hampshire*, carrying Kitchener to Russia, struck a mine west of the Orkney Islands and sank in ten minutes. This precipitated an immediate need for Asquith to decide who should replace Kitchener as Secretary of State for War. Lloyd George's task at the Ministry of Munitions had been accomplished and he was ready to move on, but there was intense opposition to his succeeding Kitchener – from the generals, from the Tories and even from the King. In the end it was Bonar Law whose quiet authority and influence prevailed on this question, as on so many others during the First World War. He insisted that Lloyd George should take over the job of War Secretary, which he duly did on 6 July. The same day Margot Asquith noted in her diary: 'We are out, it is only a question of time when we shall have to leave Downing Street.'

The military situation continued to deteriorate. The Germans strengthened their position by advancing into Romania. Lloyd George gave his famous 'knockout blow' interview to the United Press Association of America: 'There is neither clock nor calendar in the British Army today. Time is the least vital factor. It took England twenty years to defeat Napoleon, and the first fifteen of these years were bleak with British defeat. It will not take twenty years to win this war, but whatever time is required, it will be done.'

By the end of 1916 Britain's position was perhaps as grave as it would be in 1940. Much of the dissatisfaction at Westminster about the war effort began to focus on Asquith. All who knew him respected his intellect and erudition, his eloquence, his mastery of debate and his sense of justice; also his loyalty and kindness to his Cabinet colleagues. Asquith would have made a superb judge and was a great peacetime prime minister. By now, however, it was clear that he lacked the dynamic energy and dedication required in a war leader. Churchill, busily conspiring from the trenches, and Max Aitken, who enlisted the support of Bonar Law, jointly provoked the crisis of December 1916 which brought down Asquith and made Lloyd George Prime Minister.

When Churchill arrived in France in November 1915, filled with bitterness and disappointment at the way he had been treated by Asquith and the Conservatives after the failure of the Dardanelles campaign, his career looked singularly unpromising; and indeed he was to spend almost two years in the political wilderness. But it is thanks to the five months he spent in the trenches with the Royal Scots Fusiliers that we have a rich seam of correspondence with his political friends and colleagues, notably Lloyd George, and with his wife Clementine. To Clemmie, who neither liked nor trusted Lloyd George, he writes about the Welshman perhaps more candidly and openly than at any other time in their long friendship. As a counterpoint, unpublished correspondence among the Lloyd George family – Richard (Dick) and Gwilym (Gil) were both serving in the trenches – reflects their private opinions, of Churchill especially, but also of Asquith and Kitchener (particularly as many of their comments were written in Welsh to avoid the military censor).

As Churchill was on the point of departure, he received a farewell letter from Lloyd George.

> Dear Winston,
> I am so sorry that I have to leave for France this afternoon so that I cannot see you to say 'au revoir'.
> Your speech yesterday was amazingly clever both in substance and in tone.
> Under the circumstances you are right to go. All the same it is a blunder – a stupid blunder – to let you off. Here your special knowledge & gifts would be invaluable. I cannot help thinking that you must soon return.
> In a hurry. Good luck to you.
> Yours sincerely
> D. Lloyd George

With its concern, admiration and regard, this letter is a statement of Lloyd George's continuing affection for Churchill at his nadir.

In France, Churchill had hoped to command a brigade and was bitterly disappointed when this was vetoed by Asquith. He was given a battalion instead, thereby being promoted from major as far as colonel but not brigadier. He continued to be highly critical of both Asquith and of Kitchener, who had gone on a month's tour of army outposts in Egypt and the Middle East, taking with him the Seals of Office in case they were stolen by Lloyd George in his absence!

In his first letters home, Winston rejoices at being a soldier again for the first time in fifteen years. Initially attached to the Grenadier Guards, with whom his illustrious ancestor Marlborough had served, he is relieved to be away from the political mêlée – 'Lloyd George and McKenna and the old block [Asquith] are far away & look like the mandarins of some remote province of China . . .'

Ever hungry for political gossip and news, in the intervals between his regimental duties Churchill continually wrote to Lloyd George, scheming and plotting, urging him to take his chance, to achieve power and put new energy into the war effort. Both men were convinced that Asquith had to make way for a more dynamic administration and there is evidence from their correspondence that Lloyd George kept Churchill abreast of secret political developments within the Cabinet. For instance, on 27 December 1915 Churchill wrote:

> My dear David
> I shall be glad to hear how things go. Archie Sinclair (who you know) comes to France on Thursday. He will ring you up and fix a time to see you on Wedy. Give him any letter you may have for me. It will reach me surely.
>    Don't miss your opportunity. The time has come.
>    Yours ever
>    W

In his absence Winston wanted Clementine to stay in close touch with Lloyd George rather than with Asquith, whom he did not expect to remain as Prime Minister. At his urging, therefore, she invited Lloyd George round to lunch at 41 Cromwell Road, where she was living with her sister-in-law Goonie, and reported to Winston: 'He expressed great distress at you not being in the Government – He said repeatedly – "We must get Winston back".' This was certainly Lloyd George's sincere intention but Clemmie still felt that 'LG is a strange man. He was very polite & civil & most friendly, but for the moment the chance of working with you is gone & so his fire is gone and he is more detached . . .' For her part, she tended to feel more comfortable socially with Asquith, who despite his romantic dalliance with Venetia Stanley (Clementine's cousin) was really more of an avuncular figure:

The PM has not treated you worse than LG has done, in fact not so badly for he is not so much in your debt as the other man [referring to the Marconi scandal]. I feel sure that if the choice were equal you would prefer to work with the PM than with LG – It's true that when association ceases with the PM, he cools & congeals visibly, but all the time you were at the Admiralty he was loyal and steadfast while the other would barter you away at any time and in any place – I assure you he is the direct descendant of Judas Iscariot. At this moment although I hate the PM, if he held out his hand, I would take it (tho' I would give it a nasty twist) but before taking LG's I would have to safeguard myself with charms, touchwoods, exorcisms, and by crossing myself . . .

This mistrust of an alien Welshman was shared by the economist John Maynard Keynes who once described Lloyd George as 'this bard, this half human visitor from the Celtic Woods'.

Winston, though perhaps also suspicious of Lloyd George at times, replies in a much more down-to-earth manner: 'Lloyd George is no doubt all you say: but his interests are not divorced from mine, and in those circumstances we can work together – if occasion arises. After all, he always disagreed about D'lles [Dardanelles]. He was not like HHA [Asquith], a co-adventurer – approving & agreeing at every stage.'

In February 1916, Clementine invited Lloyd George to open a canteen for munitions workers at Ponders End in the East End of London. She reported to Winston: 'It is developing into a public meeting and the manager of the works is arranging for him to speak to the day and night shifts at the same time . . . about 2,000 men . . . I feel like a Chief Whip! He will get a very good reception I hope, a pleasant change from the Clyde.' She later reported that the meeting was a great success although she was annoyed with Lloyd George for not mentioning Winston in his speech.

Winston replied: 'I highly approve of your LG meeting . . . I am sure his setback [over conscription] is merely temporary . . . I expect we shall be working together someday – if no accident intervenes.' And after meeting F. E. Smith and Lloyd George on their visit to the Front (the arrival of two Cabinet ministers was a major break from the monotony of front-line life), Churchill wrote to Clementine, 'The group I want to work with & form into an effective governing instrument is LG, F. E., Bonar Law, Carson & Curzon.' It was a typically self-confident and prophetic view of the Coalition of 1916–22.

On 8 March 1916 Churchill, home on leave, spoke in the Commons debate about the naval estimates, attacking the dilatory direction of the Admiralty by his successor as First Lord, Balfour, with a clarity and incisive force derived from his own long experience and intimate knowledge of the Navy. Unfortunately he ruined the good impression he had made by closing his peroration with the extraordinary suggestion that his nemesis, Lord Fisher, should be recalled to the Admiralty. By the following day Churchill was aware that he had made 'a great error', as Lloyd George put it when they met. Clearly Lloyd George was still supportive and he and Churchill must have had a long and detailed discussion about the political situation: the evidence lies in the letter which Churchill subsequently wrote to Lloyd George from the trenches.

IOTH APRIL 1916                    6th Royal Scots Fusiliers
                                   In the Field

My dear David

It seems to me, from what I hear, that the situation we had in view before the Derby effort and again at Christmas is now again maturing. A decision on the recruiting question is now vital, and the repeated postponements cannot surely be tolerated longer. I think that Asquith will probably give way again at the last moment and thus the crisis will be averted for the time. But if not, the moment for you to act has come. We are jeopardizing our chances of winning by a continuance of a Governing instrument which never acts except upon political expediency, which never initiates anything and which utterly fails to do justice to the resolution and spirit of the country. You have let several good chances go by in hope of a better. I cannot judge events and forces so thoroughly from here, but I am inclined to think that this is the best opportunity that has yet offered; and that unless a decision to adopt universal conscription is taken forthwith you ought to resign. The party of the future might then be formed; and in that party we should be strong enough to secure those special political interests and principles with which we have been identified after the war is over, as well as driving the war forward with the utmost vigour.

I intend shortly to return to the House and I am only delaying from day to day on account of small ties out here.

On the whole I believe our interests are likely to lie together in the near future as they have done so often in the past, and certainly we have a common object which overrides all others.

Yours very sincerely
Winston S. Churchill

Churchill is clearly the supplicant; he was desperate to get back into the political arena and he saw Lloyd George as his best chance to do so.

Lloyd George remained a loyal friend to Winston throughout these months of exile in France, but he was himself under pressure, and asked Churchill to be patient. The Conservative Lord Derby had written to him in August 1916, convinced (as was more and more of the political world) that the time had come for a new administration and that Lloyd George must play a leading role in it:

I know your feelings about [Winston] and I appreciate very much that feeling which makes you wish not to hit a man when he is down, but Winston is never down . . :

If as I hope there will be a new Party formed at the end of the

War which shall break down all the old Party ties, Winston could not possibly be in it. Our Party will not work with him . . . and nothing would induce me to support any Government of which he was a member. I like him personally. He has got a very attractive personality but he is absolutely untrustworthy as was his father before him, and he has got to learn that just as his father had to disappear from politics so must he, or at all events from official life.

This was the fierce Tory opposition to Churchill that Lloyd George knew he would have to deal with and he would choose his own time in which to do so.

Meanwhile Richard Lloyd George was writing from the front in April 1916:

My dear Tada and Mammie,
I got a letter from Olwen tonight written on the 16th and from that I gathered you were all in condition. The weather here is delightful and our troubles have lessened considerably in consequence – everyone is very cheerful, I have never seen Tommy in better spirits. They had a bit of a dust up south of us judging by the noise last night and I understand we held the Germans back. However I hope we shall soon begin to push them out of it, so they must be weakening very much with these pushes of theirs. Leave seems to be hopeless at present and the fellows are grumbling quite a bit especially when they see fellows like Churchill getting home as often as they like. There are some Tommies here who haven't had leave for over 10 months and not much chance of getting it now. The staff get much more than their share of leave – in fact I don't think there ever was a war in which hardships and comfort were so unevenly distributed. The more danger you are in and the more uncomfortable you are the less pay you get.

Starting with the poor miserable Tommy in the front line getting £1 per day to the staff and the pay department and the Base and lines of communication who get fat pay and very comfortable billets. Somebody will write a very funny book on the war when it's all over. *Mae pawb yn y fyddin – swyddogion a'u dynion – wedi diflasu ar y dyn bach sydd yn byw drws nesa* [Everyone in the army – officers and men – is disillusioned with the little man who lives next door (i.e. Asquith)]. If some of these fellows get home I believe they should go there and kick him out literally. *Mae pawb wedi colli pob ymddiried yn K hefyd ond mae ganddynt feddwl go lew o'r prif ddyn yn y maes yma* [Everyone has lost all faith in K (Kitchener) too but they have a reasonable opinion of the chief man (Haig) in this field.]

This of course is just what you hear generally from officers and men. *Mae Churchill wedi gwneud mwy o ddrwg iddo ei hun gyda'r dynion drwy fynd adre ar leave rwan na wnaeth oerioed* [Churchill has done more harm to himself with the men by going home on leave now than he's ever done before]. I hear he is very popular in his battalion . . .

I saw Gil [Gwilym] last night with the General – both looking very well. If you are sending anything out don't send any tinned or potted stuff – you can get any amount of that cheaper here – but what we would like is some Welsh butter occasionally or a *torth laidd* [fruitcake] or something you can't possibly get here. Thank you so much for the bath. It is fine.

Your boy,
Dick

Despite all these criticisms of Churchill, Lloyd George's affection for him never wavered. He knew that it was only a matter of time before Churchill's genius and strategic thinking would again be called upon in Britain's hour of need.

# 5

## 1916–18: At His Zenith

'There are no friends at the top.'
Benjamin Disraeli, Earl of Beaconsfield,
Conservative Prime Minister 1868, 1874–80

WINSTON CHURCHILL RETURNED from the trenches in the
spring of 1916, hoping to regain office. However, he had
underestimated the opposition he faced, especially in Conservative circles – opposition that was intensified by the failure of the
Dardanelles campaign.

Lloyd George had helped Churchill to collect evidence to
present to the Dardanelles Commission, in order for his friend to
clear himself of responsibility for the military disaster of Gallipoli.
But Asquith was unwilling, in the middle of the war, to release
key documents relating to the Dardanelles, and until the
Commission published its report Churchill had no hope of being
readmitted to the inner circles of power. However, as 1916 progressed, with the heavy losses on the Somme in July and August,
there was growing criticism of the Coalition Government and of
Asquith himself.

In his book *Politicians and the War, 1914–1916*, Lord Beaverbrook
details the final months of the Asquith Government, with all the
complex discussions, negotiations and plotting between Bonar
Law and 'the Three C's' of the Conservative Party (Lord Curzon,
Lord Cecil and Austen Chamberlain) and Asquith, Lloyd George

and himself. Beaverbrook also describes finding Lloyd George in a vast room at the War Office in November 1916. He refers to him as a 'tremendous worker, and a man of limitless energy' and remarks on his informality and lack of pomposity. (A trait he had in common with his friend Winston was that they would both take a siesta after lunch.)

Lloyd George was also unhappy with the way in which the war was being conducted. He saw the need for a small and decisive War Cabinet rather than the sprawling Liberal Cabinet of twenty ministers which Asquith had maintained after August 1914, and put forward a plan for a new executive War Council of five ministers. Initially Asquith resisted the proposal but when it became clear that the Conservative members of the Coalition were behind Lloyd George, he agreed to consider a reorganisation.

The figure at the centre of the drama was Bonar Law, who formed a close alliance with Lloyd George. Their common purpose was not only to create a more effective War Council but to supply it with a more dynamic leadership. Lloyd George never expected to become Prime Minister and, indeed, Asquith had been assured of the loyalty of his leading ministers before offering his resignation, which he did on the evening of 5 Deccember.

On the night of 5 December, while Churchill was having a Turkish bath with F. E. Smith at the Royal Automobile Club in Pall Mall, Smith rang up Lloyd George to remind him that they were supposed to be dining together; he mentioned that Churchill was with him. Lloyd George immediately suggested that Winston should also be invited along. This perhaps careless suggestion gave Churchill the impression that he was regarded as one of the new Cabinet of war ministers who were about to grasp the helm. Surely Lloyd George would not wish him to be included in a dinner party, on this of all nights, if he did not mean to offer him a part in directing the war effort.

At the dinner that night, Lloyd George, Smith, Max Aitken (as Lord Beaverbrook still was then) and Churchill discussed who would play a part in the new Government. Lloyd George then left to meet Bonar Law, who had just returned from seeing the King at Buckingham Palace, having informed him that he was unable to form an administration and recommending Lloyd George as the new leader of the Coalition.

Driving with Aitken to the Palace, Lloyd George agonised over the fate of his closest political friend. Churchill, as the other radical minister in Asquith's pre-war Liberal administration, had been his rival for power. Max Beerbohm had depicted them in a famous cartoon, spinning a coin for the leadership and maliciously having Churchill say: 'Will either of us abide by the result?' (see page 98) Once, while playing golf at Walton Heath in 1910, they had arrived at the final hole all square. According to club legend, Churchill had said, 'Right – now I'll putt you for the premiership.' When the First World War began there had been wide expectation that it would be Churchill, not Lloyd George, who would become the wartime premier; in fact, their fellow Cabinet minister John Morley had predicted that, if war broke out, Churchill would 'beat Lloyd George hollow'; after all, he was the one with the military experience and the strategic vision. It was Churchill who had brilliantly reorganised the Navy in the three pre-war years. This was not to be, however, and after two years at war there still remained the question of whether to include Churchill in the new Government.

Churchill had been abandoned by Asquith because of his restless energy and capacity for innovation. Asquith had later turned against Lloyd George for developing precisely the same traits. Who then could better employ Churchill than Lloyd George, especially now that he was to become Prime Minister and could keep the young maverick under control? As Aitken well understood:

Churchill's pugnacity, his exuberance of imagination, his mental and physical restlessness and keenness, were great national assets.

What they needed, were pruning and directing. Was not this the natural task for the calmer mentality of an older man? Churchill, checked here and guided there by a man who was his official superior, could have been kept in office and his invaluable qualities turned to the most useful national purposes.

Aitken also said, 'Churchill was in fact a natural Lloyd Georgian' and, indeed, he had supported the idea of Coalition Government from the outset (as evidenced by his frequent letters to Lloyd George from France).

As they approached the Palace, Lloyd George told Aitken that he was particularly worried about Churchill since there was enormous pressure from his new Conservative colleagues to keep Winston out of government. Although he fully recognised Churchill's great abilities, he did not believe this was an opportune moment for his return to office. He asked Aitken to convey a hint to this effect to Churchill. (Aitken was himself expecting a ministry, the Board of Trade, but would be offered a peerage instead.)

On returning to Smith's dinner party, Aitken smiled at Churchill and said, 'The new Government will be very well disposed towards you. All your friends will be there. You will have a great field of common action with them.' Churchill 'suddenly felt that he had been duped by his invitation to the dinner' and was furious. He rose from his seat and said to F. E. (a man he had never formerly been known to address by his surname), 'Smith, this man knows that I am NOT to be included in the new Government.' With that, Churchill marched out into the street, carrying his hat and with his coat over his arm. Smith rushed after him and tried to persuade him to return, but in vain. Churchill's disappointment was the cause of a rift between him and Lloyd George that lasted for several months.

Churchill's version of the December 1916 change of government was that it was a *coup d'état*: 'Lloyd George seized the headship of the Government,' he said in the House of Commons

('Lloyd George seized the main power in the State,' he would repeat in his eulogy of 1945). 'Seized?!' responded indignant Members of Parliament. 'Yes,' said Churchill, 'seized, although perhaps the place was his, as Carlyle said of Cromwell.' But judging by Beaverbrook's insider's account of the so-called 'coup', this was not, in fact, the case.

The next day, Lloyd George met a Tory deputation consisting of Curzon, Walter Long and Austen Chamberlain and gave them the promises that they demanded – to keep Haig in command of the Army and Churchill out of the Cabinet. The Labour Party also threw in its lot with the Coalition Government, their representative Arthur Henderson joining the War Cabinet together with Carson, Curzon and Bonar Law. (Carson later said that more was decided within a few hours at the first meeting of the slimmed-down War Cabinet than in the previous twelve months.)

Asquith was clearly mistaken in thinking that no one but himself would be able to form an administration. However, it is of interest that he had a conversation with Sir Robert Donald, the editor of the *News Chronicle*, on 7 December, the day after the 'coup'. Asked whether he thought Lloyd George had caused the fall of the Government, Asquith replied that he had always been most friendly to him and that no rift had occurred in their personal relations; that Lloyd George possessed unique gifts – a real flair for politics, foresight and inspiration. Asquith did not say that Lloyd George owed a great deal to him: he had supported him over the People's Budget in 1909, and again during the Marconi scandal in 1913. Frances Stevenson would record in her diary for 22 July 1921 that she was introduced to Margot Asquith at a royal garden party: 'Mrs A. . . . mentioned Megan [LG] and I said the P.M. always said how kind Mrs A. was to her. "Not so kind as my husband was to him" was her retort.' Nevertheless, it was clear that Asquith would not accept Lloyd George's offer to be Lord Chancellor in the new administration, so F. E. Smith took the job instead (and became Lord Birkenhead).

In forming his new Cabinet, Lloyd George sought out the most experienced and influential Conservative leaders, among them Arthur Balfour and Lord Curzon. Balfour had been Prime Minister from 1902–5 and was a statesman of international repute. Curzon too had achieved his summit early in life, by becoming Viceroy of India before the age of forty. However, while Lloyd George treated Balfour with great respect and deference, with Curzon he was somewhat dismissive and often acted on his Foreign Secretary's behalf rather than allowing Curzon to enjoy the full power of office. Churchill's perceptive summary of the relationship between the two men in his book *Great Contemporaries* (1937) also tells us much about his own perception of Lloyd George.

> You could hardly imagine two men so diverse as Curzon and Lloyd George. Temperament, prejudices, environment, upbringing, mental processes were utterly different and markedly antagonistic. There never of course was any comparison in weight and force between the two. The offspring of the Welsh village whose whole youth had been rebellion against the aristocracy, who had skipped indignant out of the path of the local Tory magnate driving his four-in-hand, and revenged himself at night upon that magnate's rabbits, had a priceless gift. It was the very gift which the product of Eton and Balliol had always lacked – the one blessing denied him by his fairy godmothers, the one without which all other gifts are so frightfully cheapened. He had the 'seeing eye'. He had that deep original instinct which peers through the surfaces of words and things – the vision which sees dimly but surely the other side of the brick wall or which follows the hunt two fields before the throng. Against this, industry, learning, scholarship, eloquence, social influence, wealth, reputation, an ordered mind, plenty of pluck, counted for less than nothing. Put the two men together in any circumstances of equality and the one would eat the other.

In his first address as Prime Minister on 7 December 1916, to a group of Labour MPs, Lloyd George made some remarks that would be echoed in Churchill's own 'Blood, toil, tears and sweat' speech in the House of Commons in May 1940.

Don't let us make any mistake – for the war for the moment is going badly; the country and all the nations which hang upon the triumph of Great Britain are in great peril. Bucharest falling is not merely a question of one city passing into the hands of the enemy; it means, for the moment, the blockade broken; the work of the fleet to that extent neutralised, and we are face to face with the grimmest and most perilous struggle that this country has ever been engaged [in] . . . *I hate war, I abominate it.* I sometimes think, Am I dreaming? Is it a nightmare? It cannot be a fact. That is a thing to consider before you go into it; once you are in it, you have got to go grimly through it, otherwise the causes which hang upon it will all perish. Delay in war is as fatal as an illness . . . We cannot send men to carnage without seeing that, at any rate, everything is being done to give them a fair chance to win through to victory . . . I do not believe any Prime Minister, whoever he is, even if he has the strength of a giant mentally and physically and morally, can possibly undertake the task of running Parliament and running the war . . . Whoever undertakes to run the war must put his whole strength into it . . . I wish myself there were no parties during the war . . . I think the country is looking out for something else; it is looking out for a Government that will prosecute the war efficiently.

Alluding to a movement headed by Lord Lansdowne, which was seeking a negotiated peace with Germany, Lloyd George, in his first speech as Premier in the House of Commons, quoted his hero Abraham Lincoln: 'We accepted this war for an object, and the war will end when that object is attained.' This sentiment, too, was echoed by Churchill at the end of May 1940 in his struggle with Halifax to maintain the morale of Britain under the threat of invasion. Both Prime Ministers started their premierships by insisting that Britain would not agree to peace negotiations but would fight on until victory was won.

After the Coalition Government was announced on 10 December 1916 Lloyd George asked the newspaper proprietor, George Riddell, to tell Churchill that he would endeavour to find him a suitable position, such as Chairman of the Air Board, once the report of the Dardanelles Commission had been published. Churchill received the news, which could hardly have been a surprise, with painful anger. Afterwards Riddell confided to his diary, apparently not telling Lloyd George:

> Winston made me a little speech. He told me that for twelve years he and LG had acted in concert and that he had almost invariably subordinated his views to those of LG, the exception being the dispute on the Naval estimates in 1913. At the Marconi time he (W) had stood loyally by LG, and had debased himself to Northcliffe in order to secure his neutrality. LG had repaid him by bringing about his downfall when the Coalition was established, and now he had passed him by. Winston had determined on the first occasion never to speak to LG again, but had succumbed to his advances. Mrs Winston remarked that LG had said in her presence that he would do his bit to atone for what had been done.

Churchill threatened Riddell:

> I am still a member of the Liberal Party, and an event may happen at any moment which will lead me to alter my position. I will take any position which will enable me to serve my country but I have had enough soft soap and can only judge by actions. Had he [Lloyd George] stood by me, he would have had a loyal and capable colleague whom he could trust. Instead he has allied himself with associates who are not really in sympathy with him, and who, when he has served their purposes, will desert him without compunction.

After their interview Riddell reported that Churchill had demanded to know who had objected to his presence in the Government. Riddell had replied that he did not know, reasoning later that no matter what he said Churchill would blame his

*Right:* David Lloyd George aged 16, 1879. The previous year he had started work as a trainee solicitor and was already involved in politics through the local debating society

*Below:* Lloyd George's childhood home, Highgate in the village of Llanstumdwy near Criccieth, North Wales. The sign over the door reads 'Richard Lloyd – Manufacturer', in Welsh, and includes a picture of a boot; he was the village shoemaker

*Left:* Winston Churchill in his uniform as an officer in the 4th Hussars shortly before his embarkation for India, 1895

Below: Blenheim Palace, Churchill's birthplace, one of the largest private family homes in Britain. It was built between 1705 and 1722 by the architects Vanbrugh and Hawksmoor, as a gift from the nation to John Churchill, first Duke of Marlborough, victor of the Battle of Blenheim, 1704

*Right:* David Lloyd George photographed in 1903 as a 40-year-old backbencher, later to take Cabinet office when the Liberals returned to power in December 1905

*Below:* Winston Churchill pictured when he first stood for Parliament in 1900 after his return from South Africa at the age of 25

*Above:* Meeting of the Colonial Prime Ministers, London, 8 May 1907: Lord Elgin (*seated centre*), H. H. Asquith (*far left*), David Lloyd George (*far right*), Winston Churchill (*behind Asquith*). This may be the first photograph showing Lloyd George and Churchill together

*Left:* David Lloyd George and Winston Churchill at an air show before the First World War

In the month before Churchill's wedding, Lloyd George invited him to attend the Royal National Eisteddfod, in Llangollen. This was also the occasion on which Lloyd George introduced Churchill to the bishop who would officiate at his wedding. *From left to right:* Bishop A. G. Edwards of St. Asaph, David Lloyd George, Megan Lloyd George (aged 5) and Winston Churchill

Winston Churchill and Clementine Hozier on their engagement, 1908

*Opposite page, above left:* Lord Randolph Churchill, 1880. His career rose and fell rapidly as he achieved the high office of Chancellor of the Exchequer in 1886, only to resign within nine months. His example cast a long shadow over the young Winston *Above right:* Herbert Henry Asquith as Chancellor of the Exchequer, 1905. He served as Liberal Prime Minister from 1908 to 1916, and offered calm and steady support for the radical policies of Lloyd George and Churchill

*Left:* Winston's first day at the Admiralty, October 1911. It is probably true to say that Winston owed his elevation to the Admiralty to Lloyd George's intervention with Asquith. It was to be one of Churchill's most rewarding appointments over the next three and a half years

*Below:* Budget Day 1910. David Lloyd George, Chancellor of the Exchequer walks with red dispatch case containing the People's Budget, nervously watched by Winston Churchill. Lloyd George's wife Margaret (*left*) also looks anxious

First Sea Lord, Admiral John Fisher, 1905. An eccentric but brilliant tactician who built up Britain's fleet of Dreadnoughts, his irrepressible unpredictability cost Churchill dearly in the Gallipoli crisis of 1915

Max Aitken, Lord Beaverbrook, 1930. A Canadian financier and newspaperman, he was a go-between in both world wars, especially in the political crisis of December 1916 when he carried messages between Lloyd George, Bonar Law, Churchill and Asquith

David Lloyd George, unidentified, Clementine Churchill, Margaret Lloyd George and Winston Churchill in Criccieth, 1910. This photograph was probably taken on the occasion of the Churchills' visit to the Lloyd Georges at their new house, Brynawelon ('House of the Breezes')

Winston Churchill, Margot Asquith, H. H. Asquith, David Lloyd George and Sir Edward Grey in Scotland, 1913. This photograph was almost certainly taken during a voyage of the Admiralty yacht HMS *Enchantress* before the First World War

Lloyd George pictured on the Criccieth golf course with his brother William George (*far left*), 1910. Golf was a shared pastime of many of the Liberal leaders including Lloyd George and Churchill

Winston Churchill playing golf at Cannes, 1913. He famously described the game as 'like chasing a quinine pill round a pasture with weapons ill-designed for the purpose'

Notes passed during Cabinet meetings in August 1914 reflect Churchill's passionate effort to persuade his closest friend in the Liberal Cabinet to agree to the fateful Declaration of War

*Left:* First Lord of the Admiralty (WSC) to Chancellor of the Exchequer (DLG): 'All the rest of our lives we shall be opposed. I am deeply attached to you and have followed your instinct and guidance for nearly 10 years'

*Right:* Lloyd George: 'If patience prevails and you do not press us too hard tonight we might come together'. Churchill: 'Please God – It is our whole future – comrades or opponents. The march of events will be dominating'

*Right:* David Lloyd George and Clementine Churchill at the opening of a Munitions Workers' canteen at Poynter's End in East London, February 1916. Mrs Churchill looks uncomfortable and afterwards wrote to Winston, 'before taking [his hand] I would have to safeguard myself with charms, touchwoods, exorcisms, and by crossing myself'

*Below:* Lloyd George, giving a speech at Poynter's End, February 1916. Clementine Churchill (*far left*), Margaret Lloyd George (*far right*) and Megan Lloyd George (*left of her father*)

Sir James Guthrie, *Statesmen of World War One*, painted in 1925 Lloyd George sits on the left beneath Lord Kitchener, Asquith at the opposite end of the table beneath Bonar Law and Balfour. In a prophetic insight, Churchill – the future Prime Minister – captures the light and focus at the centre of the group portrait

*Above:* David Lloyd George and A. J. Balfour leaving the Quai d'Orsay, 1919. Balfour was at the Foreign Office during Lloyd George's premiership and gave his name to the famous 'Balfour Declaration' in support of a Jewish homeland in Palestine

*Right:* David Lloyd George and Andrew Bonar Law at the Allied conference at St James's Palace, 1921. Bonar Law had been the quiet, steady number two to Lloyd George throughout his premiership, and had kept the Conservative majority in support of the coalition

David Lloyd George with Lord Birkenhead and Winston Churchill leaving No. 10 Downing Street during the negotiation of the Anglo-Irish Treaty, October 1922. Having been a diehard Ulster supporter, Lord Birkenhead was a key figure in the coalition at this time, bringing Tory support for the settlement with Ireland

Lloyd George and Churchill at the Printers' Pension Fund dinner, 1934. Aged 70, Lloyd George wrote to Churchill beforehand that the duty of making the speech was turned into a pleasure by knowing that Winston would be there. This photograph shows how much fun they had together

*Right:* David Lloyd George and Winston Churchill in Cannes, 1938. The photograph may have been taken shortly after the party thrown by Winston and Clementine Churchill in honour of the Lloyd Georges' golden wedding in January 1938

*Below:* David Lloyd George at home in Churt, 1942, in front of Churchill's painting of the South of France. He was greatly touched by Churchill's gift: 'your picture is a joy and a delight and will cheer an old fellow'

Winston Churchill making a speech at a meeting of the members of the Lords and Commons to hear Field Marshal Smuts, 21 October 1942. As Father of the House, Lloyd George sits on the right. This is probably the last photograph of the 'Two Fathers of Victory' together

Churchill at Lloyd George's Memorial Service, April 1945. Never self-conscious about displaying his emotions, Churchill's grief is visible

exclusion on Lloyd George. The Prime Minister became somewhat angry on hearing Riddell's account: Churchill had no right
to ask such a question; he was 'unreasonable'.

On 20 December Balfour wrote: 'I am sorry Asquith is not still
PM. That was what I wanted. But I was all for Lloyd George
being given a free hand.' He knew the need for desperate measures and earlier, on being informed that Lloyd George 'wants to
be a dictator', had remarked: 'Let him be. If he thinks he can win
the war, I am all for him having a try.'

Nevertheless, for the moment Lloyd George's political position
was perilously dependent on the support of the Coalition
Conservatives led by Bonar Law, since most Liberals had followed
Asquith into Opposition. As Richard Lloyd George recalled:

> Father needed the Tory support . . . Yet he had not the least inten-
> tion of keeping his promise to the Tories [about keeping Churchill
> out]. When I reproached him about his promise he flashed at me,
> 'If I can't convince them, I'll outflank them. If I can't outflank
> them, I'll smash them.' . . . He nursed the determination to get
> Winston back as soon as he was strong enough. A year later [1917]
> he made the first moves.

The key decisions that Lloyd George took during the nearly two
years in which he ran his wartime administration flowed directly
from his experience in building up the Ministry of Munitions.
That was where he learned how to wage total war; how to organise production to meet the needs of the huge conscription army;
and how to harness the reservoir of British labour and manufacturing skills, as well as key industrial leaders, to help in executive
roles of management.

Lloyd George had taken over the direction of the war at a very
low point in the nation's fortunes. His biographer John Grigg
argues persuasively that Britain in 1917 was in no less peril than
in her better-known 'finest hour' of 1940. The biggest problem
was the growing rate of merchant shipping losses as a result of the

German U-boats which threatened the British people with star-vation. During the worst month, April 1917, nearly 800,000 tonnes of Allied shipping were sunk. Lloyd George saw that his primary task was therefore to rebuild the shipping fleet.

On his first day as Prime Minister, Lloyd George telephoned the shipping magnate Sir Joseph Maclay and brought him down, post haste, from Scotland to organise the production of merchant steamers. Maclay did for shipping what Geddes had done for munitions: a million tonnes of new ships were launched in 1917, a large number of which were powerful 8,000-tonners that could outstrip most German warships.

Lloyd George then requested the Admiralty to come up with a plan to protect merchant shipping. They suggested a corridor of fast naval vessels at the approaches to British harbours but the Prime Minister's response was that this would play straight into the hands of the U-boats. He told the naval strategists that perhaps a moving corridor or convoy of naval vessels would help. The admirals were apoplectic at the radical idea of the Navy acting in this 'wet-nurse' capacity for merchantmen (although they had done so during the Napoleonic Wars). They dismissed the plan as impossible because over 2,500 merchant vessels entered British ports every day.

Without warning, the Prime Minister visited the Admiralty and confronted the statisticians who had compiled the figure of 2,500 merchant ships. When this figure was broken down and shown to include every available fishing smack and ferry boat it became apparent that the convoy system *could* be made to work. As a result, less than 1 per cent of British merchant vessels were sunk in the final eighteen months of the war.

But to begin with, in the early months of Lloyd George's prem-iership, the situation worsened. The Germans declared that they would follow a policy of unrestricted U-boat attacks. At least this had one desirable effect: namely, by April 1917, of prompting the reluctant US President, Woodrow Wilson, to declare war on the

Germans and begin the slow process of mobilising American troops and transporting them to France.

Britain was in dire straits both on the naval front and on the Western Front, where the French Army had taken heavy losses and was close to mutiny. The next major decision facing the new Coalition was the command of the British Army at the Front. The job had already gone to Sir Douglas Haig who had a close personal friendship with King George V and was a good deal more adept at political intrigue than his military demeanour suggested.

Lloyd George put pressure on the French general Nivelle to launch an offensive in April 1917 but it failed. Haig argued that he could break through the German lines with a large-scale offensive. Politically, Lloyd George was not in a strong enough position to restrain Haig and the British generals from mounting frontal attacks. The result in 1917, at Passchendaele, was a terrible repetition of the heavy losses taken in the summer of 1916 in the Battle of the Somme.

Churchill gave his opinion of Lloyd George's military competence in a letter to Beaverbrook of November 1926:

> I am grieved that the story should produce the impression on your mind of hostility to LG. I think now, as I said then, that he was utterly wrong about Nivelle, about not stopping Passchendaele and about not reinforcing the army in the winter of 1918. He would have had far more authority over GHQ if he had not chopped and changed so much about offensives in the west. Every three or four months he was in a new mood. They at any rate were consistent about always wanting to attack. I was consistent in always trying to stop them. LG figures on both sides of the account with a contradiction which history is bound to note, because all the documents exist. In the upshot he was always wrong. He encouraged the Nivelle offensive which ended in disaster. He discouraged the final advance in 1918 which ended in success. He gave way about the prolongation of Passchendaele against a true conviction. Still there is no doubt he was much

better as No 1 than anybody else. The same may be said of Haig. The truth is that Armageddon was quite beyond the compass of anybody, even including you and me.

However, by 29 May 1917, the former Foreign Secretary Edward Grey, at least had 'a feeling we are winning the war', as he wrote to Lord Buxton. 'If so, Lloyd George deserves great credit . . . he really did push a lot of things through and get them done.'

The same month, after an intense debate in the House of Commons, Lloyd George and Churchill ran into each other at the Bar of the House of Commons, as they had done in February 1901. Following this meeting, Churchill began to bombard the Prime Minister with military strategies and ideas. Lloyd George found him to be not only a helpful ally but also a cheerful, life-enhancing companion at a time of great stress and heavy losses on the front. To their relationship Churchill also brought his intimate knowledge of the Army and his friendships with the generals, with whom Lloyd George had never felt comfortable.

Frances Stevenson gives us an insight into Lloyd George's thoughts at this time:

19TH MAY 1917
Meanwhile D. is seriously contemplating some changes in his Ministry. He says he wants someone in who will cheer him up and help & encourage him . . . I think D. is thinking of getting Winston in in some capacity. He has an intense admiration for his cleverness, & at any rate he is energetic and forceful. D. has seen him once or twice lately & I think they have talked things over . . . I don't know whether D. is seriously thinking of taking Churchill on, as he knows his limitations and realises that he is eaten up with conceit. 'He has spoilt himself by reading about Napoleon,' said D. to me.

After that second significant meeting at the Bar in May 1917, Lloyd George came to depend upon Churchill's advice on a daily basis. As was his wont, he carefully sounded out his Tory colleagues on the question of bringing Churchill back into the Cabinet. Did they not think that a man of such energy and imagination was needed in the Government? Was not Churchill wasted outside office? 'No' was the resounding answer. Bonar Law, now Lloyd George's closest ally, was asked whether he would prefer to have Churchill on his side or against him. The Scotsman replied, 'I would rather have him against me.' Lord Derby, the War Secretary, wanted none of Churchill and nor did the other Conservative members of the Cabinet. 'Some of them felt stronger about Churchill than about the Kaiser,' Lloyd George later told his son Richard. The press was also against his return to office.

Nevertheless, despite his promise to keep Churchill out of the Cabinet, Lloyd George sent Bonar Law's close friend, Beaverbrook, round to talk to him. Beaverbrook, who was also a friend of Churchill, was one of the few people who were not envious of his dynamic energy and genius. After two days Bonar Law was finally won round. Richard Lloyd George described the ensuing uproar: 'As the news swept through Parliament of Churchill's impending appointment as Minister of Munitions, scores of MPs gathered in furious conclave. "Down with Churchill! Down with Lloyd George! Have them both out!" "He's tricked us!" "He's broken his promise! Out with Lloyd George and his amateur strategist, Winston Churchill!"' More than a hundred MPs formed an anti-Churchill Coalition Front. But there was no organised leadership and there were no resignations. Lloyd George's gamble paid off. As one contemporary observer put it, 'His throne tottered but did not fall.'

Lloyd George observed privately, 'I have got back Winston. That was not easy . . . but I *have had my way*.' The Conservatives clearly understood that his reinstatement was an act of friendship. The *Morning Post* commented that 'by appointing Churchill the Prime Minister had proved to be a man who allows private partiality to overcome public duty'.

In his *War Memoirs* of 1933, Lloyd George described Churchill as:

One of the most remarkable and puzzling enigmas of his time . . .
His fertile mind, his undoubted courage, his untiring industry, and
his thorough study of the art of war, would have made him a useful
member of a War Cabinet. Here his more erratic impulses could
have been kept under control and his judgment supervised and
checked, before plunging into action. Men of his ardent temperament and powerful mentality need exceptionally strong brakes . . .
Even the Tory antipathy to him was so great that for a short while
the very existence of the Government was in jeopardy . . .

Why were they so bitter and implacable? His political record
naturally exasperated his old Party. He does nothing by halves, and
when he left it he attacked his old associates and condemned his
old principles with a vigour and a witty scorn which rankled . . .
But Conservatives could not forgive nor forget Churchill's desertion to their enemies, and his brisk and deadly firing into their
ranks at a moment when their rout had begun. Had he remained
a faithful son of the political household in which he was born and
brought up, his share in the Dardanelles fiasco would have been
passed over and another sacrifice would have been offered up to
appease the popular anger . . .

It was interesting to observe in a concentrated form every phase
of the distrust and trepidation with which mediocrity views
genius at close quarters. Unfortunately, genius always provides its
critics with material for censure – it always has and always will.
Churchill is certainly no exception to this rule . . . His mind was
a powerful machine, but there lay hidden in its material or its
make-up some obscure defect which prevented it from always
running true . . .

I took a different view of his possibilities. I felt that his
resourceful mind and his tireless energy would be invaluable under
supervision. That he had vision and imagination, no one could
doubt. The Dardanelles idea and his early discernment of the
value of tanks (Churchill had had the imagination to sponsor their
development, having seen for himself the deadly effect of
machine-gun fire) clearly demonstrated his possession of these
faculties. Men with such gifts are rare – very rare.

I took the risk, and although I had occasionally some reason to regret my trust, I am convinced I was right to overrule the misgivings of my colleagues, for Churchill rendered conspicuous service in further increasing the output of munitions when an overwhelming supply was essential to victory. As to Churchill's future, it will depend on whether he can establish a reputation for prudence without losing audacity.

This is one of the rare instances where Lloyd George expressed his true opinion of his friend. Unlike Churchill, he hated writing letters (he was the first Prime Minister to dispense with the weekly handwritten letter to the King, describing Cabinet discussions) and even in this passage from his memoirs, he writes with a typical Edwardian reserve and detachment. Yet his admiration for Churchill's 'genius' and 'powerful mind' shines through. There is no doubt that in the prosecution of the war effort in 1917 and 1918, it was with Churchill (both before and after his appointment as Minister of Munitions) that Lloyd George discussed every military and political problem.

July 1917 was a turning point for Churchill: he was back at the centre of power after two years in the wilderness. To celebrate his return he dined with Lloyd George at Number 10. When the Prime Minister took him into the sitting room after dinner Lloyd George brought out of the cupboard a placard produced by the *Daily Express* at the time of the Marconi affair. It read: CHURCHILL DEFENDS LLOYD GEORGE. Lloyd George had repaid his debt. For his part, Churchill would never forget that he owed his political resurrection to the Welshman.

Lloyd George appointed Churchill to the Ministry that he himself had created in 1915 – Munitions – which he knew intimately, and where, as Churchill described in his 1945 eulogy: 'There was the usual talk about the war being over in a few months, but he did not hesitate to plan on a vast scale for two years ahead. It was my fortune to inherit the output of those factories

in 1917 – the vast, overflowing output which came from them.'
When Churchill arrived at the Ministry of Munitions, production was already overflowing because Lloyd George had foreseen
that the war would continue beyond the expectations of others.

He was once asked who he would have in his ideal Cabinet.
He replied: 'Rothschild as Chancellor, Smuts as Foreign
Secretary, Philip Snowden for the Labour Department and Billy
Hughes as Colonial Secretary, and an Executive Committee with
myself as Chairman and two Ministers without Portfolio –
Winston Churchill and Max Beaverbrook.'

Unlike Bonar Law and his Conservative colleagues, Lloyd
George realised that it was safer to have Churchill inside the
Cabinet than outside. As a solicitor he used to say that he would
rather hire the best barrister to be his counsel, in case the other
side employed him first. It did not matter too much to him which
Ministry he put in Churchill's charge. The important thing for
Lloyd George was to have Winston at his side to discuss every
issue and problem as it arose. Churchill himself was never in any
way bounded by his departmental responsibilities; his mind
ranged freely over the whole spectrum of political and military
issues. Lloyd George frequently used him as a secret or special
emissary, whether to brief the generals at the front or to liaise with
the French leadership. After visiting Clemenceau in 1918,
Churchill recounted in his memoirs how deeply impressed he was
by the French Prime Minister's 'fighting speech' in the days when
the Germans were advancing on Paris. It was a speech from which
Churchill himself drew inspiration in 1940 ('We shall fight in the
streets . . . we shall never surrender').

The greatest significance of Churchill's close alliance with Lloyd
George between May 1917 and the end of the war lies in the
lessons that the younger man learned from him, and was able to
apply when he became Prime Minister himself in 1940: the need
to provide dynamic leadership by means of inspiring oratory as

well as efficient administration; the need to have a strong but small and decisive War Cabinet with all-party representation; the need (perhaps one that Lloyd George often forgot) to maintain close contact with the House of Commons; and the need to have a strong, unified command on the military front. In the First World War this was provided by Marshal Foch; in the Second World War, by General Eisenhower.

Never in the whole of Britain's history has the Prime Minister commanded so much power as during the two World Wars. Lloyd George effectively became a dictator, with more power in his own hands than any parliamentary leader since Cromwell. He inaugurated an era of presidential government in England by means of a vastly expanded staff (the famous 'garden suburb') at 10 Downing Street. Churchill, on the other hand, may not have had quite as much personal power in the 1940s, despite his image as the greatest Briton and saviour of his country. The generals often resisted his strategic ideas. However, there was a profound difference between the political situation in 1917 and that in 1940. Lloyd George began his war premiership with a highly critical military hierarchy and a coalition composed mainly of Conservative ministers, with a small rump of the Liberal Party and Arthur Henderson representing Labour. Churchill, on the other hand, started his term of office with the generals in anxious submission and a House of Commons majority for his own party, even though his position between May and November 1940 was by no means a strong one. And whereas Asquith had declined to serve as Lloyd George's Lord Chancellor in 1917, the previous Conservative leader, Neville Chamberlain, accepted office under Churchill in 1940. Daily in 1917–18 Lloyd George had to face an even more fearful casualty list than Churchill during the Second World War, although they both shared the same anxiety about the steady sinking of Britain's shipping. Finally, Churchill enjoyed the strong support of the United States and the intimate friendship of Franklin D. Roosevelt, whereas Woodrow Wilson was a reluctant ally and even after the Americans declared war on Germany in April 1917, it took twelve months for US troops to arrive in France.

There are some similarities in the way that Lloyd George and Churchill arrived at the premiership. Both their predecessors, Asquith and Chamberlain, had proved themselves indecisive and unequal to the demands of a growing national emergency. Lloyd George and Churchill, on the other hand, were exceptionally well equipped to inspire the country at a time of national crisis. Such was their administrative energy and capacity for leadership that Britain, alone of the major powers, survived a full participation in two world wars without its traditional institutions being destroyed. The House of Commons continued to operate in an almost habitual manner until 1940, when Churchill instituted 'Secret Sessions' of Parliament in order that strategic and military issues could be discussed in detail with members of the House without their being published for the benefit of the enemy.

A key to their success as war leaders also lay in the power of oratory. Owing to the role of radio Churchill's wartime speeches are much better known than Lloyd George's. However, a careful analysis of these will demonstrate his debt to Lloyd George both in spirit and very often in detailed phrasing. Lloyd George's style was always more populist and down-to-earth than that of Churchill. In his first great wartime speech at the Queen's Hall in October 1914, Lloyd George's homely images of life in a Welsh village – 'I know of a sheltered valley . . . I see the mountains arising beyond it' – contrast strikingly with Churchill's grand rolling phrases: 'Never in the field of human conflict, was so much owed by so many to so few'. . . 'the Battle of France is over, the Battle of Britain is about to begin.'

In forging the government and administrative structure to wage the Second World War, Churchill was the more fortunate of the two leaders in that he already had Lloyd George's achievements of 1917–18 behind him. He himself often acknowledged a debt to Lloyd George in respect of the small but powerful War Cabinet, 'the unified military command' which he established in 1917 and his occasional willingness to override the advice of the GHQ military staff and to experiment with new strategies in different theatres of the war. The 'Eastern' strategy which had dominated Cabinet discussions in early 1915, and resulted in the Gallipoli disaster, came back into focus in 1942–4 when Churchill pushed the Americans to launch Operation Torch in North Africa; also during the 1943 landings in Sicily, the ill-fated Crete expeditions and the successful D-Day landings in Normandy in June 1944.

The war situation in early 1917 was in many ways as perilous as in the summer of 1940, with colossal merchant marine losses posing a serious threat to Britain's vital food supply, but with the Nazi forces reaching Dunkirk in May 1940, the possibility of invasion in the Second World War was much more real. However, whereas Churchill knew that victory was assured once the Americans had joined the Allies in December 1941, Britain could have lost the First World War even as late as 1918 without the arrival in the spring of US troops on the Western Front.

As Churchill himself described it, Lloyd George's ascent to power in 1916 imparted a whole new dynamism to the war effort. He commended Lloyd George's 'power to live in the present, yet without taking short views' and also his 'power of drawing from misfortune itself the means of future success'. Churchill himself always took long historic views, as when he contrasted the Battle of Britain in the summer of 1940 with the Armada of 1588 or the Battle of Trafalgar in 1805. When he became Prime Minister in 1940 he followed Lloyd George's example of appointing businessmen and other non-political experts to key ministries. He described Lloyd George as the greatest man of action he had ever known. He had been exemplary in remaining constantly nimble and flexible, challenging military orthodoxy and old-fashioned thinking to find new means of defeating the enemy. Lloyd George imposed the convoy system upon a reluctant Admiralty. Churchill's many unorthodox wartime strategies included setting up British Security Coordination (BSC) for the unofficial exchange of security information with the Americans in 1940, more than a year before the United States entered the war; establishing the Special Operations Executive or 'department of dirty tricks' to infiltrate agents into occupied Europe; inventing the Mulberry harbours for D-Day; and supporting scientific innovations such as radar.

Churchill was continuously aware of the precedents set by Lloyd George in the First World War. He said, for example, 'I won't make the same mistakes as Lloyd George in 1918 [in calling the Coupon Election and maintaining Coalition Government for another four years]'. Instead, immediately after the victory over Nazi Germany in May 1945, Churchill allowed a return to normal peacetime party politics and promptly lost the July election to an unexpected Labour landslide. When his wife, Clementine, commented, 'It may be a blessing in disguise', he replied, 'Well, at the moment it's certainly very well disguised.' Unlike Lloyd George, who fell from power in 1922 never to return, Churchill succeeded in staging a comeback in 1951 and continued as Prime Minister until 1955 when he was over eighty.

Also unlike Lloyd George, Churchill was very effective at moulding his own legend by publishing detailed memoirs of both wars: *The World Crisis* in six volumes, which Balfour described as 'Winston's brilliant Autobiography disguised as a history of the universe'; and *The Second World War*, also in six volumes, which recounts the war from the point of view of his personal experience and impressions quite as much as his autobiographical work, *My Early Life*. Lloyd George's *War Memoirs*, on the other hand, appeared more than fifteen years after the end of the First World War, and he never succeeded in projecting his personality as a national leader after leaving office in 1922. He did try to justify himself in his book *The Truth about the Peace Treaties*, published in 1938, but his image faded during the era of Baldwin, MacDonald and Chamberlain, whereas Churchill's was burnished by the wilderness years of the thirties because of his prophetic rightness about the Nazi menace.

In conclusion, it is clear from Churchill's writings that there was nobody to whom he felt he owed a greater debt than to Lloyd George. His introduction to the Liberal Party in 1904 was by the side of this radical mentor; his participation in the great reform period of 1908–11 owed its inspiration and direction to Lloyd George's broad vision of social reform and, as Churchill put it in his eulogy, his love of the people and compassion for the poor. Churchill even owed his appointment as First Lord of the Admiralty, which gave him his greatest early achievements in office, to Lloyd George's intervention with Asquith. Lloyd George had tried to save him from disgrace after the Dardanelles in 1915, and had brought him back into the Cabinet in the teeth of Tory objections in July 1917. Churchill's gradual move to the right during the Coalition years of 1917–22, and his return to the Conservative Party, took place under Lloyd George's stewardship. And, finally, he owed much of the vision and dynamic energy which make for successful wartime leadership to the example set by Lloyd George in 1917–18 and to the stirring oratory which accompanied it.

# 6

## 1917–21: Shaping the Peace

*IN WAR*: RESOLUTION

*IN DEFEAT*: DEFIANCE

*IN VICTORY*: MAGNANIMITY

*IN PEACE*: GOODWILL

              Winston S. Churchill, *The Second World War*

O N THE DAY the First World War ended, 11 November 1918, Winston and Clementine Churchill went to 10 Downing Street to congratulate the Prime Minister. In his informal way Lloyd George invited Winston to dinner. As Churchill recorded in *The World Crisis*:

> On the night of the Armistice I dined with the Prime Minister at Downing Street. We were alone in the large room from whose walls the portraits of Pitt and Fox, of Nelson and Wellington and – perhaps somewhat incongruously – of Washington then looked down . . . [Lloyd George] was always natural and simple . . . One could say anything to him, on the terms that he could say anything back . . . The conversation ran on the great qualities of the German people . . . At that time we thought they were actually starving . . . I suggested that we should immediately, pending further news, rush a dozen great ships crammed with provisions into Hamburg.

Much of the discussion between Lloyd George and Churchill

that month must have been about the 'Coupon Election'* that was to be held in December. The two men had exchanged letters on 8 and 9 November on the subject of the post-war Cabinet and Winston's possible inclusion in it, Lloyd George writing: 'I should deeply and sincerely regret if anything came to sever a political and personal friendship which has now extended over fourteen years.' Churchill's reply concludes:

> . . . am I unreasonable in wishing to feel that yr principal Conservative colleagues are genuinely willing to have me act with them? Do please remember what has taken place in the past, when yr Government was formed or later, when Lord Salisbury's deputation waited upon you [two occasions when the Conservatives successfully had Churchill excluded from the Cabinet]. I do not desire to be brought simply by yr goodwill into a hostile circle. It wd only lead to much unhappiness. I understand fully the many difficulties you surmount with unfailing courage. May I not count on yr sympathetic comprehension of mine?
>
> Yrs always,
>
> W.

Lloyd George was used to handling much more difficult men than Churchill. As Margot Asquith's diary entry for 30 November records:

> LG can *walk around Winston in astuteness*! The latter always keeps the peace, the former breaks it with as much regularity as the man on the road breaks stones in front of a quarry [she appears to have confused the latter and the former here]. LG has much more character than Winston; I don't mean a *better* character, or even a better nature, but *much* more of both.
>
> Winston is a *far* better fellow with a far nicer nature tho his genius is a clumsy one . . . The bedrock of his inability to debate

---

*It was so called because members of the Liberal/Conservative coalition were given a coupon that ensured that the two parties would not compete for certain constituencies.

is a noisy inelastic mind . . . Poor Winston is shallow of soul and boyish of heart . . . Everyone he works with likes him and dislikes LG – but the latter has made an amazing success of his life – charming and camouflaging & taking in quite remarkable men, the other takes in *no* one! Winston is like the bull & LG . . . need not take either a very quick or a very long step to escape his charge!

Difficulties overcome and assurances no doubt given, Churchill wrote a long memorandum to the Prime Minister about the forthcoming election, in which he also made a strong appeal for a magnanimous settlement with the defeated Germans. He referred to the mistakes of the punitive 1871 settlement in which Germany had forcibly annexed Alsace and Lorraine. He also commented that it was impossible for Germany to pay the full expenses of the war, which even at that time were calculated at £2 billion.

Churchill was closely involved in drafting Lloyd George's manifesto for the Coupon Election. Apart from the Prime Minister, he was in fact the only remaining Liberal in the Coalition Government. Of the other eight ministers in the War Cabinet, five were Conservatives and two were Labour; the South African General Smuts did not belong to a British political party. Churchill continued to have a fairly Liberal outlook, including in the manifesto a clause to punish war profiteers and promising his Dundee constituents that the railways would be nationalised (this would finally come about under the Attlee Government in 1945).

In 1918 there were – as there would be in 1945 – strong demands for social justice and reforms to reflect the enormous social changes which had occurred during the war years. One of these was to give women the vote, as a result of their tremendous contribution to the war effort, especially in the munitions factories. More generally there was a clamour throughout Europe for greater equality: Russia was in the throes of civil war; Germany was in revolution; France had a more left-wing government.

Churchill was always sensitive to public opinion; and no one was more conscious than Lloyd George of the need for social reform and equality. He, after all, had been the architect of the pensions and unemployment benefits introduced in 1908–11. One of his electioneering slogans in December 1918 was 'Homes Fit for Heroes'. But equally, both men shared a deep suspicion of the Communist experiment which had begun to take shape in Russia, and a horror of the anarchy and violence which came in its wake.

The decision by the Coalition Government to lend its support to those candidates, Liberal and Conservative, who had voted in favour of the Government in the Maurice Debate of May 1918 had the calamitous effect of dividing and, ultimately, finishing off the Liberal Party.

General Frederick Maurice had retired as Master of the Ordnance to the British Army in France at the end of 1917. He then began to agitate behind the scenes for an attack on Lloyd George's Government because he believed that it had deliberately starved the generals of soldiers. It was true that both Lloyd George and Churchill felt that manpower was being wasted on the Western Front and that it would restrain Haig's military ambitions if fewer fresh troops were sent into battle after the disasters of the Somme and Passchendaele. Also, even at this stage of the war, the arrival of the American Army was still awaited.

General Maurice managed to convince Asquith to propose a vote of no confidence in Lloyd George's administration and to challenge the figures published by the Government as to the numerical strength of the British Army in France in the twelve months between the spring of 1917 and that of 1918. Although Asquith's vote failed and the Coalition Government survived, this was the first time since the 'coup' of December 1916 that the Lloyd George Liberals and the Asquith Liberals had been visibly opposed. This was to have a calamitous effect on the party in the Coupon Election of 1918, in which their parliamentary strength fell by over 250 seats.

Churchill's appreciation of Lloyd George's support and will-ingness to risk political opprobrium by including him in the Coalition Cabinet in 1917 was fulsomely expressed. He had written to his friend on 4 May 1918, 'It was a very warm-hearted & courageous act of yours to include me in yr Government in the face of so much Conservative hostility.' After his appointment as War Secretary in January 1919, Churchill was able to express his appreciation in a tangible form by presenting Lloyd George with three awards: the 1914–15 Star, the British War Medal and the Victory Medal. He referred to Lloyd George as a wonderful man even when he was in the Prime Minister's presence.

At the War Office Churchill was responsible for the demobil-isation of the 3.5 million British troops at the front. It was a time of great social unrest and economic deprivation. The suffering which was so visible all over Europe (and which led Herbert Hoover to launch food programmes in the nations of Central Europe), was reflected in high unemployment in England. Churchill and Lloyd George were particularly sensitive to the social upheavals because of the reforms they had introduced before the First World War and this increased their sense of responsibility for the returning soldiers, many of whom were wounded and disabled. Despite the fact that the new Coalition Government had a Conservative majority, Lloyd George was able to pass a number of radical measures, including a housing act, unemployment insurance and, under the leadership of the Education Minister, H. A. L. Fisher, a far-reaching reform of the education system. Churchill was involved in all these projects and shared Lloyd George's vision of post-war Britain.

The Paris Peace Conference opened in January 1919 with the arrival of President Woodrow Wilson in France. Georges Clemenceau represented the French Government, Lloyd George the British and Empire delegation. Together with Prime Minister Orlando from Italy, these constituted the 'Big Four'. It took almost six months for the victors of the First World War to discuss, among other issues, German reparations, the new frontiers that were to be established in Europe, the Middle East, Japan and China, and the League of Nations. Among the new countries which were carved out in this seminal year was Czechoslovakia; Hungary and Poland had new borders, as did Romania and Bulgaria. Yugoslavia became for the first time a distinct nation even though it had within it separate regions such as Slovenia, Bosnia, Serbia, Macedonia and Montenegro, with their own languages and ethnic groups. Although most of the 'fourteen points' which Woodrow Wilson brought to the conference table are now forgotten, he did introduce one powerful, popular idea to the proceedings: the right to self-determination. This appealed to small countries as far apart as Hungary and Ireland and had an impact on the new Arab countries and on the developing situation in Palestine.

Lloyd George's approach to the French Prime Minister was very much in character. Having discovered that Clemenceau had been an expert duellist in his youth, and was known as 'The Tiger', he took the first opportunity to have a major row with him and, in so doing, gained the Frenchman's respect. He often said that he had learned this technique as a young solicitor, when he would challenge a judge by being extremely disrespectful and aggressive towards him in order to establish his position. In some ways his relationship with Churchill was similar: following their parliamentary 'duel' in February 1901 they were always rivals for power and for office yet they respected and liked each other. Many of the acerbic exchanges recorded between the two men, both in the House of Commons and outside, reflect the dominant role that Lloyd George was determined to maintain. The story of their 'Master and Servant' meeting when Churchill became Chancellor in 1924 suggests that the dynamics of their relationship never really changed, even after Lloyd George fell from power.

While Lloyd George was working on the peace settlement in Paris, T. E. Lawrence (of Arabia) made the observation that Churchill was a completely different man when he was with Lloyd George: he would listen (and be subservient) to the Prime Minister whereas in other situations he would dominate the conversation. Churchill confided his own view of their relationship to Clementine on 24 January 1919: 'I breakfast lunch & dine with the PM . . . It is a good thing to get in touch again. We were diverging a good deal. I think I influence him in a considerable degree, & there is no one with whom he talks so easily.'

Nevertheless Churchill was excluded by Lloyd George from the inner councils of the peacemakers. The Prime Minister was clearly irritated by the War Secretary's constant harping on about the Bolshevik menace and the need for military intervention on the part of Britain. And perhaps he did not want to include Churchill in discussions about the new political map of Europe because he was finding it difficult enough to reach agreement with the French and to satisfy President Wilson, without having to deal with Churchill's constant flow of new ideas.

In fact, by the early 1920s the two friends had begun – and would continue – to drift apart politically. Although it was Churchill himself who had been the architect of labour exchanges and social insurance before 1914, now – perhaps wary of Bolshevism – he was gradually moving towards the right in his political outlook. In foreign policy, too, Churchill was at odds with his leader: by 1920 he was complaining that Lloyd George had virtually taken over the running of the Foreign Office. It is true that, with his wide-ranging knowledge and control of ministries at this time, historians have viewed Lloyd George as inaugurating a new era of 'presidential government'. But Churchill's complaint was probably triggered by his opposition towards the Prime Minister's desire for diplomatic recognition of the Soviet Union.

Lloyd George was fascinated by the Russian Revolution, with which he drew parallels with one of his favourite periods in history, the French Revolution. In the Russian revolutionary, Alexander Kerensky, he saw shades of Mirabeau, the florid, eloquent but ineffectual French aristocrat; in Lenin, he saw traces of Robespierre, the cold intellectual dominating the Terror. Churchill's eloquence, on the other hand, was fired by what he saw as the horrors of communism. In this he was, as usual, many years ahead of most of his countrymen who preferred not to look too closely at Bolshevism, just as they would later prefer not to see Hitler's threat to Britain. In *The Aftermath* (the penultimate volume of *The World Crisis*), Churchill declared:

> Russia had fallen by the way; and in falling she had changed her identity. An apparition with countenance different from any yet seen on earth stood in the place of the old Ally. We saw a state without a nation, an army without a country, a religion without a God. The Government which claimed to be the new Russia sprang from Revolution and was fed by terror . . .
>
> Lenin was the Grand Repudiator. He repudiated everything. He repudiated God, King, Country, morals, treaties, debts, rents, interest, the laws and customs of centuries, all contracts written or implied, the whole structure – such as it is – of human society.

The question was: how was Britain to deal with the new regime?

During the 1914–18 war, the collapse of Russia had had an extremely serious effect on the Western Front. Following the Treaty of Brest-Litovsk between Germany and the new Soviet Union in March 1918, the Germans were able to move sixty divisions from the Eastern Front to face the British and the French in Belgium and northern France. The Americans had not yet arrived to help in the fighting so the Allies were, for several weeks, badly outnumbered.

There had also been the problem of what to do about the Romanov family. The Tsar was the first cousin of King George V and the initial impulse of both the British Government and the Royal Family was to offer them shelter in Britain. However, the Tsarina was German and with the country in the grip of the First World War, there was little popular support for doing so. In the climate of the time, monarchies everywhere were under threat and felt bound to bend to the popular will. King George V himself had just changed his family name from Saxe Coburg to Windsor. As a consequence of the British Government withdrawing its offer of sanctuary to the Romanovs, in July 1918 the Tsar, his wife and their five children were murdered by the Bolsheviks at Ekaterinburg, the capital of the Urals.

The civil war that had broken out after the Armistice in Russia between the 'White' Russian armies and the Bolsheviks began to dominate the newspaper headlines. Churchill was determined to 'strangle Bolshevism at its birth' and, when trying to persuade Lloyd George to intervene, he expressed the hope that 'you will not brush aside lightly the convictions of one who wishes to remain your faithful lieutenant'. Lloyd George firmly rebutted Churchill's argument about the need to attack the Bolshevik regime and reminded him, 'I have worked with you now for longer than I have probably co-operated with any other man in public life and I think I have given you tangible proof that I wish you well. It is for that reason that I write frankly to you.'

Lloyd George later commented:

> The trouble with Winston is that he's always taking action. *He will insist on getting out his maps.* In 1914 he got out his map of the Dardanelles, and think where that landed us. And after the war I had to think what to do with him. I wanted him in my Cabinet, of course: but what's the safest place *after a war* for a man who will get out his maps? The *War Office*, of course, I thought. He'll be safe there. But was he? Before I could look round, he's got out his maps of Russia and we were making fools of ourselves in the Civil War.

A cartoon in *The Star* entitled 'Winston's Bag' showed a characteristically pugnacious Churchill surveying a rather cruel list of his 'blunders'.

Lloyd George was against intervention in Russia both because it was politically dangerous – the growing Labour movement in

Britain was supportive of the new Communist Party – and, more importantly, because so soon after the 'war to end all wars', there was little appetite for further British military adventures.

WINSTON'S BAG

HE HUNTS LIONS AND BRINGS HOME DECAYED CATS

Churchill was insensitive to this, writing to Lloyd George on 24 March 1920:

Since the armistice my policy wd have been 'Peace with the German people, war on the Bolshevik tyranny'. Willingly or unavoidably, you have followed something vy near the reverse. Knowing the difficulties, & also yr great skill & personal force – so much greater than mine – I do not judge yr policy and action as if I cd have done better . . .

... My suggestion involves open resolute action by Britain under yr guidance, & if necessary *independent* action. In such a course I wd gladly at yr side face political misfortune. But I believe there wd be no misfortune, & that for a few months longer Britain still holds the title-deeds of Europe . . .

. . . I am most sincerely desirous of continuing to work with you. I am all with you in our home affairs. My interests as well as my inclinations march with yours, & in addition there is our long friendship wh I so greatly value.

The two friends had several heated arguments on the subject of Russian intervention, provoking Lloyd George to comment: 'The most formidable and irrepressible protagonist of an anti-Bolshevik war was Mr Winston Churchill. He had no doubt a genuine distaste for Communism . . . His ducal blood revolted against the wholesale elimination of Grand Dukes in Russia.'

Churchill, who was generally in a minority in the Coalition Cabinet, was especially so over this issue. Nevertheless, it helped him a few years later to return to the Conservative Party (as Chancellor in 1924), since it burnished his credentials as a right-winger and a strong 'anti-socialist'. In fact, there is an amusing cartoon showing Lloyd George and Churchill as jockeys, both trying to mount the same horse, 'Anti Socialism'. In the end, although supplies were sent to help the White Russians, and British officers were despatched to advise on tactics, Lloyd George as Prime Minister prevailed over Churchill's belligerence.

Churchill not only felt strongly that Britain should not establish diplomatic relations with the Bolshevik regime; he also disagreed with Lloyd George's policy regarding Turkey and Greece. He wrote to the Prime Minister in 1920: 'We seem to be becoming the most Anti-Turk and most Pro-Bolshevik power in the world: whereas in my judgement we ought to be the exact opposite. Your policy these last two years has been 100% pro Russian and anti Turk. I would have counselled the opposite.'

After Turkey had been defeated in the First World War, Greece was given much of the territory on the Turkish coast and along the Aegean Sea, including the city of Smyrna, which had a predominantly Greek population. Turkey's attack on Smyrna under

THE FIGHT FOR THE FAVOURITE.

Mr. Lloyd George. "HERE, I SAY, THIS IS MY MOUNT."
Mr. Winston Churchill. "NO, IT ISN'T. I THOUGHT OF IT FIRST."

Mustafa Kemal – later to be known as Ataturk – and massacre of its Greek civilians was one of the causes of the 'Chanak crisis' in October 1922 which helped to bring down Lloyd George's administration after the Conservatives refused to go to war.

Throughout Lloyd George's post-war premiership Churchill argued that Britain did not have the troops to subdue the Middle East. He resented having to ask Parliament for funds for this purpose when, in his opinion, it was only Lloyd George's 'vendetta against the Turks' which made it necessary. He wanted Britain to propose terms which Turkey was willing to accept, and he wanted the Ottoman Empire to be resurrected, strengthened and placed under international supervision, seeing it as a valuable bulwark against Russia. He worried about France invading Syria and the Jews 'whom we are pledged to introduce to Palestine and who take it for granted that the local population will be cleared out to suit their convenience'.

Lloyd George felt that Churchill was exaggerating the menace of Communism ('he has Bolshevism on the brain'), and was to write to Austen Chamberlain on 22 March 1922:

> . . . If Winston, who is obsessed by the defeat inflicted upon his military projects by Bolshevik Armies, is determined that he will resign rather than assent to any recognition . . . whatever the rest of Europe may decide, the Cabinet must choose between Winston and me. I never thought that the restoration of European trade and business was possible without bringing Russia into the circle.

Lloyd George's main concern in the post-war economic recession of 1921 was to get Britain's overseas trade moving again: one potential export market was the new Soviet Russia. He himself took a pragmatic view of the need to deal with whatever government the Russians chose for themselves and believed that intervention was justified – if Russia desired it. Regarding Turkey, he added: '[Winston] got out his maps again. This time he got out his maps of Greece and Turkey, and that brought my tottering administration to a close.'

One senses the friendly but real rivalry between these two political giants and Churchill's impatience to claim the 'top job'. In Paris, according to Frances Stevenson's diary on 20 January 1920:

> Winston, who has been fuming all the week about Russia, said to D. yesterday, 'Well you have downed me & my policy, but I can't help admiring you for the way you have gone about it. Your strat-

egy is masterly . . . I fought you, & you have beaten me, yet I cannot help admiring you for it.' 'The worst feature of Winston,' said D. – & I believe he said it to Winston himself – 'is his vanity! Everything that he does points to one thing – self.'

TROTSKY—LIMITED.

Our Mr. George. "GOOD MORNING, GENTLEMEN. I'M AFRAID I'VE CALLED ON YOUR BUSY DAY."

Lloyd George realised that it was in Churchill's nature to climb as high as possible. Nevertheless, he 'had not the least doubt that he would be willing to pick me up' if he (Lloyd George) ever fell behind (just as he himself had picked Churchill up after the disaster of Gallipoli and his self-exile in the trenches). This was to prove just as true in 1940 as it had been in 1917 – each tried to help the other when in a position of power.

Although the two men argued and quarrelled from time to time, and were certainly jealous of each other's success on occasion, for the most part they worked together in a spirit of comradeship and shared excitement. They understood the importance and power of their alliance. And so did their opponents. In 1921 Lenin himself referred to the 'united forces of Lloyd George and Churchill' because he recognised that each was the other's closest and most important political ally.

This is not to say that Lloyd George could not be quite rude to Churchill in conversation when he chose. On 17 January 1920 (Lloyd George's fifty-seventh birthday), while the two men were playing golf at St-Cloud outside Paris and discussing the plan for yet another coalition, Frances Stevenson recorded in her diary that Churchill said, 'If you are going to include all parties [in a new coalition], you will have to have me in your new National Party.' 'Oh no!' was D.'s retort. 'To be a party you must have at least one follower. *You* have none.' Lloyd George often seems to have treated Churchill as a younger brother – with irritation but with affection – and such remarks never caused any breach in their friendship. (Speaking of his difficulties with his two First Lords of the Admiralty, Churchill and McKenna, he once compared them to trees in the forest: 'Churchill was like the Oak, gave warning before crashing, whereas McKenna was like an Elm, the branch falls without any notice.')

On New Year's Day 1921, Lloyd George moved Churchill from the War Office to the Colonial Office and Churchill insisted on being given complete responsibility for the Middle East. To understand the significance of the part both men played there, it is necessary to look at the history of the Zionist movement.

This was founded in Vienna in 1896 by Theodore Herzl with the objective of securing a homeland for the dispersed Jewish people. In the early years it was by no means certain that this would be their ancient home, Palestine, which lay, in any case, under the Turkish yoke of the Ottoman Empire, as it had done for over five hundred years, with little hope of emancipation.

The eyes of the Zionists therefore turned to other areas of the world, and in particular to the less inhabited corners of the British Empire. In 1903, Herzl had approached the Foreign Office of the Balfour administration to enquire whether the Sinai Peninsula might be considered as a permanent Jewish settlement; and, when this was rejected by the Egyptian Government (represented by Her Majesty's Consul-General in Cairo), whether Uganda might perhaps be a suitable alternative.

Herzl then decided to enlist the aid of a British intermediary and wrote to a firm of London solicitors – Messrs Lloyd George, Roberts & Co. – at 63 Queen Victoria Street in the City. The principal of that firm was, of course, the rising young Liberal backbencher, David Lloyd George, who had made a national name for himself as a leading critic of the Boer War and a stout defender of the rights of small nations and peoples.

The Zionist movement was no more than one among Lloyd George's many clients, but representing it as it sought to define itself during its formative years gave him an insight – unique among British political leaders – into its character and goals (and perhaps an idea of what to do with Palestine, should Britain ever find herself in a position to dispose of it).

Nearly thirty years later, Herzl's biographer Alex Bein wrote to Lloyd George, seeking information about this episode and adding: 'Your name is always mentioned by Zionists and Jews throughout the world with the greatest reverence and gratitude, therefore it would be of great interest if I could reveal your connection with the founder of the political Jewish nation.'

When the Sinai Peninsula was rejected by the British Government, and the Zionists themselves rejected Uganda, for nearly a decade before the First World War the movement continued to agitate for the return to the Jewish people of their biblical home-land of Palestine. This depended on the future fate of the Ottoman Empire, in which Britain would be a key instrument.

Ever since Gladstone's campaign in 1878 to remove the Turks from Bulgaria, the traditional Liberal view had been that Britain should resist Turkish encroachment on Greek territory. Perhaps also under the influence of Eleftherios Venizelos, the Greek Prime Minister who had so impressed British Cabinet ministers during the war, the Government in London took a consistently pro-Greek stance.

Having lost Bulgaria, the Ottoman Empire was shrinking. The Balkan Wars of 1912 and 1913 also saw the loss of Macedonia, Albania and the strategic port of Salonika. At the outbreak of war in August 1914, Turkey had two battleships nearing completion in British shipyards. As First Lord of the Admiralty, Churchill decided to impound the two ships before they could be used in alliance with Germany, to whom Turkey was presumed to be friendly.

Asquith noted: 'Winston in his most bellicose mood all for sending a torpedo flotilla into the Dardanelles . . .' As a result of talks between the Turkish leader Enver Pasha and the Germans, which the British Secret Service had intercepted on 31 October, Churchill despatched, on his own initiative, an order to the Mediterranean fleet to commence hostilities against Turkey. On 3 November, British warships bombarded the outer forts of the Dardanelles. The declaration of war against Turkey, which was not made until 5 November, suggested that, in Whitehall, Turkey was seen as a minor problem compared to the heavy fighting on the Western Front.

In November 1914 it was still not known in London that Enver had taken the initiative in proposing and signing a secret treaty of alliance with Germany *before* the Admiralty's seizure of the two Turkish battleships. Lloyd George believed that Churchill had precipitated Britain's war with Turkey and he was to level this

charge at him until 1921. After the failure of the Gallipoli expedition in 1915, the Cabinet stepped back from any further military
adventures against the Turks. In the small War Cabinet Lloyd
George continued to press for action on the Eastern Front
through Salonika but in 1915–16 the focus remained on the
Western Front, with the priority being to increase the flow of
munitions to the trenches.

When Lloyd George established the Ministry of Munitions in
1915 he found there was an acute shortage of acetone, a key
ingredient in the making of shells. His trusted friend C. P. Scott,
who was editor of the *Manchester Guardian*, had heard about a
chemist called Dr Chaim Weizmann who was able to manufac-
ture the missing acetone from chestnuts. When this indeed proved
to be the case, Lloyd George invited Weizmann to visit him in
London. 'You have done a great service to the State for which we
would like to give you an honour,' he told the chemist. To which
Weizmann replied: 'I require no honour for myself but I would
like to ask something for my people.' Through his charisma and
eloquence he was able to win over to the cause of the Zionist
movement, not only the future Foreign Secretary, Balfour, but
also the future premier.

When Lloyd George became Prime Minister in December
1916, a dynamic new war policy emerged and this included the
strategy of once again attacking the Ottoman Empire. Lloyd
George wanted to save lives on the Western Front and, for political reasons, he needed a military success in the East. The year 1917
therefore saw a rapid deployment of troops, mainly from Egypt, to
attack first Palestine and then Mesopotamia. Simultaneously T. E.
Lawrence was bringing to fruition British plans for the Arab revolt
so that the Turks were faced with a war on two fronts.

In March 1917 Lloyd George had written to his brother
William: 'Then comes the news from Palestine, which is thoroughly cheerful. We are not far from Jerusalem and although it is

not going to fall yet, I am looking forward to my Government achieving something which generations of the chivalry of Europe failed to attain.'

Two months later, in a speech in the House of Commons, the Prime Minister surprised even his closest collaborators by stating unequivocally that Turkey would not be allowed to keep Palestine or Mesopotamia (Iraq). Lloyd George was the only man in his government who had always wanted to gain Palestine for Britain and he also wanted to encourage the development of a Jewish homeland there. His colleagues failed to understand how strongly he held these views. There was a background to his beliefs of which they were mostly ignorant. Lloyd George was not, like Asquith or the other members of the Cabinet, educated at a public school on Greek and Latin classics; he was brought up on the Bible. Repeatedly he remarked that biblical place names were better known to him than those of battles and frontiers in the European war. This led him to believe that it was not worth winning the Holy Land only to 'hew it to pieces before the Lord'. Unlike his colleagues, he was aware that there were age-old tendencies in British evangelical and nonconformist thought that favoured the return of the Jews to Zion, and a line of Christian Zionists which stretched back to the Puritans.

The future return to Zion had remained a largely Messianic vision until the ideology of nineteenth-century Europe converted it into a contemporary political programme. One of the ideas of the age was that every nation ought to have its own independent homeland; it was thought to be a fundamental cause of the world's ills that some nations were being kept from achieving unity or independence. And a Jewish state seemed to many to be the answer to the beleaguered position of Jews in many European countries. The entry of the Ottoman Empire into the war in 1914 appeared to have brought about the political circumstances in which the Zionist dream could at last be fulfilled: 'What is to prevent the Jews having Palestine and restoring a real Judaea?' asked H. G. Wells in a letter to a newspaper.

During the summer and autumn of 1917, as British troops were advancing towards Palestine, there was furious debate between the Zionists and their opponents within the British establishment. Weizmann had successfully converted Lloyd George and Balfour to his point of view. Herbert Samuel (Postmaster-General during the Marconi scandal) also shared the vision of the Jewish home-land, but it was vociferously opposed by the Liberal Minister Edwin Montagu, another British Jew, who wrote to Lloyd George:

> I appreciate your motives – your generosity and desire to take up the cudgels for the oppressed. Did I believe as you believe in a Jewish Nation, could I hold the opinion that you hold that great idealism overcomes all practical difficulties, I might have been less opposed . . . you are being misled by a foreigner, a dreamer, an idealist [Weizmann] . . . I believe firmly that if you make a state-ment about Palestine as the national home for Jews, every anti-Semitic organisation and newspaper will ask what right a Jewish Englishman, with the status at best of a naturalised foreigner, has to take a foremost part in the Government of the British Empire. The country for which I have worked ever since I left the University – England – the country for which my family have fought, tells me that my national home, if I desire to go there . . . is Palestine. How can I maintain my position?

Montagu's objection held up the Foreign Secretary's letter to Lord Rothschild outlining British policy towards Palestine – which came to be known as the 'Balfour Declaration' – for several weeks. But feelers were extended to President Wilson and the reply from Washington was favourable. Nearly all the Jewish leaders consulted by the British Government were also strongly in favour of it. There seemed to be clear strategic benefits to the British war effort in making this generous declaration to Jewish communities in America, Britain, Germany and also Russia. All these factors came to a head at a meeting of the War Cabinet on

31 October 1917, at which Lloyd George managed to win over Montagu, Curzon and Grey. One of the strongest proponents of the Declaration was Sir Mark Sykes, a leading British diplomat who had signed the secret Sykes-Picot Agreement with the French, dividing up spheres of influence within the crumbling Ottoman Empire. After attending the historic meeting he came out smiling to greet Chaim Weizmann with the words: 'Dr Weizmann, it's a boy!'

And so the Declaration was published in the first week of November 1917. As Max Egremont noted in his biography of Balfour:

> For Balfour, diplomatic opportunism and personal idealism came together in the declaration. In Weizmann he had met an inspirational articulator of a message which took him back to the stern Old Testament tenets of his mother's low church faith and the Presbyterianism of the Scottish Lowlands. Near the end of his days, he said . . . that on the whole he felt that what he had been able to do for the Jews had been the thing he looked back upon as the most worth his doing.

If this were true of Balfour, whose name as Foreign Secretary appeared on the Declaration, how much more true was it of Lloyd George, who had been raised on 'stern Old Testament tenets' by his uncle, Richard Lloyd; who, as a young solicitor, had acted as legal adviser to the early Zionist movement in Britain; who had made a principled stand as a defender of the rights of small nations as a rising politician during the Boer War; who had been persecuted in the Marconi case alongside his Jewish friends Rufus and Geoffrey Isaacs; and who proudly boasted in 1921 that he had made the Zionist Herbert Samuel the 'first procurator of Judaea since Pontius Pilate' (in other words, High Commissioner in Jerusalem).

Lloyd George was the moving force behind the statement that 'His Majesty's Government looks with favour on the establishment of a National Home for the Jewish People in Palestine . . . provided of course that the rights of the indigenous inhabitants are protected'. The letter was written to Lord Rothschild, as the leader of the British Jewish community, for political and strategic reasons: to win the support of American Jews; to forestall any attempt by the Kaiser to make a similar declaration (an unlikely event, given his anti-Semitic views); as a reflection of gratitude for Weizmann's contribution to the British war effort; and in the belief that the financial and moral support of the world-wide Jewish community might be equally crucial.

It can be argued – as some historians have – that the Balfour Declaration was an ill-considered move by the British Government. But it had taken into account the factors and peoples involved by mentioning that the rights of the indigenous inhabitants of Palestine would be protected. As Lloyd George later wrote: 'We made an equal pledge that we would not turn the Arab off his land or invade his political and social rights.' On the contrary, although there was a clear sense of the benefits to the British Empire of having a British Protectorate with a Jewish homeland in a strategic location as far as Egypt and the Suez Canal were concerned, everything written by Balfour and Lloyd George suggests that the Declaration originated from idealistic motives – and this is endorsed by the comments of their Cabinet colleagues and friends.

Only the exigencies of the First World War could have brought the Balfour Declaration to fruition. With the defeat of the Turks and the collapse of the Ottoman Empire, the way was open for a new empire – the British – to control the Middle East. In the Treaty of Versailles Lloyd George insisted on Britain retaining full authority over Palestine.

So it was that on 13 February 1921 Churchill took up his appointment as Colonial Secretary to sort out the warring factions in the Middle East. Churchill's own history had also been that of a pro-Zionist. His early opposition to the Aliens Bill of 1904 was reinforced by the fact that he represented the heavily

Jewish constituency of Manchester North-West. And there is a constant thread of sympathy and admiration for the Jews running through his powerful oratory.

When Churchill arrived for the Cairo Conference in March 1921 he quickly convened a panel of experts, including T. E. Lawrence, General Allenby and the diplomat Sir Percy Cox. The problem was that in the heat of battle the British had promised the same territory to two groups of peoples. The Arabs believed that Palestine would be theirs; the Zionists, although still a minority of the population, had begun to purchase land and irrigate the dry uplands of Judaea for agricultural use and on which to settle immigrants.

Lloyd George had put Churchill, as Colonial Secretary, in the invidious position of having to make some Solomonic judgements about the future of the conquered and mandated territories. Notwithstanding the tortuous history of the Middle East in the last fifty years, it is difficult to imagine that Churchill and the British Government of the time could have devised a better plan for Palestine. In order to satisfy the aspirations of the Hashemite dynasty Churchill decided to carve out two new kingdoms: in Eastern Palestine he created the Kingdom of Trans-Jordan (later Jordan), which he gave to King Hussein's son Abdullah. Mesopotamia he renamed Iraq and gave to Abdullah's brother, Feisal. Then he visited Jerusalem, where he planted a tree at the new Hebrew University and made a speech in which he praised the efforts of the Zionist settlers. Despite opposition from the Grand Mufti of Jerusalem and the Arab community, Churchill refused to discountenance in any way the British commitment to the Balfour Declaration.

As he reported to the Cabinet on 22 July: '. . . Palestine is complicated by the pledge which was given by the late Foreign Secretary, Mr Balfour, in a most critical period of the War, that a Jewish National Home would be favoured by Great Britain in Palestine. There are 550,000 Arabs, 60,000 Jews and 60,000

Christians living in Palestine. The Zionist ideal is a very great ideal, and . . . one that claims my keen personal sympathy . . .'

It can thus be said that the 1917 Declaration and the resultant territorial settlement of 1921 were the joint work of Lloyd George and Churchill, and that the two men shared the same vision of the historic task of the British Empire while it temporarily held mandated power over the conquered Turkish territories: to provide the foundations for a Jewish state in the historic biblical lands.

Having enjoyed himself carving up the Middle East and thereby laying the foundations for many of today's intractable ethnic and religious problems in the region, Churchill hurried home with the expectation of becoming the new Chancellor of the Exchequer. When he arrived back in London on 10 April 1921, he found to his dismay that the undistinguished Sir Robert Horne had been appointed Chancellor instead. As in December 1916, Churchill was extremely angry with Lloyd George and gave up all social contact with the Prime Minister: no more dinner parties, no more intimate conversations – formal relations only. As Frances Stevenson confided to her diary on 26 April:

> Winston still very vexed with the PM as a result of, as he thinks, having been neglected in the recent promotions. D. says Winston fully expected to be made Chancellor of the Exchequer . . . when all the changes were made, & he has not been to see D. since his return. D. has only seen him in Cabinets & meetings of the kind, & Winston writes him 'Dear Prime Minister', whereas it used to be 'Dear Ll.G.' or 'My dear David' even.

# 7

## 1921–9: Still His Friend and Lieutenant

'The past stood ever at his elbow and was the counsellor upon whom he most relied.'

Lord Rosebery, 1930

AT THE BEGINNING of the First World War Ireland had been teetering on the brink of civil war; indeed, the Conservative & Unionist Party had threatened to support a rebellion in Ulster if the Liberals pressed ahead with plans for Home Rule. Feelings ran high and Churchill in particular was viewed as a traitor because his father had been such a strong supporter of the Ulster cause. In March 1914, in his capacity as First Lord of the Admiralty, he had signalled the 3rd Battle Squadron to sail to a position off the coast of Ireland during the so-called 'Curragh Mutiny'; this arose when a group of British officers stationed at the Curragh in County Kildare, the Army's major base in Ireland, threatened to resign their commissions rather than quell a rebellion in Ulster (many of them were Ulstermen). In July 1914, following the round-table conference at Buckingham Palace, Lloyd George pressed Prime Minister Asquith and his fellow Liberal Cabinet members to make Ulster an exception to Home Rule. That, then, was the position when the First World War began.

In April 1916, when the Easter Rising occurred in Dublin, Ireland again drew the attention of the Coalition Government. Asquith hurried over to Dublin to see for himself what was happening and then turned to Lloyd George, whose sympathies with Ireland had never yet been challenged:

My dear Lloyd George,

I hope you may see your way to take up Ireland; at any rate for a short time. It is a unique opportunity and there is no one else who could do so much to bring about a permanent solution.

Yours very sincerely,

H. H. Asquith

In response, Lloyd George convened an Irish round table with two Ulster representatives – Edward Carson and James Craig (later, as Lord Craigavon, Prime Minister of Northern Ireland) – and from southern Ireland the Nationalist Party leader, John Redmond, Joseph Devlin and T. P. O'Connor, his old friend and neighbour in London. Lloyd George proposed that there should be Home Rule for Ireland immediately, with an amending act to retain the six counties of Ulster as part of Britain. But although his proposal seemed acceptable to the Irish delegates, it was rejected by the House of Lords. Lloyd George, however, owed Asquith an unexpected debt: had it not been for the Prime Minister's request that he handle the Irish situation, he would have been with Kitchener on the cruiser HMS *Hampshire*, which sank off the Orkneys in 1916.

One of the most pressing tasks which awaited the Coalition Government after the war was therefore the solution of the Irish 'problem'. But while Lloyd George was signing the Peace in Paris, civil war was declared in Dublin.

The Sinn Fein MPs who had been elected in December 1918 had refused to take their seats in Westminster and gathered in Dublin to form an assembly (in fact, nearly fifty of the total number of seventy-three were in prison). The new Irish leaders had been warmly received in the United States – Eamon de Valera of Sinn Fein was hailed in New York as 'the President of the Irish Republic'. The influence of America upon the Anglo-Irish situation in 1919–21 was, though not always visible, profound. The Irish set particular store by President Woodrow Wilson's contribution to the Treaty of Versailles, the 'fourteen points', which included the right to self-determination. Hence the various Home Rule movements merged into a military rebellion and the Irish Republican Army made its first appearance.

The Irish civil war became increasingly violent and the British Government responded with the 'Black and Tans', mostly British ex-servicemen, wearing black-and-khaki tunics, who became auxiliary members of the Royal Irish Constabulary, the local police force. They soon acquired a reputation for being as violent and ruthless as the IRA, whom they were trying to suppress. A situation of lawlessness developed in the Irish countryside and the police force was forced to withdraw from everywhere except major towns and army barracks.

Although Lloyd George had written to Churchill on 10 May 1920, 'I am very anxious about Ireland, and I want to help you', he and Winston were not to give it their full attention until the situation got out of control in the latter part of that year. In November Lloyd George introduced a new Home Rule Bill in the House of Commons, but the violence continued, with fourteen British officers killed in reprisals in Dublin in the same month. Although most of the country was under martial law by the beginning of 1921 and there were five hundred casualties in the first three months of that year, Lloyd George continued to seek peace and indicated that he was prepared to meet with de Valera and his Sinn Fein colleagues. Churchill, who – as Secretary of State for War and later Colonial Secretary – had responsibility first for the military situation in Ireland and later for the peace settlement, was opposed to any attempt to treat with the rebels: 'they must surrender or be destroyed,' he said. But then, typically, he was in favour of a magnanimous settlement with the people of southern Ireland. He differed from Lloyd George in method only, not in purpose. Both men, as prominent British leaders, were under threat of assassination during this period. Field Marshal Sir Henry Wilson, an Ulsterman who had led the British Army's attempts to quell the Irish rebellion, would be gunned down on the steps of his home in Eaton Square, London, the following year.

In June 1921 King George V made an influential speech in Belfast, asking the Irish leaders to 'stretch out the hand of conciliation', and in July a truce was effected. Lloyd George sent General Smuts to talk with de Valera and the republican leader Arthur Griffith in Dublin. Smuts tried to persuade them, on the basis of the South African constitutional settlement, that Ireland would gain its independence under a Dominion status within the British Empire. Lloyd George and de Valera finally met at 10 Downing Street on 14 July. After hours of negotiation Lloyd George said that talking to de Valera was 'like trying to pick up mercury with a fork'. Hearing this, de Valera retorted: 'Why doesn't he use a spoon?'

In October de Valera sent the Irish delegation, headed by Arthur Griffith and Michael Collins (the charismatic IRA leader) to London. The British delegation was led by Lloyd George, Churchill and Lord Birkenhead. Birkenhead's role was significant because he had been an out-and-out Tory Unionist since 1910. In exchange for his support for a Home Rule settlement, Lloyd George had brought him into the inner Coalition Cabinet. Although the Coalition included men of stature such as Curzon, Beaverbrook and Carson, Lloyd George's Government was for the next year in effect dominated by a triumvirate of himself, Churchill and Birkenhead. Of these three, Lloyd George and Churchill were the central figures.

The negotiations dragged on for several weeks. On the British side, the three key demands were that Ireland should remain within the British Empire; that the Irish ministers should swear an oath of allegiance to the British Crown; and that Ireland should allow the British Navy to control Irish ports where the strategic defence of Britain was affected. For their part, the Irish wanted full independence and the essential unity of the whole of Ireland. On the night of Sunday 30 October, Lloyd George met Arthur Griffith, the senior Irish delegate, privately at Winston Churchill's house in Sussex Square, Bayswater. The Prime Minister was due to face a vote of censure in the House of Commons the following day. If Griffith was prepared to recommend recognition of the Crown and partnership within the British Commonwealth to the Irish delegation, then Lloyd George would try to carry a measure making Ulster subordinate to an all-Ireland Parliament. They agreed.

Michael Collins meanwhile was downstairs, chatting with Birkenhead and Churchill about his hair's-breadth escapes from the police. When Collins complained that Churchill had been responsible for putting a price of £5,000 on his head, Churchill left the room and returned with a framed placard, the Boers' offer of reward for his own capture. 'They only thought me worth £25,' he said sorrowfully. It was a bond between the two men, and they were becoming friends. Later Collins sent a message, 'Tell Winston we could never have done anything without him'.

The next day the House of Commons upheld Lloyd George's plan. Ulster, however, was not so easy to manage. There was still the difficulty of where to set the frontier between North and South. In the final days of the negotiations at Downing Street, Lloyd George deployed all his skills of argument. Finally, he issued an ultimatum to Arthur Griffith and his Irish colleagues: if Sinn Fein refused to be party to the agreement there would be civil war within three days. Arthur Griffith promised to recommend the agreement to his colleagues. Michael Collins signed it at 2.30 a.m. on 1 December, 'looking for all the world', as Lloyd George said, 'as if he was signing his own death-warrant'. Indeed he was: he was to be assassinated six months later in Dublin.

Lloyd George and Churchill had again worked successfully together – to bring a settlement to the age-old Irish problem. The peace would hold in Ireland for the next fifty years, despite the division of the island. Birkenhead's role – and that of Churchill – was important in bringing Tory and Unionist support to what had traditionally been a Liberal policy of Home Rule, and in defying the diehards by making a generous and magnanimous settlement with the Irish Republican leaders. Churchill often remarked that this was similar to the way in which Britain had dealt with the Boers in South Africa after their defeat. The Irish were not to prove so biddable, however, and did not lend their support to the British in the Second World War, as the South Africans had done in 1914–18.

At the beginning of 1922, Beaverbrook wrote of the extraordinary political position occupied by Lloyd George, who was effectively 'Prime Minister without a party'. This fact was obscured by the Prime Minister's constant activity: the Versailles Treaty, the Irish question, unemployment, Bolshevik Russia, war reparations, the Middle East – and also by a series of international conferences which Lloyd George convened in Cannes. *Punch* commented on this conference mania, while poking fun at his penchant for golf and Churchill's for painting.

There was a price of to pay for the Government's apparent success in signing the treaty with the Sinn Fein leaders. It is probable that the demise of the Conservative–Liberal Coalition led by Lloyd George, in October 1922, was hastened by the Irish settlement, about which many Conservatives were deeply unhappy.

In the autumn of 1922 the new Turkish Government under Ataturk began to adopt a more belligerent policy towards the remaining Greek colonies on the coast of Asia Minor. After the massacre at Smyrna the Turks drove out most of the Greek colonists from other towns along the coast. As the Turkish forces approached the Dardanelles they encountered the British forces which were still occupying forts at Chanak and on the Gallipoli peninsula. General Harington, who was in charge of the British forces in the region, adopted a diplomatic stance and kept open communications with Ataturk and the Turkish commanders in order to avoid military confrontation.

Churchill, with his usual prescience, foresaw the danger of Britain's involvement in a Turkish–Greek conflict and advised

THE CONFERENCE HABIT.

Mr. Winston Churchill. "JOLLY PLACE, CANNES.   WHERE'S YOUR NEXT CONFERENCE?"
Mr. Lloyd George. "WELL, I'M TOLD THE SCENERY'S PRETTY GOOD IN HONOLULU."

Lloyd George to avoid it at all costs. At this point there was a revolt by Conservative backbenchers, who were equally opposed to Britain getting entangled in another war in the Middle East less than four years after the end of the Great War. Since then British forces had fought in Palestine, Turkey and Mesopotamia and there had been a high number of casualties in all three theatres of war. Until now, as the former Foreign Secretary, Sir Edward Grey, put it, 'the leaders of the Conservative Party [had sworn] by Ll.G in public, however much they may [have sworn] *at* him in private'. The so-called 'Chanak crisis' was perhaps the straw that broke the camel's back. It provoked the meeting at the Carlton Club on 19 October 1922 at which Stanley Baldwin warned his fellow Tories that Lloyd George was a 'dynamic force' that had already broken up the Liberal Party and, if they did not take care, would break up the Conservative Party too. This speech effectively brought down the Lloyd George Government.

At least one historian has identified a consistent policy by the Conservatives during the interwar years of keeping Lloyd George and Churchill divided or, latterly, keeping them both out of office. Baldwin, a man of small vision but much political astuteness, clearly saw the need to exclude Lloyd George from any future Coalition Government. Less politely he nicknamed him 'the Goat'.

A general election was held in November 1922; although the Labour Party became considerably stronger, it resulted in an overall victory for the Conservatives. The Liberals suffered from their ongoing internal divisions and their secular decline became yet more visible.

Lloyd George was still only fifty-nine years old and in good health. Many expected that one day he would return as prime minister. A prime minister of sixty or seventy was quite unremarkable; Churchill was to be sixty-five when he assumed the premiership in 1940, and would continue in office until after his eightieth birthday. And Gladstone had held the office at the ripe old age of eighty-four.

Despite his reservations about Lloyd George's pro-Greek policy, and the fact that he had lost his seat in Dundee, Churchill was the most conspicuous supporter of the fallen Prime Minister. He sent the following message, from the hospital where he had undergone an emergency appendectomy, to his former constituents:

> In the political confusion that reigns . . . I take my stand by Mr Lloyd George. I was his friend before he was famous, I was with him when all were at his feet. And now today, when men who fawned upon him . . . who climbed to places in Parliament upon his shoulders, have cast him aside . . . I am still his friend and lieutenant.

Soon after the 1922 election Churchill went to live for six months in the South of France, where he spent much of the time writing his book about the First World War, *The World Crisis*. Victor Cazalet recorded in his diary:

> 5 JANUARY 1923
> Winston has taken to gambling with terrible earnestness. He plays twice daily and is now *20,000* francs up after a month's play. He does not play very high. He works very hard all day, either at his book or painting. I had a very long talk with him one night, from *11* p.m. to *1* a.m. I roused him on Free Trade. We had discussed Lloyd George and his last Cabinet. LG, he said, had made one howler after another during the past *18* months, especially in foreign policy. He (Winston) had disagreed with him on all.
>
> Apropos of the Versailles Treaty, Winston told me he said at the time to LG he would not put his name to it for £*1,000*. It was cruel and relentless and spelt chaos. But still he maintains that we could not have got through the four critical years after the war except under a Coalition. The year *1919* when there was nearly a revolution was, he thought, the danger year.

Churchill's dismissive view of the Versailles Treaty may perhaps reflect his bitterness at having been excluded by Lloyd George from the inner councils of the peacemakers in Paris in 1919. However, he soon put any lingering bad feeling behind him. In the latter half of 1923 Lloyd George had gone on a three-month trip to the United States and Canada, still in the afterglow of his fame as 'the man who won the war'. In November, when he landed at Southampton after his triumphant tour, a note from Churchill awaited him: 'We are in for a big fight – and I am glad to think *together*.' Both men had pugnacious temperaments and relished a fight against the odds. Lloyd George loved storms because they mirrored his mercurial, changeable temperament. Churchill was at his best with his back against the wall.

After Lloyd George's coalition of Liberals and Conservatives lost power in November 1922 the split within the Liberal Party became wider. Andrew Bonar Law succeeded him as Prime Minister, but failing health led to his resignation in May 1923 and he died on 30 October. Bonar Law was replaced as Conservative leader by Stanley Baldwin, who announced at the beginning of November that he would impose protective tariffs on manufactured imports. This brought the Liberals together again on the free trade platform and was what prompted Winston's cryptic note to Lloyd George of 9 November. The same political issue had resulted in a landslide victory for the Liberals in January 1906.

In the snap election of early November, which Baldwin called on the issue of tariff policy, the Conservatives fell from 344 to 258 seats. Labour was in second place with 191 seats and the combined Liberal Party came third with 158. In this triangular situation, both Asquith and Lloyd George agreed to give the Labour Party a chance to form a government since they could no longer support the Conservatives. In January 1924 Ramsay MacDonald therefore took office as Britain's first Labour Prime Minister twenty-four years after the party was formed. However, the Liberals found it difficult to support the Labour Government, which negotiated a treaty with Soviet Russia and published the infamous 'Zinoviev Letter' giving the British Communist Party directions for organising an armed insurrection.

The Labour Government fell after only nine months of uneasy existence and there was talk of reviving the coalition between the Liberals and the Conservatives, with the object of keeping Labour out of power. Churchill tried hard to bring Lloyd George back into the Coalition fold, and wrote to Balfour on 3 April:

> I have had a long talk with LG. He has greatly altered his point of view, and seems inclined to lean towards those National Liberal elements which he somewhat precipitately dispersed after the last General Election. I think that if things are steered and driven in the right direction, he might well be a buttress of a future 'Conservative and Liberal Union' Administration in which the colleagues who stood by him in 1922 were influential. He has not shown the slightest resentment at the open lobbying which Freddie Guest [Churchill's cousin] and others have been doing to recreate the National Liberal wing. In short, the movement towards the reconstruction of a strong instrument of government with an adequate majority, and with a proper subordination of Party and personal interests, is making steady headway.

But there was still strong Tory opposition to Lloyd George, particularly in view of the lingering scandal about the honours which had been awarded in exchange for political funds while he was Prime Minister in 1921–2. The so-called 'honours scandal' was in reality little different from the practice which had been followed by all previous British governments – to raise party funds by rewarding businessmen and supporters who had contributed to the cause. Lloyd George merely organised the system in a more open way. But although the responsibility was not entirely his, some fairly disreputable characters (such as the swindler Horatio Bottomley) were involved in the sale of honours between 1918 and 1922. Many of the new peers and knights of the time had made their money in unsavoury ways, for instance in war profiteering, and this contributed to the popular criticism of the so-called 'Lloyd George Liberal fund'. The fund continued its life for twenty years after the Coalition ended in 1922 and was used mainly to pay for the pamphleteering and election campaigns undertaken by the diminished Liberal Party in the 1929, 1931 and 1935 elections. It does not appear to have bothered Churchill unduly and he certainly made no private or public criticism of it.

Even as late as the autumn of 1924 Churchill believed that he could bring Lloyd George back into a Liberal–Conservative alliance. He wrote to Clementine in August: 'I had a long and very satisfactory talk with LG, and we were closer together politically than we have been since he took part in putting in the Socialists.'

In September Churchill wrote to the leading Conservatives Arthur Balfour and Edward Carson: 'I visited LG at Churt on Sunday . . . [LG] is quite ready to try to turn the Government out on the Russian Treaty [the Labour Government's recognition of the Soviets as the legitimate government in Russia].' This may, however, have been Churchill's interpretation of Lloyd George's position, since he did not share Winston's strong anti-communist views; he had indeed taken the pragmatic step of establishing trade relations with the new Russian Government. Nevertheless it had taken the first Labour Government in Britain to fully recognise the Soviets. In this respect Lloyd George supported the Labour Party. Churchill, of course, did not.

Churchill realised what a bleak prospect the election of November 1924 offered to the Liberals, who were squeezed between Labour and Conservative. He tried hard to get Lloyd George to agree to a deal that would allow the Liberals and Conservatives not to stand against each other in constituencies where doing so would allow Labour to win.

As late as mid-October, although he was clearly moving towards rejoining the Conservatives, Churchill replied to questions at a public meeting by saying: 'I am a Liberal, opposed to the official Liberal leaders [i.e. Lloyd George] on account of their putting socialists into power. I am a Liberal working shoulder to shoulder with the Conservatives in a national emergency.'

Baldwin was to further his policy of dividing the two friends when, in November 1924, the Conservative Party returned to power with a massive majority and he unexpectedly appointed Churchill to be his Chancellor of the Exchequer. Churchill recorded in his memoirs that he was 'so astonished by the offer that I would have replied "Will a bloody duck swim?", but it was a formal occasion so I accepted graciously' and took out Lord Randolph's robes, carefully preserved since his father's Chancellorship in 1886.

On his appointment, the first telegram he received was from his old colleague: 'Warm congratulations on your appointment to a great office. Best wishes. Lloyd George.'

Churchill invited Lloyd George to visit him at the Treasury, partly to seek advice on his new role from a former chancellor, but also to discuss some points about the First World War for *The World Crisis*. The event was described by Bob Boothby:

When Churchill joined the Conservative Party and Baldwin's Government, he and Lloyd George inevitably drifted apart. One day, after I had become his Private Parliamentary Secretary, Churchill said to me: 'I know you are a great friend of Lloyd George. I am now writing the last volume of *The World Crisis* and there are certain questions that he alone can answer. Do you think you could persuade him to come and see me?' I said: 'It is not a question of persuasion. He would be delighted.' I then went to see Lloyd George and said: 'Winston wants to see you.' He replied: 'Splendid. Fix up an appointment.' I did, for the following evening at six o'clock. Lloyd George arrived punctually and I showed him into Winston's room. They were alone together for about an hour. After that I heard Lloyd George leave by the outside door, down the corridor. I sat alone in the secretary's room. Nothing happened. No bell rang. After about ten minutes curiosity overcame me and I went in to find the Chancellor sitting in an armchair, gazing into the fire, in a kind of brown study. I said to him: 'How did it go?' He looked up and replied: 'You will be glad to hear that it could not have gone better and he answered all my questions.' Then a hard look came into his face and he went on: 'Within five minutes the old relationship between us was completely re-established. The relationship between Master and Servant. And I was the Servant.'

It is nevertheless clear that, from 1924 onwards, the 'Master' and 'Servant' roles began to reverse. During the next five years, when Churchill held the high office of Chancellor of the Exchequer, Lloyd George, despite his reputation as 'the man who won the war', was out of office, and his prestige and influence inevitably diminished.

That December Baldwin wrote in his weekly report to George V: 'Five years ago a prophet would have been totally without honour if he had foretold that in December 1924 the House would see Mr Lloyd George leading a vigorous attack on the Safeguarding of Industries Act, and on the other side Mr Winston Churchill appearing a doughty champion in its defence.'

The truth was that throughout the 1920s the two former colleagues were moving in opposite political directions: Churchill to the right; Lloyd George to the left. That this may be an oversimplification is borne out by Lloyd George's withering criticism of the Labour Party at the Albert Hall on 20 January 1925:

> You cannot trust the battle of freedom to Socialism. Socialism has no interest in liberty. Socialism is the negation of liberty. Socialism means the community in bonds. If you establish a Socialist community it means the most comprehensive, universal and pervasive tyranny that this country has ever seen. It is like the sand of the desert. It gets into your food, your clothes, your machinery, the very air you breathe. They are all gritty with regulations, orders, decrees, rules. That is what Socialism means.

Churchill, perhaps eager to affirm his renewed Tory allegiance, gradually became more critical of his former mentor. As Beaverbrook wrote to the newspaper proprietor Lord Rothermere on 12 February 1925:

> Winston came to dine with me the other night. He is a firm supporter of Baldwin and his debt settlement. He criticises [Lloyd]

George very freely for the wicked Irish Treaty and declares that the Coalition Government ought to have continued to prosecute the war against Sinn Fein for another winter. I tried to shame him into acknowledgment of his leading part in making the Treaty. It is not easy to succeed.

Winston himself wrote to Clementine on 25 March 1925:

LG has returned – washed out – to Westminster – I had a pleasant talk with him. He is going to the Canaries for a cruise. He said he ought not to come to the House – but it was like not being able to keep away from the 'pub'. He made a speech on foreign affairs full of truth & knowledge – but lacking any clear purpose.

And in May 1925, Stanley Baldwin's weekly letter to the King contained some gleeful comments on how his new Chancellor had routed the former Prime Minister in the debate on the Russian Treaty:

He opened his attack on the Liberal amendment by challenging Mr Lloyd George to say whether he had taken any part in drafting that amendment, whether he approved of it, or whether he had even read it. Mr Lloyd George's spontaneous action in endeavouring to obtain a copy of the Order Paper from the friends around him, and the look of guilt on his face were quite sufficient to convince the House that Mr Churchill had made a very accurate guess.

Churchill's view in 1926 was that Lloyd George would move even further to the left. Dining with him, he found the Welshman quite 'astonishingly empty of knowledge and ideas but very genial and plucky'. Clearly they retained a great affection for one another, but politically they had less and less in common. Lloyd George was, Winston wrote to Clemmie,

tragically isolated in the present House, with hardly a friend and still fewer supporters . . . tied up as he is in this wretched bundle of squabbling Liberal factions, he never gets the chance to speak with the clear bold counsel of a great Statesman thinking only of the merits of the question and his country's good. He has all the disadvantages of Party politics, without a Party to back him up.

The divergence between their politics would become even more marked and apparent at the time of the General Strike in May 1926.

After Lloyd George had fallen from power in 1922 he earned his living – as indeed did Churchill – as a journalist, writing weekly articles criticising the Government of the day (usually Conservative) for its handling of the nation's affairs. Churchill had come into his sights in April 1925 when, as Chancellor of the Exchequer, he decided to put Britain back on the gold standard, in other words to restore the pre-war parity of the pound sterling with the gold sovereign.

Churchill's grasp of economics was not perhaps his strongest point as Chancellor of the Exchequer. However, he had taken advice from economic experts before making this decision; moreover, he was not following his own instincts in this matter but giving in to pressure from the City, and in particular from Montague Norman, the Governor of the Bank of England.

Perhaps they were harking back to the glory days of the Victorian era when sterling and the gold sovereign were the cornerstones of the world monetary system. After 1918, Britain's massive debt to the United States for the purchase of war *matériel* meant that the pound would never again enjoy the leading role that it had done before 1914. The main effect of the restoration of the gold standard was to make Britain's exports uncompetitive and cause growing unemployment.

Lloyd George had hurried home from a holiday in Madeira to be in the House of Commons when his old friend and former colleague presented his first Budget. He warmly praised Churchill's plans to extend national insurance benefits to widows and orphans, but condemned the decision to return to the gold standard. He declared: 'It has made Sterling dearer and artificially put up the price of British goods . . . Coal owners and miners have been driven to the brink, largely through this deed of egregious recklessness by the Chancellor of the Exchequer.'

In his sustained opposition to the return to the gold standard, Lloyd George was supported by Maynard Keynes, who wrote a series of articles entitled 'The Economic Consequences of Mr Churchill', echoing the title of his book on the Treaty of Versailles, *The Economic Consequences of the Peace*. Sterling's value had been raised by 10 per cent, and Keynes said that Churchill's policy effectively reduced British wages by 10 per cent or about two shillings in the pound.

Within weeks, unemployment started to rise. As Lloyd George had pointed out, the coalmining industry was particularly hard hit. Baldwin at first resisted subsidising the coal industry, but was finally persuaded to make a wages subsidy. However, when this came to an end in April 1926, the coalminers went out on strike.

The General Strike began on 3 May 1926. Lloyd George and Churchill had widely differing attitudes towards this drastic action by British workers.

Lloyd George pleaded in the House of Commons for a settlement and sharply criticised the 'do nothing' and 'strong-arm' policies advocated by Baldwin and the Tory Cabinet. Initially, Asquith (still leader of the Liberal Party) was as anxious as Lloyd George to keep the door open for talks with the strikers. But when the Liberal Shadow Chancellor Sir John Simon declared in the House of Commons that the General Strike was illegal and that trade union funds should be confiscated, Asquith and Grey backed the Government.

Churchill, meanwhile, was busy editing and publishing the *British Gazette* (the only newspaper that appeared during the General Strike). On 8 May the *British Gazette* announced that the armed forces of the Crown would receive the full support of the Government in – a Churchillian phrase – 'any action that they may find it necessary to take in an honest endeavour to aid the civil power'. The Crown, however, in the form of George V, objected to this statement, and with good reason because no strong action by the police, much less the military, had proved necessary. Lloyd George was highly critical of the *British Gazette* because it excluded contributions from leading Liberals such as Asquith or himself, or from neutral figures such as the Archbishop of Canterbury.

The Liberal Shadow Cabinet met without Lloyd George, who dissented from their pro-Government view. He said that the action of the Government was 'precipitate, unwarrantable and mischievous. But for that, we might now have had peace . . . I prefer the Liberal policy of trusting to conciliation rather than to force.' (Churchill preferred force.) As a result of Lloyd George's alignment with the workers, another breach opened up in the Liberal Party.

The positions of Lloyd George and Churchill were polarised by the labour issue in 1926. Lloyd George's sympathy for the striking workers was consistent with his radical views in the great reforming era of 1908–11 and explained his success at resolving so many of the industrial disputes of that time. Churchill, with his tough, somewhat military response to industrial anarchy and loss of production, also remained true to himself.

The General Strike lasted a week, and was orderly and good-tempered. There was no real threat of revolution, as the Conservatives tried to claim. But one of the sad results of the rift in the Liberal Party was the final estrangement of Lloyd George and Asquith, who resigned as leader in October 1926 and died two years later. The relationship between Lloyd George and Churchill, meanwhile, continued to be one of warm friendship in private and fierce political divergence across the floor of the House of Commons.

In February 1927 Clementine Churchill commented to Winston: '[Asquith] is of course rather sad about [William]

Wedgwood Benn's defection. It seems unreasonable to be driven into the Labour Party by Lloyd George, when Lloyd George will so very soon join him there!' Of course there was no chance of Lloyd George ever joining the Labour Party, but it was a common perception among upper-class English people in the post-war years that he was a man of the left.

Such opinions were fuelled, for instance, by his reluctance to endorse the Conservative Government's decision to sever diplomatic relations with Russia in 1927 and to send the Soviet diplomats home to Moscow. In May, Churchill wrote to E. L. Spears: 'Mr Lloyd George who used to be so sure of himself and gave us such able leadership in bye-gone years cannot even make up his mind which Lobby to vote in. On the blunt question – Should the Russians go or stay? he could vote neither "Aye" nor "No".'

How, on the other hand, did Lloyd George see Churchill at this time? He described the Chancellor's Budget speech of 1927 as providing 'over two and a half hours of extraordinarily brilliant entertainment'. Whether or not this was written in irony, more generally he used to say that Churchill was a Tory at heart. And it does seem that Churchill's gradual move to the right during the 1920s and 1930s – his hatred and fear of communism, his resistance to political reform in India and his constant return to the theme of military rearmament (which of course in the end turned out to be justified) – did indeed reflect his inherited prejudices.

During the later 1920s the political skirmishing between the two former colleagues was at a rather low and trivial level and never affected their deep affection for each other. Their friendship mirrored that of the two characters at the centre of Churchill's novel *Savrola*: 'We are on opposite sides, but we will fight under the rules of war. I hope we shall remain friends even though –' 'We are officially enemies.' Whether inside or outside the House of Commons, Churchill defended himself stoutly against Lloyd George's attacks on the Government, but in private he was always very complimentary to his old chief.

T. E. Lawrence wrote to Churchill on publication of *The World Crisis* in 1929:

18 MARCH 1929

I particularly like your fairness toward Lloyd George. The future is going to flay our generation for its unfairness to him. He's ever so much bigger than the statesmen of the Napoleonic times. He's said magnificent things, & his own performances, with that team, were marvellous. You give him, not full marks, but more than's the fashion: and so you do yourself great credit. It makes me glad, all through 1920 and 1921, to find him and you so close together. Of course your later advantages over him are partly due to your being young enough to try again: and partly to your greater strength. But Ll G has been a very grand figure. He was a big man in Paris.

Of course the Greek business was awful. Venizelos stole the wits of Harold Nicolson, & so cajoled the Foreign Office: and Ll G's nasty little Nonconformist upbringing fell for him. It was the ruin of a Middle East situation that was a clear gift to us.

By this time Lloyd George was very much out of favour in political circles. Nevertheless, Churchill's memoirs prove that he was consistently loyal and fair to the great achievements of the Coalition Government of 1916–22, the Anglo-Irish Treaty among them.

# 8

## 1929–38: In the Wilderness

'There is scarcely any more abundant source of error in history than the natural desire of writers . . . to discover or provide simple explanations for the actions of their characters.'
Winston Churchill, *Lord Randolph Churchill*, 1906

ON 18 FEBRUARY 1929 Lloyd George had a long talk with Churchill, who was still Chancellor of the Exchequer, about the likely outcome of the next general election, to be held in May of that year, and the possibility of reviving the Conservative/Liberal alliance in order to keep out the socialists. (There is a note of their conversation in the Lloyd George papers in the House of Lords.) Beaverbrook commented in March: 'Churchill has no intention whatever of allying himself with Lloyd George, although rumours to this effect in Conservative circles are doing him a great deal of harm.' In any case, the Prime Minister, Baldwin, was not interested; his slogan was 'Safety First'.

The Liberals themselves had considered the possibility of an alliance with Labour but Lloyd George concluded: 'If it means that the Liberals in the House of Commons are to carry the ladder and hold it in its place for five years whilst the Socialists are up on the scaffolding doing all the building . . . this would be the final blow to the Liberal Party.'

In the May election it was above all Lloyd George who, although in opposition and leading a small minority party, led the campaign of ideas. Even before the Wall Street crash in October 1929, and the economic depression that followed, there were two million unemployed British workers. The inspired theme of the Liberals' campaign was therefore 'We Can Conquer Unemployment' and this was also the title of a remarkable pamphlet which Lloyd George commissioned from Maynard Keynes and other leading economists, to be funded by the party. It proposed putting idle men, materials and money to work to solve the problem of the Depression, a plan very similar to the one that Franklin D. Roosevelt was to enact with his New Deal after 1933.

Yet despite an innovative campaign, the election proved to be yet another watershed for the Liberals. As Lloyd George had forecast, Labour moved into first place with 288 seats, with the Conservatives gaining 260 and the Liberals only 59. Baldwin refused to seek Liberal support on the kind of terms which Lloyd George had discussed with Churchill earlier in the year, and so Ramsay MacDonald again formed a minority administration.

In the eyes of Aneurin Bevan, the newly elected Member for Ebbw Vale who had himself worked as a miner at the age of thirteen, Churchill and Lloyd George were in 'a temporary re-alliance' in their attack on the Coal Bill, which Labour introduced at the end of 1929, for failing to tackle the basic problems of the British coal industry. The strength of Bevan's criticism in the parliamentary debate on the Bill disconcerted Lloyd George who, in the words of one observer, 'was confronted with the ghost of his own angry youth'.

During the summer of 1930, as the economic climate in Britain worsened, the Liberals had a long conference with the Labour Government of Ramsay MacDonald, but Lloyd George was still not prepared to sacrifice his party's independence. By the spring of 1931, the cost of keeping two million men on the dole drove the Labour Chairman, George Lansbury, to appeal to the Liberal leader to join the party:

Your coming would crown a professional life with the knowledge that as the world of thought and action moved on, you never closed your mind, and when the hour came and you were needed, you flung aside all thought of self and came over to the new groupings of true liberalism.

But the most that Lloyd George would concede was a pledge by the Liberals to back the Labour Government in their unemployment plans.

The recession steadily deepened until, in August, the country's financial situation was so acute that Ramsay MacDonald was forced to resign when he was unable to gain the support of a majority of his Cabinet over measures to rescue the British economy. A temporary National Government was formed to deal with the emergency, under MacDonald's leadership and including Baldwin and Neville Chamberlain from the Tories, Sir Herbert Samuel and Lord Reading (Rufus Isaacs) from the Liberals, and two socialists, Philip Snowden and J. H. Thomas.

In October 1931 another general election was held, resulting in an overwhelming victory for the National Government which won 554 seats (471 of which went to the Conservatives). Labour emerged with an ignominious 52.

A fortnight before the political crisis Lloyd George had been struck down by illness and had to undergo an operation for prostate cancer. MacDonald wrote to him: 'At this moment you are first in my thoughts. We all feel what a loss is your absence.' Lloyd George replied from his sickbed, 'I am sorry I have not been able to give you any real help, but if the promise of the doctors is redeemed I may be of some use later on'. Behind the scenes it was Baldwin who was really in control of events. Had it not been for Lloyd George's sudden illness, it was he rather than Baldwin who would have dominated the National Government.

On 12 August Churchill had paid tribute to Lloyd George in the *Daily Mail*:

History will re-turn her pages back to [Lord] Chatham to find his parallel in achievement. No one has consciously shaped the details and routine of British daily life as he has done. The great systems of Insurance against old age, sickness, invalidity, and unemployment which affect the whole social life of the British nation, and distinguish them in degree at least from every other country, are his characteristic contributions.

The system of progressive taxation . . . dates from the Lloyd George budget of 1909. The splendid motor roads which lace the British countryside . . . are the products of his original Road Fund.

No hand more than his carried the Irish Settlement . . . But it is upon his actions in the crisis of the greatest and most terrible of wars that his fame will rest.

. . . individual leaders . . . played a far smaller part in Armageddon than in any former war . . . There are, however, a number of definitive actions and decisions of Lloyd George which exercised cardinal influence upon the final result.

He first of all, before the end of 1914, proclaimed to the Cabinet the impending failure of Russia . . . from the beginning of 1915 [he] imagined the gigantic scale upon which the production of munitions of all kinds must be undertaken . . . and drove forward the universal mobilization of British industry for war purposes.

Facing the daunting threat of German submarine attacks in spring 1917 he did not lose heart and he did not tolerate defeatism in others . . . Nothing broke the German submarine attack so much as the convoy system. Mr Lloyd George's personal share in forcing that upon the Admiralty is a noteworthy and indisputable page in his record . . .

It may well be that the chief and most damaging cause of Mr Lloyd George's decline is his identification with the petty political exigencies of a small and dwindling party. Let us hope that when he is restored to health he will stand squarely upon his own feet and, untrammelled by party ties and weak, discordant associates, give his own true counsel upon National and Imperial questions to Parliament and the nation as a whole.

Whether such a course would lead to power may be uncertain. But that it will afford him the only pedestal worthy of his past is sure.

The movement for independence in India had been gathering momentum since 1900 and by 1930 it had become clear that the British Government had to anticipate changes there. Though he held no position and carried no title, Gandhi had become, in the eyes of the Indians, their anointed leader. He had led the famous March to the Sea to gather salt – protesting against the British monopoly on salt production – and had been imprisoned by the British for leading other such peaceful, non-violent protests. The Viceroy, Lord Irwin (who later became Lord Halifax), took the initiative and set up a meeting with Gandhi in Delhi in 1931. Few British observers or residents in India thought that the Indians were ready for self-government; nevertheless, the move to Dominion status, which was proposed by the British Government in 1930–1, received support that went far beyond the ranks of the Conservative Party.

Churchill took a completely different view of the Indian situation. He did not regard the Indians as capable of, or ready for, self-government. It cannot be said that he was uninformed about India – he had lived there for nearly four years; he had studied the caste system; he knew something of the complex ethnic geography of the subcontinent with its many different languages and tribal groups, and more particularly the role of the princes and maharajas who presided over a number of provinces under the overall aegis of the British Raj. Baldwin and the other party leaders made every effort to bring Churchill round to their point of view for the sake of solidarity. Churchill's stand against the 'Irwin reforms' not only alienated him from his colleagues in the Conservative Party but also from the Tory leadership.

From today's perspective, it may be said that Churchill, with his usual prescience, may have understood that the Hindu–Muslim divide was an overwhelming obstacle to a peaceful evolution to self-determination in India; indeed, the massacres of 1947 bore out his prophetic vision. On the other hand we can look upon Churchill's view of the Indians (and particularly his refusal to meet Gandhi) as being not merely old-fashioned but somewhat racist.

Lloyd George, by contrast, had not yet visited India but instinctively had sympathy with the right of the Indian population to self-government. So it was that on a cold wet night in November 1931 Gandhi arrived to visit Lloyd George at Churt, his home in the country. He wore his native dress, with bare legs and sandals. In his diary A. J. Sylvester reported that he was swathed in a heavy blanket like a bathrobe and the only sustenance he took was a bottle of goat's milk and a handful of dates. Lloyd George welcomed him warmly and, with Gandhi curled up on the sofa, they talked for hours, ranging over the vast field of Indian politics. A stray cat that had turned up at Churt a few days earlier took a great fancy to the visitor and was named after Gandhi. The Indian did much of the talking, Lloyd George as ever the good listener. Gandhi opposed giving separate votes to the Hindu and Muslim communities, as he was to oppose partition fifteen years later. Lloyd George put the same question to Gandhi that he had to the Irish delegation in 1921: was he willing for India to remain within the British Empire? Gandhi said yes – within a British Commonwealth of free nations. 'Well, Gandhi may be a saint,' said Lloyd George, 'but he is certainly a first-class politician.'

While Lloyd George hailed Gandhi as the most brilliant man he had ever met, Churchill was fulminating against him as a 'half-naked fakir of a type well known in the East, parlaying with the Viceroy or the representative of the King Emperor'. He was still poking fun at Gandhi (among other targets) in 1933 when, on 24 April, he stood up to make an after-dinner speech to the Royal Society of St George, which was to be broadcast by the BBC: '. . . We can picture Sir John Reith, with the perspiration mounting on his lofty brow, with his hands on the control switch, wondering, as I utter every word, whether it will be his duty to protect his innocent subscribers from some irreverent thing I might say about Mr Gandhi, or about the Bolsheviks, or even about our peripatetic Prime Minister [Ramsay MacDonald].' The issue of 'political correctness' was already a sensitive one with the media, as Churchill's uncharacteristic self-restraint shows.

Following Gandhi's visit, Lloyd George travelled by sea to India and Ceylon. During the voyage he read Churchill's history of the First World War, *The World Crisis*, which stimulated him to write his own war memoirs.

En route to Ceylon in December 1931 Lloyd George heard that Churchill had been involved in a car accident in New York. He was deeply concerned and immediately sent him a cable. Churchill, who had suffered shock, concussion and bruising, replied that 'he had momentarily forgotten that traffic in the United States goes on the right side of the road'.

Churchill had lost the Exchequership in the 1929 defeat of the Conservatives to Labour and would not be recalled to government for more than a decade. So, during the 1930s, he, like Lloyd George, was out of office, mistrusted and shunned by the politicians who presided over what W. H. Auden called that 'low dishonest decade'. MacDonald, Chamberlain and Baldwin would do anything to keep Lloyd George – 'the Welsh wizard' or, less flatteringly, 'the Goat' – out of Downing Street, and Baldwin refused to let Churchill back into his Shadow Cabinet because of his 'hundred-horsepower brain'.

Consequently, the two men renewed their friendship. They spent a great deal of time visiting each other in their country homes, Churt (near Guildford in Surrey) and Chartwell (near Westerham in Kent); coincidentally, both houses were designed by the same architect, Philip Tilden (who was driven to distraction by both clients). The Chartwell Visitor's Book is full of visits by Lloyd George for lunch, but never to stay the night.

In 1934 Lloyd George and Churchill were invited to the dinner of the Printers' Pension Fund, at which they were both expected to speak. For Lloyd George, this duty was turned into a pleasure by the fact that his old friend Winston would also be present; photographs show them in sparkling form, exchanging jokes and banter while the chairman of the Printers' Pension Fund stands between them. Perhaps one of the secrets of their enduring friendship was that they had so much fun together.

The two men also spent their holidays together, mainly in Morocco or the South of France. Margaret and Clementine usually stayed at home, and their husbands met up with friends such as Beaverbrook and Riddell. However, on 24 January 1938, Winston and Clementine Churchill hosted a Golden Wedding lunch for David and Margaret Lloyd George at the Carlton Hotel in Cannes. Churchill made a speech saying that Lloyd George would figure prominently in the history of the world, and Lloyd George replied that there was no one with whom he would sooner have celebrated this occasion than Winston and Clemmie. Winston afterwards told Dick and Gwilym Lloyd George how pleased he was with these remarks because he knew they were sincere. Their father was then seventy-five and clearly his memory was becoming faulty for he announced that he had first met Churchill in 1890 and that their friendship had lasted for forty-eight years. Churchill would have been a sixteen-year-old schoolboy at the time, and although a meeting was theoretically possible on a visit from Harrow to the House of Commons, it seems unlikely.

Another holiday was especially memorable for a young Cambridge don (later a novelist), Charles P. Snow, who happened to be spending Christmas in the same hotel in Antibes as the Lloyd George family. In his colourful portrait of Lloyd George he recalls his surprise at receiving an invitation to join the family party and how warmly he was received. A couple of days later he plucked up the courage to ask Lloyd George why he had invited a complete stranger to share their Christmas dinner. Lloyd George replied, with a mischievous glint in his eye, 'Well, as a matter of fact, I thought you had an interesting head.' Phrenology had become fashionable in the early 1900s and Snow did indeed have a remarkable domed head that an amateur like Lloyd George found fascinating. He used to judge his colleagues in the political world accordingly. Churchill evidently had a distinctively large cranium, a fertile imagination and a bump of perception; Neville Chamberlain and Halifax had thin craniums with a narrow perception of the world.

In January 1936, when the two friends were staying at the Mamounia Hotel in Marrakesh, Lloyd George was asked to intervene in a dispute between Winston and his son Randolph. Against his father's wishes, the headstrong twenty-eight-year-old wished to stand as an independent Conservative against Baldwin, embarrassing Winston's hopes of a rapprochement with the Tories. Lloyd George tried to prevent Randolph from standing, but without success.

At the time both elder statesmen were busy writing: Lloyd George his *War Memoirs*, and Churchill completing *Marlborough: His Life and Times*. Both also continued to supplement their income by writing newspaper articles.

One day they found it hard to concentrate on their work because, as Lloyd George recalled, some fellow started practising on a ukulele. Presently he heard a terrific yell from Winston (who had the room on the floor above him in the hotel). The yell was long and continuous and the ukulele stopped.

On another occasion, while Lloyd George and A. J. Sylvester were enjoying an evening aperitif, there was a knock on the door and in walked Churchill with a picture which he proudly declared he had painted in an hour. It was a little gem, depicting a Marrakesh building coloured in ochre, with the red setting sun on it, tall palms, a Moor in the middle of the road and a native woman at the well. Lloyd George said it was an inspiration. Churchill, wearing his blue boiler suit and with paint smeared all over the sleeve, was as pleased as a child. He later presented his friend with an oil painting of the Mediterranean on which he had also been working and which was given pride of place above Lloyd George's desk at Churt. Lloyd George said 'Your picture is a joy and a delight and will cheer up an old fellow who is a friend and an admirer of your genius.'

To celebrate his seventy-third birthday, on 17 January, Lloyd George gave a dinner that Churchill attended. Sylvester recalled:

There is no doubt that Winston and LG stimulate each other. I was immensely interested watching the facial expressions of these two brilliant men . . . Winston rose and made a speech: 'This is a memorable occasion . . . Ours is a very long political friendship. It is now forty years or more [*sic*] since we began to be friends in the House of Commons. There have been many vicissitudes in public life during that period, and all the time I have thanked God that he [Lloyd George] has been born to work for our country, for the masses of those poor people in times of peace, and for our strength and security in the great days of the war. I ask you to join with me in drinking his health . . . for I can assure you we shall need his counsel and his efforts in the years which lie before us.' LG replied, thanking him and saying 'I have the good fortune to have present with me my oldest political friend. It is the longest political friendship in the life of Great Britain. It is a friendship which has not depended in the least upon agreement, even on fundamentals. I doubt whether there is any other country where it would be possible for men to fight, and fight very hard, as we have done, more particularly throughout the last 10 or 15 years, without for one moment impairing the good feeling and the warmth, and if I may be allowed to say so no one knows better than my family the affection with which I return my friendship. It is to me a very great delight that he should have been here today to propose this toast. I thank you from the bottom of my heart.'

Two days later King George V died. Lloyd George and Churchill discussed the position. Both of them were friends of the new King, Edward VIII, and decided to return at once to London.

When staying at Balmoral with King George V and Queen Mary during the summer after the death of Edward VII in 1910, Lloyd George had suggested that it would be well received, especially in Wales, if the royal family reinstated the ancient custom of investing the Prince of Wales at Caernarvon Castle (an event which had last taken place in 1300 after Edward I's conquest of Wales). Their Majesties readily agreed; the consequence was that the young Prince, David (later Edward VIII), who was then sixteen years old, used to come regularly to 11 Downing Street for lessons in Welsh with the Chancellor. He came to be much loved for his easy and unpretentious manner with the Lloyd George family and the domestic staff.

At the investiture itself, in July 1911, it was Churchill as Home Secretary who took a leading role and made a speech, whereas Lloyd George, the architect of the whole event, was, as Constable of Caernarvon Castle, in the background (and his uniform was a good deal more traditional than the Earl of Snowdon's in 1969!). Both Churchill and Lloyd George remained close to the young Prince of Wales during the next twenty-five years (there is an appealing photograph of Churchill in 1920 evidently giving advice to the Prince).

On 18 November 1936, Edward VIII paid a visit to the abandoned steelworks of Dowlais in South Wales. Surveying the devastated industrial scene and the evident poverty of the Welsh families before him – 75 per cent of Welsh miners were unemployed – the new King was obviously moved and, turning to the Minister of Labour, said, 'These steelworks brought the men hope . . . something must be done to see that they stay here – working.'

At this time, unknown to the British public because of the deference shown by the press towards the royal family in the 1930s, the King was passionately in love with an American divorcée, Mrs Wallis Simpson. The National Government led by Stanley Baldwin and Neville Chamberlain, and the leaders of the Church of England, objected to the King's infatuation; there may also have been a hostile political element in their judgement, disapproving, as they certainly did, of Edward's utterances in Wales and elsewhere, and of his obvious sympathy for the poor and the unemployed.

By 7 December, when Stanley Baldwin made a statement in the House about the King's predicament, the mood of the Establishment was set against the monarch and his intention to marry Mrs Simpson once her divorce from Ernest Simpson was finalised.

In his romantic support for the monarchy Clementine described Churchill as 'the last old-fashioned Monarchist'. But he had few supporters for his 'King's party' and the one heavyweight politician who would have wholeheartedly supported him – Lloyd George – had left Britain in November for a month's holiday in Jamaica. There were many on Baldwin's side who were relieved that Lloyd George was out of the country as he and Churchill would have been a formidable team, working together on the side of the King.

When Churchill rose in the House to plead with the Government to give Edward more time to consider his position he was shouted down. Baldwin replied that the Government was not prepared to introduce legislation to allow a morganatic marriage. Churchill shouted across the floor at Baldwin, 'You won't be satisfied until you have broken him, will you?' and stormed out.

Churchill sent Lloyd George a telegram urging him to return. The Welshman's view was that it was an impertinence that Baldwin would not let the King choose his own wife; he considered the Prime Minister full of 'humbug and hypocrisy'. 'Had the King not exposed the callous neglect by the Government of distress and poverty and bad housing conditions' they would not have shown such alacrity to 'down' him. But Lloyd George was still in Jamaica when King Edward VIII gave his abdication speech on 11 December. From there he sent a sympathetic telegram: 'May I, as an old Minister of the Crown . . .'

At Christmas, when the crisis was over, Churchill wrote to Lloyd George: 'I believe the abdication to have been altogether premature and probably quite unnecessary. However, the vast majority is on the other side.'

Churchill, almost alone among his contemporaries, foresaw the dangers of Hitler's philosophy and the National Socialist movement in Germany. Even before Hitler became Chancellor in March 1933, he had read *Mein Kampf*; he had informants who told him about the brutal, undemocratic process by which the Nazis took and held power, and about their anti-Semitism. The previous year Churchill had been in Germany visiting the battlefields of the Duke of Marlborough in order to write his ancestor's biography. While in Munich he had been invited to meet Hitler, but before doing so had had a conversation with Ernst Hanfstaengl, a friend of his, who spoke good English. All was going well until Churchill said, 'Why does your boss hate the Jews? It may be a popular policy to start out with, but it is a bad one to follow on.' Hitler angrily cancelled what would have been a historic meeting.

Hitler reoccupied the Rhineland in March 1936 without provoking any serious response from Britain or France. In June, Lloyd George attacked the Baldwin/Chamberlain National Government for its policy of appeasement towards Mussolini's campaign in Abyssinia. Frances Stevenson described the situation thus:

> When Britain abandoned the sanctions which the League of Nations had imposed [upon Italy] . . . LG could keep silence no longer. In the Foreign Affairs debate which followed in June 1936, the vials of his wrath and contempt were outpoured: . . . 'Tonight we have the cowardly surrender, and *there* are the cowards [pointing at the Treasury Bench].' The speech was devastating: LG

resurrected his old fighting days . . . The House was almost hysterical . . . The Front Bench seemed to cower before this onslaught, and Baldwin's reply was pitiable . . . After the speech a young Tory member went up to Churchill and said that he had never heard anything like it in the House. 'Young man,' Churchill replied, 'you have been listening to one of the greatest Parliamentary performances of all time.'

But while he now appeared to be close to Churchill in matters of foreign policy, Lloyd George's main concern was still unemployment. He admired Roosevelt and his 'New Deal' and on the surface it appeared that Hitler, also, had achieved some measure of economic success with his vast programme of public works, especially road-building, which employed thousands of German workers. So, in June 1936, Lloyd George was flattered to receive an invitation to visit Hitler.

In July General Francisco Franco had started the Nationalist revolt against the Republican Government in Spain, which led to three years of civil war. Both Mussolini and Hitler gave Franco strong military support. At first Churchill also came out as a supporter of Franco, at least in his lack of sympathy for the Popular Front. Lloyd George, on the other hand, firmly supported the Republican cause in Spain.

In September Lloyd George spent almost a fortnight in Germany and had two meetings with Adolf Hitler. Hitler was convinced that the German collapse of 1918 had been due to the lack of effective political leadership in the country compared to Lloyd George's wartime initiatives. Lloyd George meanwhile saw Hitler, who had now been in power for over three years, as acting vigorously to eliminate unemployment in Germany with a very similar programme to the one he himself had proposed in 1929. At any rate he came away from Berchtesgaden, Hitler's Alpine retreat, not only inspired by the enormous window (which he would copy at Churt) but charmed and impressed by the Führer. In consequence he wrote a newspaper article describing Hitler as the 'George Washington of Germany'. Churchill's verdict on this whole episode, delivered to his doctor, Lord Moran, in old age, was: 'I would never have fallen into that trap.'

As an irregular radical, it was characteristic of Lloyd George that while he was busy meeting Hitler he was at the same time able to support the left-wing socialist and republican Government in Spain and also (despite Foreign Office opposition) the increase of Jewish immigration to Israel. Lloyd George had not read *Mein Kampf* and he was unwilling to see the expansionism and anti-Semitism underlying the economic improvements of Hitler's Germany. Like many others who had been through the First World War, Lloyd George was keen at all costs to avoid another war with Germany.

In his favour, while on his recent visit, Lloyd George had told German Baptist leaders that he did not like Hitler's attack on the Jews: 'England would not tolerate interference in religion.' And certainly by 1937 the scales had begun to fall from his eyes; well before the Munich Agreement of 1938, he had rejoined his old friend and comrade, Churchill, in denouncing the Conservatives, first under Baldwin, then under Chamberlain, for their delay in rearming Britain to combat the German menace. As his Parliamentary Private Secretary Bob Boothby later wrote: 'Churchill was preoccupied with air rearmament. Lloyd George deplored our military and naval weakness, which he himself would never have tolerated.'

In 1939 Lloyd George and Churchill met the Soviet Ambassador, Ivan Maisky, in the House of Commons, and their conversation was recorded by the author and diplomat Harold Nicolson in his diary. Both Lloyd George and Churchill understood that a British guarantee to defend Poland would be worthless unless Britain also had a treaty or alliance with Russia (in the event, the Stalin–Hitler Non-aggression Pact of August 1939 doomed Poland to invasion, as they foresaw).

Churchill went straight to the point in challenging Maisky to ally Russia with Britain and France; Lloyd George, by contrast, questioned the Russian Ambassador about the Polish Army. Would they be able to defend themselves, either against Nazi Germany or against the USSR? What were their armaments? How good was the officer class? This enraged Churchill, who was bent on saving Poland, and he rebuked Lloyd George sharply: 'You must not do this sort of thing, my dear. You are putting spokes in the wheel of history . . .'

This difference in outlook would again become apparent in 1940 when Lloyd George, summing up the strategic situation after the fall of France and the retreat from Dunkirk, was unable to see how Britain could win the war. Churchill, on the other hand, with his extraordinary and unique combination of prophetic vision and indomitable will, would not contemplate anything other than a British victory.

# 9

## 1939–45: Fathers of Victory

'History with its flickering lamp stumbles along the trail of
the past, trying to reconstruct its scenes, to revive the echoes,
and kindle with pale gleams the passion of former days.'

Churchill, 1940

THERE WAS A significant difference between the position
Churchill had occupied in 1914 and the situation in which
he found himself in 1939. For three years before the outbreak of
the First World War, he had been First Lord of the Admiralty and
therefore able to ensure that the Royal Navy was fully equipped
and trained to counter the German High Fleet. In 1912–13, when
nominally in charge of the Navy, he had taken many hours of
flying lessons and had come to appreciate the value of aircraft for
reconnaissance and bombing. In the 1930s Churchill therefore
understood, long before the military commanders and most of his
Cabinet colleagues, the value of an effective air force. Though out
of power, he tried to persuade the reluctant National Government – Baldwin, Chamberlain and their colleagues such as
Samuel Hoare – to maintain Britain's defences against German
attack by rebuilding the Royal Air Force, just as he had rebuilt the
fleet of battleships between 1911 and 1914. But his advice went
unheeded and so, in 1939, Britain was unprepared for war.

An interesting parallel between 1914 and 1939, on the other
hand, was that once again Lloyd George resisted the Churchillian

conclusion that war was inevitable. In April 1939, when the two men met outside the chamber of the Commons, Churchill spoke of 'smashing through' in the case of war. Lloyd George asked, 'With what?' They had been alone in the lobby but Churchill was talking so loudly that other MPs came up to learn their views on Chamberlain's statement about the international situation. Lloyd George was convinced that a Franco-British alliance with the Soviet Union would deter Hitler's adventurism. The Conservative leadership, Chamberlain and Halifax, however, were not prepared to deal with Stalin until it was too late.

Churchill's outlook was belligerent. Lloyd George has been accused of defeatism; realism might be a fairer judgement. 'Lloyd George had none of Churchill's passion for the military art: but his mind – despite, or perhaps because of, his leaps of imagination – was level, critical and quantitative'; in the same way that he had talked to C. P. Snow of the Spanish Civil War – 'Look for the prisoners! Look for the places! Pay no attention to the rest!' – he now focused on the size of the various armies and their weaponry, and the tactical and strategic situation. In the light of this he was understandably gloomy about the prospects of war with Germany.

Churchill's prescient warnings of the coming German menace and about the lack of British preparation enormously boosted his reputation in these final months before the Second World War began. On 4 August 1939 he and Lloyd George lunched with Churchill's close friend and confidant, Brendan Bracken. Lloyd George advised Churchill not to join Neville Chamberlain's Government, if invited, and Bracken agreed. 'Winston was passionately fond of office', said LG, 'yet he has made all his reputation out of office. Joe Chamberlain was the same. Bright and Cobden did likewise. Charles James Fox was the same.'

Lloyd George had no confidence in Chamberlain and Halifax. As a keen amateur phrenologist, he used to say about

Chamberlain: 'Look at his head ["a narrow mean man with a narrow thin skull"]. The worst thing Neville Chamberlain ever did was to meet Hitler and to let Hitler see him.' As for Halifax, when the Foreign Secretary went to Germany to see the Nazi leaders, Lloyd George declared that it was like 'sending a curate to visit a Tiger; he would not know if it was growling in anger or in fun, and in either case he would not know how to reply'.

Lloyd George had wholly changed his view since being 'charmed' and 'fascinated' by Hitler in September 1936. Despite his deep reservations about the National Government, typically he was the first to congratulate Churchill when the latter was recalled to the Admiralty three years later.

When war broke out on 3 September 1939 Churchill was back at the Admiralty. It was precisely where he had been on 3 August 1914, but this was an older and wiser Churchill, who was able to draw on the lessons learned during the earlier conflict with Germany, many of which he had absorbed at the side of his 'chief', David Lloyd George.

Lloyd George, meanwhile, was able to express his views in articles for the *Sunday Pictorial*

10 SEPTEMBER
Germany is again the aggressor. Once more it is a fight for international right – the recognition of the equal right of nations, weak as well as strong, to lead their own independent lives so long as they do not interfere with the rights of their neighbours . . . Russian non-intervention is . . . worrying for the Allies.

17 SEPTEMBER
[America deciding to provide war materials may prove decisive:] this will be a war of material superiority even more than the last.

24 SEPTEMBER
[LG blamed Britain for the fall of Poland; for not checking Poland's defensive capabilities before guaranteeing to stand by her.]

1 OCTOBER

Moscow documents indicate that Bolshevism has joined whole-heartedly the confederacy of menace . . . We have been completely outmanoeuvred by the German Dictator . . . The leaders of the Western democracies in Britain and France are entirely outclassed by the two great dictators with whom they have had to deal – Mussolini and Hitler. To these I may now add Stalin. This was borne out by the British bungling of the negotiations with Russia. However, Britain now has the grim, if somewhat sullen, determination to beat Hitler.

15 OCTOBER

[Although Chamberlain described Hitler as a liar, a thief and a cheat, LG still hopes to make peace.] Hitler has nothing to gain from a protracted war, as it would leave him forced to get his daily bread from Stalin. It is also in Western interests to secure peace – war would damage trade and shipping. [Lloyd George wants the President of the United States to convene a peace conference.]

22 OCTOBER

The effect on British opinion of the losses and casualties inflicted by German submarines and bombers has been exactly what would be anticipated by anyone who has made a study of the character of our people. It has perceptibly stiffened our attitude.

29 OCTOBER

The bombardment of our cities will not intimidate the spirit of the stubborn Briton. It will only exasperate him and stimulate his fighting spirit.

Churchill was in an invidious position in 1939–40 because, as a Cabinet minister, he was bound to be loyal to Chamberlain; but there were parallels between Chamberlain and Halifax, who had for so long appeased Germany and failed to prepare Britain for war, and Asquith and Grey in 1914. Although Churchill's experience of fighting in the trenches in 1916 was shared by Anthony Eden, Harold Macmillan and other fellow ministers, he was the only member of the Chamberlain Cabinet who had been in the 1914–18 War Cabinet. However, the transfer from the peacetime Liberal Government in 1914 to the wartime Coalition Government in 1915 had required a much greater adjustment than that facing Chamberlain's National Government in 1939. At least Britain had been through the experience before and Churchill knew what had to be done.

To a surprising degree, the First Lord of the Admiralty in 1939 would find himself refighting the 1914–18 war, both at sea and in the struggle to provide the troops with adequate weapons and equipment. In the early days of the Second World War, the U-boat menace loomed just as threateningly as it had in 1917–18. The answer was the same as the one Lloyd George had finally elicited from a reluctant Admiralty in 1917 – convoys – and this time Churchill made certain that Britain's merchant shipping was well protected by the Navy. Until the end of 1942, he would anxiously watch the Atlantic Ocean from his 'map room'; it was the gauntlet that had to be run for the sake of essential supplies. In one consignment 50,000 rifles were being shipped from America to arm the poorly equipped Home Guard in preparation for the German invasion which threatened the country in July 1940.

During the first few months of the 'Phoney War' of 1939–40, Churchill continually made comparisons with the First World War. He was acutely aware of Britain's lack of preparedness. Drawing on his earlier experience, on 23 January 1940 he pointed out to the Military Co-ordination Committee that the 'great shell plants' laid down by Lloyd George in the summer of 1915 had not come into full production until the autumn of 1917. The 'enormous increase' achieved then was 'solely due to the fact that the foundations had been laid early'. For this reason 'he was pressing for long-term construction to begin immediately'. Addressing an audience in Manchester on 27 January 1940 Churchill said, 'I can speak with some knowledge' having presided over the Ministry of Munitions 'in the culminating phases' in the First World War. Agriculture [another of LG's pet projects] also, he stressed, must be organised 'upon at least the 1918 scale.' All this he had learned from Lloyd George.

As the war situation became more serious in the spring of 1940, Chamberlain clearly leaned increasingly on Churchill, who proved to be a loyal colleague. In April Churchill suggested the inclusion in the War Cabinet of Archie Sinclair and Max Beaverbrook, both close friends of his. Chamberlain was surprised that Churchill had not yet suggested Lloyd George. Dating back to Chamberlain's unsuccessful tenure as Minister for National Service in 1917, there had been a deep-rooted antipathy between the two men, although Lloyd George had always been an admirer of the Prime Minister's brother, Austen, and of his father, Joe Chamberlain.

Churchill, meanwhile, was still the same excitable, impulsive schoolboy, the same armchair strategist, at sixty-five as he had been at the age of forty when the First World War began. Instead of Gallipoli, he set his sights on a landing in Narvik in Norway in April 1940. But again the parallels are striking. The Navy and the Air Force were undermanned. The Germans had already occupied the airfields by the time the expedition arrived, and British marines faced heavy opposition, just as the troops had done in the Dardanelles. As before, the expedition was badly planned and poorly executed. Churchill, as First Lord of the Admiralty, took a good deal of the blame.

On 1 May, Harold Nicolson noted in his diary that 'There is a theory going round that Lloyd George may head a Coalition Cabinet'. As Chamberlain's position weakened with the failure of the Norway campaign, inevitably there were rumours about who might succeed him. However, it seems unlikely that David Lloyd George, at the age of seventy-seven, would have entertained the possibility of becoming wartime Prime Minister again.

During the Phoney War Lloyd George was one of the few British statesmen who understood the gravity of the situation and how weak were the British defences. When Bob Boothby suggested in 1940 that 'only Churchill could save us'. Lloyd George replied:

> You are probably right, but it will be a one-man show. He has at least one great general – Wavell. I was not so fortunate. But, mark my words, he will get rid of Wavell. I will not join him. If I did, I should be the only one to stand up to him. And that would be no good for either of us. I will do my best to get rid of Chamberlain, for under him we are bound to be defeated. That is all I can do.

Nevertheless, the debate in the House of Commons on 7 and 8 May 1940 posed a dilemma for Lloyd George. How could he attack Chamberlain without damaging his old friend Winston?

The debate on 7 May included a slashing attack on the Government by Leo Amery, who as a backbench Conservative MP represented the dissident wing of the party. Echoing Cromwell's dismissal of the Long Parliament, he thundered at Chamberlain: 'In the name of God, go!'

The Prime Minister responded on 8 May: 'But I say this to my friends in the House – and I have friends in the House. No Government can prosecute a war efficiently unless it has public and Parliamentary support . . . I call on my friends to support us in the Lobby tonight . . .'

This was the signal for Lloyd George to intervene. His daughter Megan came running to his room in the House to tell him that Chamberlain had just given him an opening. The stage was set for his last great speech in Parliament: 'The Father of the House of Commons remained physically and intellectually full of vigour. He had much preparation for this role. In twenty minutes of speaking . . . Lloyd George drew upon two decades of hostility to Neville Chamberlain, four decades of love for Winston Churchill, and five decades, recently celebrated, of experience in the House of Commons.'

> I feel that I ought to say something, from such experience as I have had in the past of the conduct of war in victory and in disaster,

about what I think of the present situation and what really ought to be done . . . I try to get the facts, because unless you really face the facts you cannot overcome the difficulties and restore the position . . . First of all [in 1940 we are] strategically in a very much worse position than we were before [in 1914–18] . . .

Significantly, Lloyd George then dwelt on the impact of the European war, which had developed so rapidly, on public opinion across the Atlantic. Like Churchill, he regarded the United States as a key future ally. '. . . what has happened was a hammer blow to Americans . . . This is the first doubt that has entered their minds, and they said "It will be up to us to defend Democracy."'

He then went on to attack the military preparations, and in particular the failure of the Narvik landings and the fact that the British forces had arrived 'too little and too late' to save Norway from a Nazi invasion:

Is there anyone in this House who will say that he is satisfied with the speed and efficiency of the preparations in any respect for air, for Army, yea, for Navy? Everybody is disappointed. Everybody knows that whatever was done was done half-heartedly, ineffectively, without drive and unintelligently. For three or four years I thought to myself that the facts with regard to Germany were exaggerated by the First Lord, because the then Prime Minister [Baldwin] – not this Prime Minister – said that they were not true. The First Lord was right about it.

Lloyd George took the opportunity to praise Churchill and to bolster his political position before going on to attack the Norway campaign in detail, saying: 'I do not think that the First Lord was entirely responsible for all the things that happened there . . .'

At this, Churchill leapt to his feet to proclaim his loyalty to Chamberlain and accept his share of the blame: 'I take complete responsibility for everything that has been done by the Admiralty, and I take my full share of the burden.' Lloyd George riposted, to wide applause and laughter from the packed house: 'The right hon. Gentleman must not allow himself to be converted into an air-raid shelter to keep the splinters from hitting his colleagues.' Having thus deftly separated Churchill from the rest of the Chamberlain Cabinet and reminded the House of how right his prophetic warnings had been throughout the 1930s, the elder statesman moved on to attack Chamberlain personally.

> He said, 'I have got my friends.' It is not a question of who are the Prime Minister's friends. It is a far bigger issue. The Prime Minister must remember that he has met this formidable foe of ours in peace and in war. He has always been worsted. He is not in a position to appeal on the ground of friendship. He has appealed for sacrifice. The nation is prepared for every sacrifice so long as it has leadership . . . I say solemnly that the Prime Minister should give an example of sacrifice, because there is nothing which can contribute more to victory than that he should sacrifice the seals of office . . .

As Lloyd George said this, he pointed his finger at Neville Chamberlain, who sat sulking on the front bench. Coming on top of damning speeches by Leo Amery and Admiral Keyes, in the opinion of many observers this was the moment when the Commons changed its mind about Chamberlain's continuance as Prime Minister. Lloyd George, a successful war leader himself, spoke with a voice that was widely respected throughout Britain. In addition, he had met Hitler and taken the measure of the man. Chamberlain had met the German dictator twice, in Munich and at Berchtesgaden and, as Lloyd George observed, had been 'worsted' on both occasions. When he sat down, his message left the Commons in no doubt that Britain needed a fighter to lead her wartime effort; if this were accepted, there could be little further doubt that Winston Churchill alone could fill that role.

In the face of this withering attack, Chamberlain's position was seriously undermined and a large number of Conservative MPs voted against the Government or abstained. Although Chamberlain won the vote of confidence by a narrow margin, within forty-eight hours he had resigned as Prime Minister. Although the nation may very well have demanded Churchill as leader, Lloyd George's intervention had decisively influenced the outcome of the debate. It was the last major contribution either man made to the other's career. As Marvin Rintala wrote:

> The political careers of Lloyd George and Churchill were . . . intertwined. Those careers were eloquent evidence for the proposition that friends stand in a common world with a common destiny. If they stood together, Lloyd George and Churchill did not stand still. They moved rapidly, climbing to high cabinet offices. Without the other, neither likely would have climbed so fast so far. Their friendship was the most important factor in the political careers of both . . . They chose freely to become and remain friends, and they were never permanently estranged from each other because neither wanted to be.

When Winston Churchill unexpectedly became Prime Minister after the humiliation of Neville Chamberlain in this Commons debate, it was in the face of strong opposition from a number of Conservative Party stalwarts. Perhaps the most vocal was 'Rab' Butler, Halifax's deputy at the Foreign Office, who referred to Churchill as 'the greatest political adventurer of modern times' and 'a half-breed American'. Even King George VI let it be known that his preference was for Halifax. The King and the Foreign Secretary were close friends and Halifax had the unique privilege of having a key to the gardens of Buckingham Palace.

There would soon be strong opposition from Buckingham Palace, as well, to Churchill's proposals to include the press baron, Beaverbrook, in the War Cabinet and to make Brendan Bracken a Privy Counsellor. In the opinion of Halifax, Butler and the royal household, these characters were members of Churchill's 'gang' and, like him, 'political adventurers'. So, of course, was Lloyd George – an outsider, a maverick, and an adventurer.

As far as the premiership was concerned, however, Halifax was identified with Chamberlain's policy of appeasement. He announced that he did not think he could run the war effort and that the Prime Minister should in any case be a Member of the House of Commons rather than a hereditary peer as he was himself. In the meeting called by Chamberlain to discuss the succession on 10 May 1940, attended only by Halifax, Churchill and himself, the latter remained uncharacteristically silent.

After his appointment as Prime Minister Churchill wrote that he went to bed at 3.00 a.m. and slept soundly, with a conscious feeling of destiny and a profound sense of relief that at last he had the power in his own hands to direct the war effort: 'I felt . . . that all my past life had been but a preparation for this hour and for this trial'. Perhaps the most important part of that preparation had been during the last eighteen months of the First World War when he had worked closely with Lloyd George.

When, on 13 May, Churchill appeared in the House for the first time as Prime Minister and made his first speech in that capacity – 'I have nothing to offer you but blood, toil, tears and sweat' – it was Lloyd George who rose to respond:

Perhaps I may be permitted, as the Senior Member of this House, to say a few words in support of this Motion. May I, as one of the oldest friends of the Prime Minister in this House – I think on the whole that we have the longest friendship in politics in spite of a great many differences of opinion – congratulate him personally upon his succession to the Premiership. But that is a small matter. I congratulate the country upon his elevation to the Premiership at this very, very critical and terrible moment. If I may venture to say so, I think the Sovereign exercised a wise choice. We know the right hon. Gentleman's glittering intellectual gifts, his dauntless courage, his profound study of war, and his experience in its operation and direction . . . it is fortunate that he should have been put in a position of supreme authority. I do not know that it is altogether a matter of personal congratulation – perhaps the reverse. He is exercising his supreme responsibility at a graver moment and in times of greater jeopardy than have ever confronted a British

Minister for all time. We all, from the bottom of our hearts, wish him well. The friends of freedom and human rights throughout the world will wish him God speed; their hopes are centred in him now because it will depend upon him more than on any of his associates. I am not criticising now, because the man who has got the supreme direction is the man upon whom most of the responsibility depends. May I say that their prayers will be for him and that, in my judgement, the sacrifices of Britain and her Empire will be at his disposal.

Churchill sat with his head in his hands, tears streaming down his face. Afterwards Lloyd George 'went to congratulate him, grasping his hand with tears in his eyes'.

One of Churchill's first difficult decisions as Prime Minister – 'to defend Calais to the last man' – was a controversial one, compared by some to the disaster of Gallipoli. Although the surrender of Calais to the Germans was overshadowed in the history of the war by the heroic evacuation of the British Expeditionary Force from Dunkirk, it is thought that Britain lost four thousand men, either killed or captured, as a direct result of Churchill's determination (reminiscent of his adventure in Antwerp in October 1914) to fight until the end. Lloyd George meanwhile saw little hope of Britain being able to prevail militarily against the advancing Panzers which had so quickly overrun France.

The upper-class complacency and moral humbug that had made Chamberlain and Halifax so confident that they could deal with the Fascist dictators had been shattered by the outbreak of war, and would be even more completely undermined by the sudden collapse of France. Halifax and Chamberlain, although part of Churchill's Coalition Cabinet, were dubbed in the press 'the Guilty Men' who had left Britain under-armed and unprepared for the Nazi onslaught. It may have been no accident that this propaganda coincided with the intense debate that was taking place within the Cabinet in the final days of May 1940; it was then that Halifax led a determined pro-peace initiative to persuade Churchill that overtures should be made towards Mussolini to try to secure an alliance with the Italians and a 'reasonable' peace with Hitler, to forestall an invasion of Britain.

In the end, Churchill won the argument by telling his Cabinet ministers that 'Every one of us would rather die choking in his own blood on the ground than ignominiously surrender to the Germans . . .' It was an emotional and patriotic appeal in the hour of maximum danger when the Dunkirk evacuations were taking place, and one which persuaded the reluctant Conservative ministers to support the new Prime Minister, perhaps because there seemed to be no alternative. But after the first few insecure weeks of his premiership – with France and Belgium surrendering to the Germans and Britain's position looking increasingly precarious – Churchill was able to grasp the reins of power more decisively. He won over his Cabinet and the public with his stirring oratory, notably in his speech on 4 June, following the Dunkirk fiasco: 'We shall fight on the beaches . . . we shall never surrender.'

Oratory was all very well, but only so long as he had the means to back it up. The provision of weapons and equipment, which had been such a contentious issue in 1915, provoking Lloyd George to establish the new Ministry of Munitions, was likewise one of Churchill's early challenges as Prime Minister. One feature of his response was similar to Lloyd George's: the willingness to appoint often unorthodox outsiders and businessmen to tackle the entrenched bureaucracy and speed up the provision of essential supplies. For instance, Beaverbrook was appointed Minister of Aircraft Production to replace Spitfires and Hurricanes faster than they were being shot down in the Battle of Britain.

During the early weeks of his premiership, Churchill repeatedly asked Lloyd George to join him in his new administration. He wanted the radical and dynamic administrator of the First World War to help him deal with the national emergency – and with the military commanders. He told Boothby: 'It took

Armageddon to make me Prime Minister, but now I am there I am determined that power shall be in no other hands but mine. There will be no more Kitcheners, Fishers or Haigs.' Again and again between the years 1940 and 1945 Churchill reflected on the experiences and mistakes of the 1914–18 war and recalled the difficulties that Lloyd George had had in controlling his generals. Churchill was true to his word and, just as Abraham Lincoln had done in the American Civil War, dismissed any general who did not deliver him a victory – often unjustly.

Lord Gort, the commander of the BEF, was summarily dismissed although he had managed to save nearly 350,000 British soldiers by ignoring Churchill's explicit directive to move the BEF south to help the French, rather than west to the Channel ports. And, as Lloyd George had predicted, Wavell was dismissed as commander of the British Army in North Africa.

Although he differed from Lloyd George in his ruthless approach to his generals, Churchill knew that the lessons of 1917 would prove invaluable and he wanted the elder statesman to be one of his inner War Cabinet of five ministers. On 29 May Lloyd George refused Winston's offer of a Cabinet post. He felt he could not join the Churchill administration because of the antipathy between him and Neville Chamberlain: 'No – Chamberlain and I will never agree. Whilst he opposes my appointment my presence will only cause friction.'

At this stage, Churchill was in no position to abandon Chamberlain, to whom he felt some loyalty and, more importantly to whom the Conservative Party was loyal. There is a parallel here with Lloyd George's position in July 1917 when he too was dependent on the support of the Conservative Party and he too had tried to bring his friend, Winston Churchill, into the Coalition Government against determined opposition.

On 6 June, Churchill again asked Neville Chamberlain whether he would allow Lloyd George to be found a place in the

War Cabinet: 'Lloyd George would', he wrote, 'be a valuable counsellor, and a help to me and to the Cabinet.' But being treated 'as an outcast', he would become, so Churchill felt, 'the focus for regathering discontents'. Churchill believed that Lloyd George was ready to put aside 'all personal feuds or prejudices', and he added: 'In this terrible hour, with all that impends, the country ought to be satisfied that all its oldest and best-known leaders are playing their part . . .' Max Beaverbrook (ubiquitous as a wheeler-dealer in any political crisis) visited Lloyd George at Churt, his home in Surrey, and told him that Chamberlain would be resigning in the near future and that Lloyd George should therefore bide his time.

Using Boothby as an emissary, Lloyd George sent a letter to Churchill saying that he thought both Chamberlain and Halifax were a liability in the War Cabinet. With his usual far-sightedness he also predicted that only with America and Russia as allies could Britain possibly win the war. Both ministers would be opposed to any alliance with the USSR, and Halifax was also distrusted in the United States.

Even after Chamberlain's death in November 1940 Lloyd George made excuses as to why he would not join Churchill's Coalition Cabinet. Frances Stevenson's eleven-year-old daughter, Jennifer, wrote to him: 'Dear Taid, Why won't you join the Cabinet, many people all around the country are disappointed that you won't join.' Lloyd George, who was now seventy-seven, responded unconvincingly that he could do much more for the country outside the Government. His son Dick wrote: 'He had lost his nerve. The old war horse had lorded it in peaceful pastures so long that the weight of armour frightened him.'

In 1939 he had told his nephew William George (as related to the author), 'Winston lacks judgement', an opinion he often repeated despite his unfailing public support for his old political colleague. He was convinced that their attitudes to the conduct of the war would be so divergent as to make a working relationship impossible. Frances Stevenson recalled:

> LG's iron will was set against working with Churchill, or taking any part in the war ... 'Winston and I would never work together. I would be certain to disagree with him, and finally I would have to resign, leaving the position much worse than if I had refused to take office, and leaving us bad friends, which would be a great grief to me ... Winston *likes* war: I don't.'

Perhaps the truth was that he did not want to play second fiddle to Churchill.

On 12 June 1940, Churchill and his War Cabinet were in Tours in the Loire valley for the last meeting with the French Prime Minister, Reynaud, and his Cabinet before they surrendered to the Germans. Churchill tried valiantly to persuade the French to fight on, but to no avail. In the middle of the meeting, Louis Spears, Churchill's go-between with the French – as he had been for Lloyd George in the First World War – reminded Churchill of the older man's habit of asking for an adjournment, in order to consult his colleagues. The eight British ministers went out into the garden to confer, desperate to find a way of bolstering the French position. Cutting through the discussion, Max Beaverbrook, whom Spears described as 'a controversial and energetic Canadian', said to Churchill, 'We are doing no good here. Reynaud and his colleagues are determined to surrender ... we should go home immediately.' It is a matter of history that although the French Cabinet held another meeting later that day, they did not invite Churchill to attend. The defeatist faction – Pétain and Weygand – prevailed.

Some commentators have interpreted Lloyd George's negative stance in 1940 as being as defeatist as Pétain's and suggested that, like Pétain, he was readying himself to negotiate with Hitler. Although in the summer of 1940 Britain was as near to being invaded as at any other time in her history, there is no evidence to support this interpretation of Lloyd George's position. On the contrary, his writings and private conversations at the time were consistently patriotic and supportive of Churchill and his administration. It is therefore unproductive to speculate that he would have led a British version of France's Vichy Government if Hitler had succeeded in conquering Britain.

On 24 July 1940, Chips Channon, a backbench Conservative Member of Parliament, with a penchant for gossip and rumour, usually collected in the House of Commons or at London dinner parties, had noted in his diary: 'Lloyd George, whose affection for Winston had noticeably cooled of late, predicts that after the PM's first great blunder, the country, now admittedly hysterically infatuated with him, will turn against him and only remember his mistakes. I wonder?' Like many observers who predicted that Churchill and Lloyd George would eventually fall out, he was to be proved wrong. Lloyd George, whatever his private criticisms and concerns – in 1941, in a meditative mood, he observed, 'Winston has never been much inclined to listen. I fear that now he will listen even less' – loyally continued to support Churchill.

On 12 December 1940, the British Ambassador to the United States, Philip Kerr, now Lord Lothian, died suddenly in Washington. He had been a close friend and colleague of Lloyd George in the First World War, and during the 1930s had led a campaign to preserve world peace. Churchill had to make an immediate decision as to whom he should appoint to replace Lothian. In defiance of conventional Foreign Office thinking, his first choice for the ambassadorship was Lloyd George. Colville noted in his diary that 'He would like to try LG . . . if he could trust him.'

Since Neville Chamberlain's death the previous month there was no longer any reason for Lloyd George to decline the offices that Churchill continually offered him. There was, however, the question of his uncertain health. Lord Dawson, the well-known royal doctor, examined him and informally reported to Churchill that considering his advanced age, he was good for six hours a day, but 'those six hours would be radium'. However, the Chargé d'Affaires at the Washington Embassy sent a telegram to the Prime Minister: 'Rightly or wrongly, Lloyd George is regarded in this country as an appeaser, and as not unwilling to consider making terms with Germany.' President Roosevelt, on the other hand, immediately approved the mooted appointment, but once again Lloyd George declined the offer on medical grounds.

According to Lord Halifax, the eventual choice as American Ambassador, Churchill had wanted to put Lloyd George through an inquisition as to whether he had 'the root of the matter in him . . . by this he means that any peace terms . . . offered . . . must not be destructive of our independence'. Churchill still wanted his old friend and colleague to join his government, even though he was aware that Lloyd George was one of the few British statesmen who would not be averse to negotiating with Hitler. He had not concealed his reservations about Churchill's Cabinet, believing its members to be mere tools of Winston's ambition. He felt that Britain ought never to have entered a war in defence of Poland and continued to be pessimistic about the outcome. In his biography of Lloyd George, *Tempestuous Journey*, Frank Owen wrote: 'Might not a day come when all the other great public figures had been discredited by personal failure and by the general hopelessness of an apparently Endless War, and a call come for a statesman who had never wanted it, or waged it, but was able and willing to wind it up?'

During the first year of the war, while Churchill was trying to persuade Lloyd George to join his Cabinet, not only was the latter's health slowly deteriorating, but he was also struck by a domestic tragedy. In January 1941, his beloved wife of fifty-three years, Dame Margaret Lloyd George, died suddenly at their home in North Wales. Lloyd George was prevented by heavy snowfalls from reaching her bedside in time. Winston sent a heartfelt message to him on his bereavement, saying that Margaret had embodied all that was 'good and great about the British race'. Lloyd George appeared as a stricken and aged figure at his wife's funeral, and in some ways his physical deterioration accelerated after this date. Clearly he would not have been able to participate in the full workload of a wartime cabinet.

A year after Churchill became Prime Minister, on 10 May 1941, there was a secret session debate in the House of Commons, at which MPs were able to voice their concerns and criticisms of Churchill's conduct of the war effort. David Lloyd George was the most prominent critic; at the age of seventy-eight he had not lost his ability to charm and dominate the House. While he did not hide his affection for Churchill, his critique was a pointed one:

> The Prime Minister must have a real War Council. He has not got it. Now the Prime Minister is a man with a very brilliant mind, one of the most remarkable men who have graced this house with his presence. There is no doubt about his brilliant qualities, but for that very reason, if he will allow me to say so, he wants a few more *ordinary* persons to look after him. The Prime Minister wants men against whom he can check his ideas, who are independent, who will stand up to him and tell him exactly what they think.

Churchill responded, 'I did not think the speech of Mr Lloyd George was particularly helpful at a period of what he himself calls "discouragement and disheartenment". It wasn't the sort of speech which one would have expected from the Great War leader of former days, who was accustomed to brush aside despondency and alarm and push on irresistibly towards the final goal.'

The respect and affection between the two men never dwindled, despite this public bickering, and Lloyd George was certainly not among the three MPs who voted 'no' in the confidence motion. His criticism of Churchill was well meant and they had lunch together again soon afterwards. As Lloyd George repeatedly said to his friends, 'I am fond of Winston and I don't want to quarrel with him', which is why he would continue to refuse any positions in his wartime Cabinet.

During the dark days of the summer of 1940 and the greater pressures that came to bear on Churchill in 1941 when Britain's merchant shipping was being sunk at an alarming rate by German U-boats, he remembered Lloyd George's capacity to look beyond the dilemmas or defeats of the present to the possibilities that lay in the future. (In his eulogy of 1945, Churchill would refer to his mentor's capacity to draw from defeat itself the sustaining power of victory.) He also recalled Lloyd George's way of looking 'two fields ahead' and seeing beyond the immediate challenge to the political and military consequences that were not yet apparent to most observers.

Richard Lloyd George described his father's influence on Churchill thus:

> Both men, of course, became Prime Minister in the very dark days of a world war; and Winston Churchill was able to profit by Lloyd George's earlier experience and activities – a unified Allied Command, the convoy system for merchant shipping, a military attack through Italy, the 'soft under-belly' of the Central Powers – one of father's schemes was to try to get in by the back door through the Balkans and Italy, the front gate being too heavily guarded. These were pages from Lloyd George's book, well thumbed over and studied by Winston Churchill.

Another key aspect of wartime leadership that Churchill had learned from Lloyd George was of marshalling his powers of oratory to raise morale and dampen defeatism. Lloyd George was the first truly 'democratic Prime Minister' who saw the need to go over the heads of his parliamentary and ministerial colleagues to the people – as at the beginning of his premiership in 1916. Churchill went further in his great wartime speeches in the summer of 1940 that did so much to bolster national morale at a time of great danger and uncertainty. Geoffrey Shakespeare worked as secretary to both wartime premiers and admired Churchill's amazing facility with words and his clarity of vision: 'Having been closely associated with Lloyd George in the preparation of his speeches, I was interested to observe Churchill's technique. "Are you ready?" he would ask the stenographer. "I'm feeling very fertile tonight"', and would then launch into the speech that he was to give to Britain and the world the following day.

But alongside attention to detail in war planning, perhaps the most essential (and overlooked) lesson that Churchill drew from Lloyd George was concern for the welfare and comfort of the ordinary soldier. He owed this to his own youthful background as a soldier in Britain's frontier wars in India and South Africa, and as a Liberal politician when he had drunk deeply at the fountain of radical ideas. So, in the constant stream of 'prayers' he addressed to his generals and ministers between 1940 and 1945, frequently headed 'Action This Day' (perhaps another idea borrowed from the First World War premier's constant dynamic stream of directives), Churchill never forgot the importance of the ordinary serviceman or woman.

As Prime Minister, Churchill constantly measured himself against Lloyd George and his successes and failures during the 1914–18 conflict. In January 1942 Anthony Eden noted in his diary that he had commented: 'LG was young when he became Prime Minister and therefore right to insure against the future. But that he [Churchill] was already sixty-five when he took office.' Two months later the editor of The Times, R. M. Barrington Ward, reported after lunching with Churchill: 'Winston said, "I am an old man" (he didn't sound it). "Not like Lloyd George, coming out of the last war at fifty-six or so [this was exactly his age, as it happened], I may be seventy before this war ends . . . No man of my age has had to bear such disasters as I have."' Even as late as

1944, Churchill was thinking about his place in history and how the electorate would treat him in a post-war election. He told Jock Colville, 'the English people throughout their history always turned on those whom they thought had served them well in hard times e.g. Marlborough, Wellington, Lloyd George.'

In 1944 Frances Stevenson (who had become Lloyd George's second wife in 1943) wrote:

MAY 27TH

D. and I discussed today Lord Acton and his phrase 'I have no contemporaries'. I said the same thing might apply to D. He agreed, & said, 'I regard Winston as my only contemporary. We have always been friends. That is the reason that I have preferred to adopt an attitude of indifference to his policy and his Government – instead of openly quarrelling.'

Between 1939 and 1944 Churchill and Lloyd George remained in regular contact. Their meetings included several long lunches, at which Lloyd George would give the Prime Minister the benefit of his reflections on the First World War and his advice on the present conflict. Harold Nicolson recorded a memorable exchange between the two men in the House of Commons on 21 September 1943:

[After Churchill's speech] Old Pethick-Lawrence [aged seventy-one] . . . rose to reply from the Labour benches. Lloyd George walked out towards the bar of the House. Winston rose in his seat, scurried along to catch him, calling out over his shoulder to Lawrence, 'It's all right, I'm coming back.' He stood for a moment at the bar, talking to Lloyd George. It was strange to see those two fathers of victory standing there together. The eyes of the House were upon them. The pink rows of faces were turned not towards poor Pethick-Lawrence, but towards the two famous men at the bar. Then Winston scurried back to his seat and the House resumed its accustomed boredom.

In old age, Lloyd George's verdict on Winston was:

239

We respected each other – We didn't agree all the time, of course. I liked Winston, he had a good sense of humour – I always thought something good would come of him – he was an inspiring young man – brilliant, original – *He rose above us all in time.* Even when we were on opposite sides of the House [in 1901–4 and in 1922–40] you can respect your opponent – Churchill was a bit impetuous when young [1908–15] but he did want to improve the lot of his fellow men – he was warm-hearted and compassionate – he had a good attitude – Maybe I helped him [at the outset of his career] – maybe I showed him the way – he moulded himself a lot on me. I was a model for him – a mentor – were we rivals? Yes, but good friends throughout. Sometimes I used to tell him what a good speech he had made. I valued his friendship – deeply – more than any other – I always knew he had a destiny.

The two veteran campaigners met for the last time on 24 May 1944, when Lloyd George made practically his last appearance in the House of Commons. Now eighty-one years old, he was already very ill with cancer. As Frances Stevenson recorded:

D. decided on Wednesday to go to hear Winston's speech, and we are both glad, for the House gave him (D.) a touching welcome. I wonder if they realise how near it may be to his last appearance. Winston, whom we met in the corridor afterwards, was nice to us both. D. was rather inclined to be critical of the Government's policy, but I thought Winston very patient & I finally managed to turn the conversation to his pictures: we parted very happily. It was a perfect spring day, but as we drove through the smiling countryside there was a heavy sadness in my heart.

# Epilogue

On 26 March 1945, the Second World War was drawing to a close. The Allied armies had reached the Rhine, and Churchill, ever eager to be at the battle front, paid a two-day visit to Generals Montgomery and Eisenhower whose troops were crossing the German frontier near Wesel. He returned to London in the evening of 26th March.

News came through of Lloyd George's death the following morning. Churchill told the House of Commons, 'I do not think we can do any more business today.' He went home and that evening spent four hours preparing his tribute to the man who had been his friend, colleague and mentor for more than forty years. His typist, Elizabeth Langton, recalled that he worked until 4 a.m. on the eulogy – which he delivered in the House on 28 March.

'Mr Speaker, shortly after David Lloyd George first took Cabinet office as President of the Board of Trade, the Liberals, who had been in eclipse for twenty years, obtained in January 1906 an overwhelming majority over all other parties. They were independent of the Irish; the Labour Party was in its infancy; the Conservatives were reduced to little more than 100. But this moment of political triumph occurred in a period when the aspirations of nineteenth-century Liberalism had been largely achieved. Most of the great movements and principles of Liberalism had become the common property of enlightened men all over the civilised world. The chains had been struck from the slave; a free career was open to talent; the extension of the franchise was moving irresistibly forward; the advance in education was rapid and continuous, not only in this island but in many lands. Thus at this moment when the Liberal Party became supreme, the great and beneficent impulses which had urged them forward were largely assuaged by success. Some new and potent conceptions had to be found by those who were called into power.

It was Lloyd George who launched the Liberal and Radical forces of this country effectively into the broad stream of social betterment and social security along which all modern parties now steer. There was no man so gifted, so eloquent, so forceful, who knew the life of the people so well. His warm heart was stirred by the many perils which beset the cottage homes: the health of the breadwinner, the fate of his widow, the nourishment and upbringing of his children, the meagre and haphazard provision of medical treatment and sanatoria, and the lack of any organised accessible medical service of a kind worthy of the age from which the mass of the wage earners and the poor suffered. All this excited his wrath. Pity and compassion lent their powerful wings. He knew the terror with which old age threatened the toiler – that after a life of exertion he could be no more than a burden at the fireside and in the family of a struggling son. When I first became Lloyd George's friend, and active associate, now more than forty years ago, this deep love of the people, the profound knowledge of their lives and of the undue and needless pressures under which they lived, impressed itself indelibly upon my mind.

Then there was his dauntless courage, his untiring energy, his oratory, persuasive, provocative, now grave, now gay. His swift, penetrating, comprehensive mind was always grasping at the root, or what he thought to be the root, of any question. His eye ranged ahead of the obvious. He was always hunting in the field beyond. I have often heard people come to him with a plan, and he would say, 'That is all right, but what happens when we get over the bridge? What do we do then?'

In his prime, Sir, his power, his influence, his initiative were unequalled in the land. He was the champion of the weak and the poor. These were great days. Nearly two generations have passed. Most people are unconscious of how much their lives have been shaped by the laws for which Lloyd George was responsible. Health insurance and old-age pensions were the first large-scale State-conscious efforts to set a balustrade along the crowded causeway of the people's life and, without pulling down the structures of society, to fasten a lid over the abyss into which vast numbers used to fall, generation after generation, uncared for and indeed unnoticed. Now we move forward confidently into larger and more far-reaching applications of these ideas.

I was his lieutenant and disciple in those bygone days, and shared in a minor way in the work. I have lived to see long strides taken, and being taken, and going to be taken, on this path of insurance by which the vultures of utter ruin are driven from the dwellings of the nations. The stamps we lick, the roads we travel, the system of progressive taxation, the principal remedies that have yet been used against unemployment – all these to a very great extent were part not only of the mission but of the actual achievement of Lloyd George; and I am sure that as time passes his name will not only live but shine on account of the great, laborious, constructive work he did for the social and domestic life of our country.

When the calm, complacent, self-satisfied tranquillities of the Victorian era had exploded into the world convulsions and wars of the terrible twentieth century, Lloyd George had another part to play on which his fame will stand with equal or even greater firmness. Although unacquainted with the military arts, although by public repute a pugnacious pacifist, when the life of our country was in peril, he rallied to the war effort and cast aside all other thoughts or aims. He was the first to discern the fearful shortages of ammunition and artillery and all the other appliances of war which would so soon affect, and in the case of Imperial

Russia mortally affect, the warring nations on both sides. He saw it before anyone. Here I must say that my hon. and gallant Friend the Member for Wycombe [Sir Archibald Knox] was a truthful and vigilant prophet and guide in all that information which we received. He was our military representative in Russia. But it was Mr Lloyd George who fixed on these papers, brought them forth before the eyes of the Cabinet and induced action to be taken with the utmost vigour possible at that late hour.

Lloyd George left the Exchequer when the Coalition Government was formed, for the Ministry of Munitions. Here he hurled himself into the mobilisation of British industry. In 1915 he was building great war factories that could not come into operation for two years. There was the usual talk about the war being over in a few months, but he did not hesitate to plan on a vast scale for two years ahead. It was my fortune to inherit the output of those factories in 1917 – the vast, overflowing output which came from them. Presently Lloyd George seized the main power in the State and the headship of the Government.

He imparted immediately a new surge of strength, of impulse, far stronger than anything that had been known up to that time, and extending over the whole field of wartime Government, every part of which was of equal interest to him.

I have already written about him at this time, when I watched him so closely and enjoyed his confidence and admired him so much, and I have recorded two characteristics of him which seemed to me invaluable in those days: first, his power to live in the present yet without taking short views; and, secondly, his power of drawing from misfortune itself the means of future success. All this was illustrated by the successful development of the war; by the adoption of the convoy system, which he enforced upon the Admiralty and by which the U-boats were defeated; by the unified command on the Western Front which gave Marshal Foch the power to lead us all to victory; and in many other matters which form a part of the story of those sombre and tremendous years, the memory of which for ever abides with me, and to which I have often recurred in thought during our present second heavy struggle against German aggression, now drawing towards its victorious close.

BRITAIN'S
GREATEST
WAR PRIME MINIS

Thus the statesman and guide whose gentle passing in the full-ness of his years we mourn today served our country, our island and our age both faithfully and well in peace and in war. His long life was, from almost the beginning to almost the end, spent in political strife and controversy. He aroused intense and sometimes needless antagonisms. He had fierce and bitter quarrels at various times with all the parties. He faced undismayed the storms of criticism and hostility. In spite of all obstacles, including those he raised himself, he achieved his main purposes. As a man of action, resource and creative energy he stood, when at his zenith, without a rival.

His name is a household word throughout our Commonwealth of Nations. He was the greatest Welshman which that unconquer-able race has produced since the age of the Tudors. Much of his work abides, some of it will grow greatly in the future, and those who come after us will find the pillars of his life's toil upstanding, massive and indestructible; and we ourselves, gathered here today, may indeed be thankful that he voyaged with us through storm and tumult with so much help and guidance to bestow.'

★

'I loved your speech about Lloyd George,' Clementine Churchill wrote to her husband from Cairo, en route to Moscow for a five-week tour to promote Anglo-Russian relations. 'It recalled forgotten blessings which he showered on the meek and lowly.'

In 1945 there was a deep undercurrent of popular dissatisfaction and a longing for social reform, which was to be expressed in the Labour landslide victory in the general election less than four months later. Churchill seems to have been dimly aware of this growing feeling of discontent (which particularly found expression among the ordinary soldiers serving in the British Army) and it is reflected in the theme of social reform and economic improvement in his tribute to Lloyd George. Coupled with this was his acknowledgement that many of the lessons in leadership which he, Churchill, had learned, came from the 'Master of them all', Lloyd George, in the final two years of the First World War.

When Lloyd George died, Churchill, in a typically thoughtful and generous gesture in the midst of a wartime government, made the necessary arrangements for Lloyd George's four grandsons, who were serving in the Army, Navy and Air Force, to attend his funeral in Wales. Afterwards, Churchill made a dismissive comment to his wife about Lloyd George's Welsh village funeral with his hearse borne on a 'farm cart'. He told Clementine that he wanted a grand military funeral with 'lots of bands'. 'You will, dear,' she replied. But it was perhaps in death (as at birth) that their unlikely friendship was again highlighted. Lloyd George went back to his native village, Llanystumdwy, to die among his own people. Churchill was buried in 1965 at

Bladon, next to Blenheim Palace, after the most memorable state funeral in modern British history.

After the death of Lloyd George at the end of the war, Churchill continued to maintain a link with his old friend's family. Even before Lloyd George had declined Churchill's pressing invitation to join the five-man War Cabinet in the summer of 1940, his younger son, Gwilym, had joined the wartime Coalition Government as parliamentary secretary to the Board of Trade; and in 1942 he became Minister of Fuel and Power. Churchill liked to have a member of the Lloyd George family in his team, and Gwilym, like Winston himself, was to move gradually to the right. After his father's death in 1945, he switched from the Liberal Party to the Conservatives, although when Churchill offered him a place on the Opposition front bench, Gwilym insisted that he would only sit as a Liberal. 'What the hell else should you sit as?' was the characteristically belligerent response from Churchill.

Several times it was rumoured that Gwilym was to become the Speaker of the House but, in the event, Churchill brought him into the Conservative Government, as Minister for Food (where he ended rationing) in 1951, and as Home Secretary and Minister of Welsh Affairs (where he presided over one of the last hangings) in 1954. In appointing him, Churchill wrote, 'It has been a great pleasure to me to submit your name for this high office, for I am sure it would have given pride and satisfaction to your Father.'

A key event of this period was the coronation of Queen Elizabeth II in June 1953. On the evening following the ceremony, my father, Owen Lloyd George, then Viscount Gwynedd, was invited back to 10 Downing Street for drinks with the Prime Minister. By a curious coincidence Churchill was also entertaining El Glaoui, the Moroccan Pasha who had invited him and Lloyd George for dinner in the Atlas Mountains in 1936 – 'a most sinister individual', my father recalled.

After giving my father an enormous tumbler of whisky the Prime Minister turned to him with a growl and asked, 'What do you do, young man?' 'I am a farmer, sir, in Berkshire,' my father replied. Churchill then made great play with the pronunciation of Burkshire and responded, with a chuckle, 'Well, I do some farming myself, but I also manage to fit in one or two other things.'

Churchill kept repeating the strong suggestion that my father should enter public life, and concluded by saying, with great relish, 'You will . . . the blood will out.' He reminisced with affection about Lloyd George and his abilities. 'He could always see into the next field,' he said.

Even when Churchill was over eighty in 1955, one of the few causes which would bring him to speak in the Chamber was the motion to erect a statue to Lloyd George in the lobby of the House of Commons.

Today Churchill and Lloyd George face each other on either side of the member's entrance to the Parliamentary Chamber. A visitor to Westminster Abbey today will be struck by the prominent inscription beneath the West door:

REMEMBER
WINSTON
CHURCHILL

It was placed there on the 25th anniversary of the Battle of Britain, 15 September 1965, about nine months after Sir Winston passed away. Nearby lies an oval tablet in Welsh slate, commemorating David Lloyd George, 1863–1945, Prime Minister 1916–22. Between these two wartime Prime Ministers, and among the pantheon of British sovereigns, heroes, and poets who are buried in the Abbey, lies the tomb of the Unknown Warrior. Both Lloyd George, as Prime Minister, and Winston Churchill, as Secretary of State for War, attended the ceremony on Armistice day, 11 November 1920, when George V dedicated the memorial. It is fitting that the two statesmen are commemorated in such close proximity in Westminster Abbey.

# Cast of Main Characters

**Max Aitken – Lord Beaverbrook** (1888–1964) A Canadian newspaper proprietor and businessman who came to England in 1910. He was elected to Parliament in 1910 and for the next fifty years was a ubiquitous kingmaker and confidant of both Lloyd George and Churchill, and perhaps most significantly, of his fellow Canadian, Andrew Bonar Law, who, unlike Beaverbrook, was a shy and austere man. Beaverbrook, like his fellow newspaper proprietors Lords Northcliffe and Riddell, loved political gossip and often entertained the leading politicians of the day. His books, *Politicians and the War* and *The Decline and Fall of Lloyd George*, were particularly important sources for this work.

**Herbert Henry Asquith** (1852–1928) Perhaps the most brilliant and certainly the most erudite of British Prime Ministers in the last two hundred years. A classical scholar at Balliol College, Oxford, he went on to become the youngest ever QC and the youngest ever Home Secretary in Gladstone's last administration in 1894; thus in his early forties he was already marked out as a future Liberal Prime Minister. He had to await the death of Campbell-Bannerman in 1908 before finally ascending to that height. In the next seven years he presided over the brilliant Liberal Cabinet in which Lloyd George and Churchill were the two leading reformers. Asquith's greatest achievement as Prime Minster was to oversee the enactment of the national insurance and old-age pension schemes and several other social reforms. On the other hand he was unable to resolve the Irish question before the outbreak of war in August 1914.

The first two years of 'total war' found Asquith, along with almost every other British political and military leader, unprepared and ill equipped to deal with the organisational needs and social and political implications of the world conflict. He wisely delegated great powers to Lord Kitchener as Secretary of State for War but this unfortunately also led to some blunders such as the Gallipoli campaign, which Asquith supported but Kitchener did not back with sufficient military force. By 1916 it was apparent that the political establishment at least had lost confidence in Asquith's war leadership. Nevertheless, his influence over both Churchill as a young minister, and his number two, Lloyd George, with whom he worked closely for eight years, was profound. He also enjoyed a close social relationship with both men, particularly with Winston and Clementine, who often dined with the Asquiths in the years before the war.

**Arthur James Balfour** (1848–1930) Philosopher and the author of *Defence of Philosophic Doubt*. He was elected to Parliament in 1874 and in 1878 became private secretary to his uncle, Robert Cecil, Marquess of Salisbury, who was Prime Minister three times between 1885 and 1902. During this period Balfour was promoted to Secretary for Scotland (1886) and Chief Secretary for Ireland (1887–91) where, despite his rather effeminate and superior manner, his policy of suppression earned him the name of 'Bloody Balfour'. After serving as First Lord of the Treasury and leader of the House of Commons he succeeded Salisbury as premier between 1902–5. Against all expectations, he achieved a number of things as Prime Minister: the Entente Cordiale with France in 1904, the Committee of Imperial Defence which was his brainchild, the Education Bill of 1902. In December 1916, his support for Lloyd George was perhaps the most crucial element in enabling him to succeed Asquith as Prime Minister.

Lloyd George's feelings for his Foreign Secretary were almost reverential, particularly when he remembered his first days in the House of Commons as a young Welsh solicitor observing the great parliamentary figures of the 1890s: Gladstone, Balfour and Chamberlain.

Balfour reciprocated the admiration of 'the little man', as he called Lloyd George. In 1917 he was responsible for the Balfour Declaration which promised Zionists a national home in Palestine. Two years later, Balfour wrote to Bonar Law about the Prime Minister: 'Our friend is, I think, the most remarkable single figure produced by the Great War.'

At the beginning of Churchill's political career, during the battles over tariff reform and free trade, Balfour regarded Winston with tolerant affection. By 1911, however, the cordiality between the two politicians had become strained and Balfour refused to appear with Churchill on a joint platform. Balfour occupied a rather unique position: although he was in opposition, he received details of the proceedings of the Committee of Imperial Defence, which he had founded, with the full approval of Asquith.

**Wilfred Scawen Blunt** (1840–1922) Poet, diarist and Arabist. He had lived in Egypt when young, knew most of the Egyptian leaders and supported their claim to independence from the British Protectorate. He also followed events in Turkey closely, and was something of an expert on the Middle East. He had been friendly with Lord Randolph Churchill, and he met Winston in 1903. His diaries form perhaps the most perceptive and accurate picture of the young Churchill in his years as an MP before the First World War. They spent several weekends together shooting and talking late into the night.

**Andrew Bonar Law** (1858–1925) A Scottish Canadian businessman with a Presbyterian background who stood for a Glasgow constituency and unexpectedly became leader of the Conservative Party in 1911. Because of his relatively unprivileged background, he made friends easily with the Liberal leaders, especially Lloyd George, and they formed a great partnership during the First World War. Bonar Law was a sad man whose wife died before the First World War and who lost a son during the First World War. Lloyd George described taking him for a drive in the South of France:

LG: 'What beautiful scenery.'
BL: 'I don't like scenery.'
LG: 'What pretty women.'
BL: 'Not interested in women.'
LG: 'What do you like, Bonar?'
BL: 'I really like a good game of bridge.'

**Violet Bonham Carter** (1887–1969) Asquith's daughter, who wrote an affectionate and deeply observed portrait of Churchill, *Winston Churchill as I Knew Him*, in the year of his death, 1965. She first met him in the summer of 1906 when she was nineteen and he was thirty-two. They sat next to each other at a dinner party where he sat staring at his plate and refused to utter a word for the first half-hour. Then he turned to her and said in a rather gloomy voice, 'We are all worms but [more cheerfully] I do believe I am a glow-worm.' From that moment on they became good friends and there is little doubt that Violet Asquith, as she then was, was in love with Winston. He married Clementine Hozier soon after this but Violet remained devoted to him. She married Maurice Bonham Carter, who was Asquith's private secretary, in 1917 and remained a pillar of the Liberal Party all her life, engaging in an acrimonious feud with Megan Lloyd George, who occupied a similar role as her father's devoted admirer and follower and guardian of his political legacy. Violet Bonham Carter comments with some objectivity about the friendship between Lloyd George and Churchill; she was critical of this development in her adored Winston but recognised the depth and importance of Lloyd George's influence over the young Churchill.

**Sir Henry Campbell-Bannerman** (1836–1908) The son of the Lord Provost of Glasgow, he joined the family drapery business and was elected as a Liberal MP in 1868. He became Chief Secretary for Ireland under Gladstone in 1884 and Secretary of State for War in 1886. Although not a great public speaker, he acquired a reputation as a good administrator and a party political operator. Alone among the Liberal leaders, he opposed the Boer War and so established himself on the more progressive wing of the Liberal Party, becoming leader in 1899 when its fortunes were at a low point. His integrity and concern for the poor and unemployed won him a wide following and the landslide Liberal victory in January 1906. He resigned because of ill health in April 1908 after serving as Prime Minister for only two years and four months, and died two weeks later. Both Churchill and Lloyd George looked up to him as a kindly, old-fashioned Liberal but were impatient to proceed with social and political reforms which accelerated under the leadership of Asquith between 1908 and 1911.

**Sir Edward Carson** (1854–1935) Along with F. E. Smith (later Lord Birkenhead) Carson was the leading barrister and Tory debater of his day. He and Smith together represented the Ulster cause in Parliament before 1914. Together with Sir James Craig (later Lord Craigavon) Carson formed the leadership of the Ulster Defence Volunteers in 1913–14. He was one of the most vehement opponents of Winston Churchill's inclusion in the Coalition Government during the First World War because, in the eyes of the Ulster leaders, Churchill had betrayed Lord Randolph's 'Orange card'. Carson became part of Lloyd George's War Cabinet in 1917.

**Georges Clemenceau, 'the Tiger'** (1840–1925) Clemenceau fought several duels in his youth, was of a fiery temperament and, as Mayor of Montmartre in 1870, had witnessed the humiliation of the French Army by the Prussians and the entry of the Kaiser into Paris. Clemenceau became Prime Minister at the nadir of France's fortunes in 1917 and was very much the leading figure at the Treaty of Versailles, where his insistence on making the Germans pay for the war overrode the idealism of President Woodrow Wilson and the pragmatism of Lloyd George. Churchill greatly admired Clemenceau and certainly borrowed some of his rhetoric and patriotism for his own speeches in 1940. Perhaps Lloyd George's relationship with Churchill was based on the same foundation: respect for each other as fighters.

**Lord Curzon** (1859–1925) 'George Nathaniel Curzon, a most superior person!' (was a popular rhyme) – and Churchill wrote in *Great Contemporaries*: 'the morning was golden, the midday was bronze and the evening was leaden'. He was an outstanding scholar at Eton and Oxford, he wrote brilliant papers about Persia and India, and became Viceroy while still in his thirties. He was in that exalted position when in, 1896, Churchill arrived at Bangalore as a young subaltern in the Hussars. Curzon returned to England in 1905 with every expectation of becoming Prime Minister but his plans were thwarted first by Balfour and then by the long Liberal ascendancy. In 1915 he joined the Coalition Government and served as Foreign Secretary under Lloyd George until 1922.

**Lord Fisher** (1841–1920) 'Jacky' Fisher had joined the Navy as a midshipman in the 1850s and worked his way up to being Admiral of the Fleet and First Sea Lord in 1900. He made many enemies in the naval establishment because of his combative and fiery temperament and his uncompromising love of the Navy, which he was determined to modernise and equip with the latest weaponry. He was the architect of the Dreadnought building programme before the First World War. Fisher was an inveterate correspondent, with a unique style: 'Yours till hell freezes over', 'Yours to a cinder'. Many of his letters were addressed to Winston Churchill, with whom he had a love–hate relationship and upon whom he had a profound influence. When Lloyd George and (ironically) Churchill initially opposed the naval building programme in 1908–10, Fisher proposed to First Lord McKenna that they should lay down four battleships and name them: *Winston*, *Churchill*, *Lloyd* and *George* ('How they would fight! Uncircumventable!').

Fisher's baleful influence on Churchill increased after he was brought back from retirement in 1914 at the age of seventy-one to replace Lord Mountbatten's father, Prince Louis of Battenberg, who resigned as First Sea Lord because of slurs on his German name. Fisher then proceeded to resign his office and vanish, in May 1915, directly causing the crisis in the Liberal Government which led to the formation of a Coalition administration and Churchill's loss of office as First Lord of the Admiralty. Churchill astonished the House of Commons by proposing Fisher's recall to the Admiralty in early 1916. Even his wife Clementine was appalled by this blunder.

**Lord French** (1852–1925) Commander-in-Chief at the outbreak of war in 1914 and a civilised and sociable general of the old school, who had fought in the Boer War. He was very friendly to Churchill when he arrived in the trenches as a colonel in the Royal Scots Fusiliers in November 1915. Unfortunately, French was replaced as Commander-in-Chief at that very time by Douglas Haig and so Churchill, instead of getting a brigade and becoming a brigadier as he had hoped, was given a battalion and remained a colonel.

**Sir Edward Grey** (1862–1933) An old-fashioned type of Foreign Secretary who spoke no foreign languages, had visited few foreign countries and did not really like foreigners. He gave one of the greatest speeches of his life on 3 August 1914, announcing Britain's decision to declare war on Germany. Like Asquith, he never really adapted his traditional Liberal mentality to the tremendous demands of the new age of 'total war'. Churchill and Lloyd George used to joke that he mainly loved fishing and the wildlife at his Northumberland estate: 'If the Kaiser wanted to get his attention, he would have had to threaten to shoot Grey's bloody squirrels!' According to Riddell's diary entry for 19 July 1913, Lloyd George described him as 'a kind fellow, the only man I would serve under except Asquith'.

**Field Marshal Haig** (1860–1925) Haig's reputation has always been controversial but there is no doubt that he was a conscientious and fine soldier and that he also had astute political antennae, maintaining a close correspondence with King George V and other Conservative political leaders. He was however immune to the criticism that he had wastefully sent thousands of men 'over the top' to their deaths at the Somme in July 1916 and again at Passchendaele in 1917. His mind was set in a certain mould and could not be changed, despite Lloyd George's attempts to influence him. In the end LG solved the problem by appointing Marshal Foch as the overall commander of the Allied army, with Haig in a subordinate position. However, Haig's final push in the summer of 1918 proved unexpectedly successful and his post-war reputation remained high.

**Clementine Hozier** (1885–1977) Although Clementine's father was thought to be Sir Edward Hozier, recent research by her daughter Mary Soames has shown it more probable that he was in fact 'Bay' Middleton. She was one of the most beautiful women of the Edwardian era, twelve years younger than Churchill. During the nearly sixty years they were married, she proved to be a firm support and wise counsellor to him. She had her suspicions about Lloyd George's character, which she fully voiced in her letters to Winston at the front in 1915–16. Churchill urged her to consider the value of an alliance with the Welsh radical statesman and during the next twenty-five years, despite Clementine's objections, they remained close friends and often holidayed together, without their wives, in the South of France. Nevertheless, Lloyd George was a frequent guest at her lunch table and they respected each other. When the Welshman died she wrote to Winston in appreciation of his eulogy, saying that his comments recalled Lloyd George's work for the poor. She had been a much firmer supporter of the Liberal Party than Churchill himself before the First World War, writing to congratulate Lloyd George on his speeches at the time of the People's Budget and again in 1912–13 when she had a notable row with the Duke of Marlborough about her left-wing sympathies. Her influence on Churchill, though often invisible to historians, must have been profound and important.

**Rufus Isaacs** (1860–1935) Isaacs led a fascinating and adventurous life. He had gone to sea at the age of sixteen and sailed round the world. He subsequently qualified as a barrister and had a brilliant career as a QC. He was Attorney-General in Asquith's Government and was identified with Lloyd George in the Marconi scandal of 1912–13 when both were suspected of 'insider dealing' as a result of buying shares at the pre-listed price on the advice of his brother, Godfrey, who was a director of the company. However, his career was not affected. He was raised to the peerage as the Marquess of Reading and was made Viceroy of India by Lloyd George in 1921.

**Philip Kerr** (1882–1940) A key figure in the Liberal Party from 1917 when he joined that part of the Prime Minister's secretariat which was accommodated in the garden of 10 Downing Street, otherwise known as Lloyd George's 'Garden Suburb'. Kerr was a foreign policy expert who was also a Christian Scientist and a great supporter of the League of Nations. He played a crucial role in helping Lloyd George to form British policy in the negotiations over the Treaty of Versailles and became Marquess of Lothian in 1930. He was also identified with the appeasement policies of the years that followed, but was really a campaigner for a peaceful solution to the Nazi threat. He became British Ambassador to the United States in 1939 but died suddenly the following year, leading Churchill to offer the position of US Ambassador to Lloyd George before the appointment of Lord Halifax. The Lothian Papers in the Scottish National Archives in Edinburgh are an important source of comment and information on Lloyd George's premiership.

**Lord Kitchener** (1850–1916) Kitchener was born in Ireland and served in the Royal Engineers in Palestine, Cyprus and the Sudan. He first became a household name as a result of his successful campaign to win back the Sudan in 1898 and avenge the murder of General Gordon. Churchill, as a young lieutenant in the 21st Lancers, took part in the famous cavalry charge at Omdurman; after the battle he criticized Kitchener who had reputedly kept the head of the Mahdi in a tin box. During the Boer War Kitchener was again a ruthless but successful general and it was his decision to destroy the Boer farms and move the women and children into concentration camps which Lloyd George condemned in the House of Commons. Kitchener then became Commander-in-Chief in India and subsequently Governor of Egypt, to which he was returning on 3 August 1914 when Asquith, at Churchill's suggestion, appointed him Secretary of State for War.

Having spent his whole life in the British Army, Kitchener was quite unused to the democratic give-and-take of the Liberal Cabinet. He became a national figure again with the famous poster 'Your country needs you', in response to which over three million men volunteered for war service between 1914 and 1916. Kitchener believed that the British Army had to concentrate its efforts on the Western Front, he initially opposed the Dardanelles campaign but later supported Asquith and Churchill. It was his decision to withdraw from Gallipoli after 100,000 casualties. Gallipoli damaged Kitchener's reputation as well as that of Churchill. In June 1916 Asquith, on the point of removing him as War Secretary, sent him to rally the faltering Russian military effort in the Allied fight against Germany. Lord Kitchener was drowned on 5 June when HMS *Hampshire* hit a mine off the Orkneys.

**Margaret Lloyd George** (1863–1941) Born Margaret Owen, the only child of a prosperous Welsh farming family, she could trace her ancestry back to Prince Owen of Gwynedd in 1100. She was very proud of her heritage, and much preferred to be in Wales than in London. After she and David Lloyd George were married in January 1888 they had a brief time together in Criccieth, where Richard and Mair were born, in 1889 and 1890 respectively; then Lloyd George became MP for Caernarvon Boroughs after a snap by-election in 1890 and was catapulted into the world of Westminster politics. Thereafter, their lives tended to diverge – especially after the death of Mair in 1907 – with Maggie living mostly in Wales and Lloyd George at Westminster. They had three more children: Olwen, born 1892, Gwilym, born 1894, and Megan in 1902. When Lloyd George became Chancellor of the Exchequer in 1908, Maggie moved with him to Downing Street. She was extremely fond of the young Winston who was a frequent guest of the Lloyd Georges, and intervened on at least one occasion (at the time of the struggle over the naval estimates in 1912), to prevent Lloyd George from quarrelling with his close friend. She was calm, sensible, full of good humour and in many ways the temperamental opposite of Lloyd George, who was highly strung, brilliant but unpredictable. She stood by him throughout his career, even when he was cited in a divorce case. The scandal that could have ended his political career was completely silenced when Maggie appeared with him in the witness box. Despite the fact that Lloyd George effectively lived as a bigamist for almost thirty years of their marriage, she faithfully kept his political career going, especially by nursing the constituency in North Wales, while he was in London or travelling overseas. When she died in 1941 he was heartbroken.

**Sir Edward Marsh** (1872–1953) A civil servant of the old school, and also an aesthete and great collector of paintings and poets. He became Churchill's private secretary when the latter served as assistant Colonial Secretary under Campbell-Bannerman in 1907 and commented with rare insight: 'The first time you meet Winston you see all his faults, and then the rest of your life you spend in discovering his virtues'. In his engaging memoir *A Number of People*, he recounts his travels with Churchill and his devotion to him until his retirement in 1937.

**Charles Masterman** (1873–1927) A strange, idealistic and evangelical young Liberal who played a key role behind the scenes in the social reforms of 1908–11 with which the names of Lloyd George and Churchill are indelibly associated. Masterman was for a short time a Liberal MP, but was much more effective as a civil servant: he was Parliamentary Private Secretary to Lloyd George, for whom he drafted much of the National Insurance Bill. Having involved himself in social work in the East End, he was familiar with many of the problems of the working classes. His wife, Lucy Lyttelton, was the granddaughter of the great Liberal Prime Minister, William Gladstone, and wrote revealing diaries and a biography of her husband who died at the age of fifty-four.

**Edwin Montagu** (1874–1924) Montagu came from a wealthy old-established Anglo-Jewish family and after Cambridge went into political life, becoming Private Parliamentary Secretary to Asquith who nicknamed him 'the Assyrian' because of his dark looks. He is a minor figure in the story of the political intrigues during the First World War. Perhaps his most important actions were, first, to marry Venetia Stanley, who had been Asquith's confidante until 1915. This greatly shocked Asquith. Secondly, he was a strong opponent of the Balfour Declaration in 1917, trying to persuade Lloyd George to delay any commitment to a Jewish homeland which he regarded as undermining his own position as an Anglo-Jewish civil servant.

**Lord Morley** (1838–1923) A disciple of W. E. Gladstone, whose biography he wrote. The young Churchill was delighted to sit next to Morley in the Liberal Cabinet between 1908 and 1914 and to draw on his long experience and wisdom. Morley believed in peace, retrenchment and reform. At the outbreak of war in August 1914, he therefore resigned from the Liberal Cabinet. Churchill wrote a charming essay about him in *Great Contemporaries*, calling him 'one of the old-fashioned Victorian Liberal statesmen'.

**Harold Nicolson** (1886–1968) Married to Vita Sackville-West and with her created the famous garden at Sissinghurst Castle in Kent. He was also a minor figure in the political life of his time. He joined the Foreign Office in 1909 and served in the embassies at Madrid and Constantinople before being seconded to the British delegation to

Versailles in 1919. Nicolson was a National Labour MP from 1935–45. His diaries form a valuable record of the interwar period and, during the Second World War, of the House of Commons debates and the gossip and rumours that flew around Westminster before and after Churchill became Prime Minister. He was a great admirer of Lloyd George and called him and Churchill 'the two fathers of Victory'.

**Lord (George) Riddell** (1865–1934) A solicitor and newspaper proprietor who became a close friend and confidant of Lloyd George. He also owned the popular golf club at Walton Heath and brought both Churchill and Lloyd George in as members, together with a number of other political luminaries including Bonar Law. He wrote very extensive diaries, both before and after the First World War; these are in the British Library and, like those of Sylvester, have only been partially published. Lloyd George put Riddell in charge of press relations during the Versailles Treaty and his record of the proceedings is a valuable document. He remained a good friend of Lloyd George until almost the end of the latter's premiership. There was, however, a famous episode when Lloyd George's Airedale terrier Bill terrified Riddell when he was left alone in a room with the dog and was discovered perched on a chair with the dog barking at him. He never forgave Lloyd George the loss of his dignity and relations between them cooled because the latter found the incident uproariously funny.

**Herbert Samuel** (1870–1963) A pillar of the Liberal Party who, along with Rufus Isaacs, had been implicated in the Marconi scandal with Lloyd George in 1913 when Solicitor-General. A strong supporter of Lloyd George, Samuel went on to become the first Governor-General of Palestine under the British mandate after the First World War. He was also a strong Zionist.

**C. P. Scott** (1905–1980) As Editor of the *Manchester Guardian* Scott was the voice of the Liberal conscience and had a wide influence and following among the nonconformist constituent of the party. He was therefore close to Lloyd George, who frequently consulted him, along with the other nonconformist leaders such as Robertson and Nicholl.

**F. E. Smith** (1872–1930) was born in humble circumstances in Cheshire, from a family of blacksmiths. Through hard work and intellectual brilliance, he won a scholarship to Oxford and was called to the Bar in 1899. His maiden speech in the House of Commons in 1906 was considered one of the most brilliant in parliamentary history, and he always maintained a vigorous wit and coruscating invective ('Mr. Smith, you are very offensive.' 'I am trying to be, My Lord, but you can't help it.'). A close friend and drinking companion of Winston Churchill, he was asked by Lloyd George to be Lord Chancellor in 1919, becoming Lord Birkenhead, and lending his valuable support to the Irish Treaty (he was a well known Unionist on the right wing of the Tory Party). He died young, in 1930. His son was godson to Churchill, whose biography he wrote in 1933.

**Jan Christian Smuts** (1870–1950) Born in South Africa and educated at Cambridge. Smuts then returned to South Africa and became a member of Paul Kruger's Transvaal Government. He was the most brilliant, if not the most bitter, opponent of Britain during the Boer War, in which he proved himself a guerilla leader of exceptional talent. He never forgot the aftermath of the war, when the Transvaal and the Orange Free State were handed back to the Boers in the new Union of South Africa under the Vereeniging peace treaty of 1902, which he regarded as an extraordinary example of far-sighted statesmanship and in which he played a crucial role. Smuts served as Defence Minister under President Botha until 1914, when he led the successful campaign of the British South African Army in German South-West Africa (Namibia). In 1917, soon after becoming Prime Minister, David Lloyd George convened an Imperial War Cabinet, inviting Sir Robert Borden, the Canadian Prime Minister, Billy Hughes of Australia and Smuts, among others, to join. Smuts was in fact the only colonial leader to serve in War Cabinet and had a high reputation in England. He played a leading role in the formation of the RAF and he was an influential figure in the Paris peace negotiations in 1919.

Smuts was Prime Minister of South Africa from 1919 to 1924 and again from 1939 to 1948 when he worked closely with Churchill. He was the only person to sign the peace treaties at the end of both the

First and Second World Wars. There is a well-known story that Lloyd George sent Smuts down to South Wales in 1918 to quell a strike. When he arrived in Swansea, Smuts did not make a speech. He simply said to the angry Welsh miners, 'I believe that your people are famous for singing.' The miners immediately responded by spontaneously singing a number of hymns. When the Prime Minister inquired how he had settled the strike, he replied: 'I simply asked them to sing.'

**Frances Stevenson** (1890–1972) From an Anglo-French family, Frances Stevenson had been a teacher at Mair Lloyd George's school in Wimbledon and met the Chancellor of the Exchequer while working as a summer tutor to his daughter Megan in 1911. She gave up teaching to become Lloyd George's private secretary in 1912, drawn to him by 'a magnetism which made my heart leap and swept aside my judgment', his mistress in 1913, and for the next thirty years devoted her life to him, becoming his second wife in 1943. Her record of events in the First World War is particularly valuable for the light it casts on the relationship between Lloyd George and Churchill, although her role in Lloyd George's life meant that she was not acknowledged by Churchill. Her comments on him are thus often somewhat waspish, although she readily acknowledged the true friendship and love that existed between the two men. To a great extent her diary entries are the most accurate record we have of how Churchill was perceived by his closest friend.

**A. J. Sylvester** (1885–1984) Sylvester was a champion shorthand stenographer, reputedly the fastest in the British Civil Service, who was seconded to work for Maurice Hankey, the First Secretary of the Liberal Cabinet, appointed by Asquith in 1915. He went on to become Lloyd George's private secretary, and almost his manservant, for the next thirty years. His diaries, which are more than a million words long, constitute a detailed day-to-day record of Lloyd George's life, mainly during his premiership. Sylvester is a reliable amanuensis but his diary nevertheless tends to get bogged down in trivialities. It was published in an abridged form as *Life with Lloyd George* (1975) and is deposited in the National Library of Wales, where it has never been fully deciphered because of the antiquated form of shorthand which he used. Sylvester lived to nearly the age of 100.

**Chaim Weizmann** (1874–1954) Originally from Poland, Weizmann was a chemist, who came to Manchester in the early 1900s. During the First World War he developed a process of producing acetone from chestnuts, which formed a key ingredient in the explosives so badly needed by the British Army. Lloyd George, as Minister of Munitions, invited Weizmann to meet him in London. Both he and Churchill were actively sympathetic to the Zionist cause and so when Weizmann requested their support, his plea fell on fertile ground. He was perhaps the most charismatic and brilliant of the Zionist leaders, who single-handedly enlisted the support of Balfour, Lloyd George, Churchill and other key British politicians for the Jewish homeland and thus for the state of Israel.

**Field Marshal Sir Henry Wilson** (1860–1922) Probably the most brilliant and insightful of the British Army generals, Wilson had been in charge of military intelligence before the First World War and drew up many of the battle plans and manoeuvres that were put into practice by the British Expeditionary Force in 1914. He was an inveterate gossip and diarist who gave many of the political leaders nicknames, such as 'Titwillow' and others that were less complimentary. As CIGS (Chief of the Imperial General Staff) Wilson was one of the few generals trusted by Lloyd George. He did not, however, return the trust and, like many of the First World War generals, indulged in political intrigue. He was cut down by IRA gunmen on the steps of his house in Belgravia in 1922, perhaps because, being an Ulsterman, he had taken an uncompromising stand on the reprisals against Irish Republican atrocities during the previous year's civil war.

# Chronology
## relating to Lloyd George's and Churchill's Lives

| | |
|---|---|
| 1863 | *17 January* David Lloyd George (LG) born in Manchester |
| 1864 | LG's father dies; the family moves to Llanystumdwy to live with Uncle Richard (Lloyd) |
| 1874 | *30 November* Winston Spencer Churchill (WSC) born at Blenheim Palace |
| 1878 | LG starts work in a solicitor's office, aged fifteen |
| 1884 | LG qualifies as a solicitor |
| 1886 | LG makes first speech |
| | Lord Randolph Churchill resigns as Chancellor of the Exchequer |
| 1887 | WSC goes to Harrow School, aged thirteen |
| 1888 | LG marries Margaret Owen |
| 1890 | LG elected as Liberal MP for Caernarvon Boroughs |
| 1895 | Lord Randolph Churchill dies; WSC joins the 4th Hussars |
| 1896 | WSC goes to India |
| 1897 | WSC take part in the Malakand Field Force expedition to Afghanistan |
| 1898 | WSC works as a journalist attached to the 21st Lancers during the Battle of Omdurman in the Sudan |
| 1899 | *October* The Boer War breaks out. LG becomes the most outspoken opponent; WSC goes to South Africa as a correspondent for the *Morning Post* |
| 1900 | WSC is captured, escapes, and becomes famous 'from London to Ladysmith via Pretoria' |
| | *October* WSC is elected Conservative MP for Oldham, Lancashire |
| 1901 | *January* Queen Victoria dies |

*18 February* Winston's maiden speech, and first meeting with Lloyd George, in House of Commons

*December* LG is almost lynched in Birmingham

1902 Arthur Balfour becomes Conservative Prime Minister

1903 The Colonial Secretary, Joseph Chamberlain, announces his Protectionist policy. Churchill moves towards the Liberals

1904 *31 May* Churchill crosses the floor to join the Liberals. Runs as Liberal candidate for North-West Manchester

1905 *December* Balfour resigns as Prime Minister. Campbell-Bannerman forms a Liberal administration with LG as President of the Board of Trade and WSC as Under-Secretary of State for the Colonies (under Lord Elgin)

1906 *January* Landslide victory for the Liberals (Liberals 397 seats, Unionists 157, Irish Nationalists 82, Labour 51)

1907 *June* Colonial Prime Ministers meet in London. WSC goes on a four month tour of British colonies in Africa

*November* LG's eldest daughter Mair dies, aged seventeen

1908 *April* Campbell-Bannerman resigns and Asquith takes over as Prime Minister. LG appointed Chancellor of the Exchequer; WSC succeeds him as President of the Board of Trade

WSC loses by-election in North-West Manchester but is adopted as a Liberal candidate for Dundee

*September* WSC marries Clementine Hozier

1909 *April* LG presents the 'People's Budget'. Churchill becomes president of the Budget League

*November* House of Lords rejects the People's Budget

1910 *January* Liberals win the general election by a narrow margin (Liberals 275, Unionists 273, Irish Nationalists 82, Labour 41)

*February* WSC moves to the Home Office

*April* King Edward VII dies. George V succeeds him as King

*May–Dec* 'Truce' between the Liberal and Conservative parties

*December* Liberals again narrowly win general election (Liberals 272, Unionists 271, Irish Nationalists 84, Labour 42)

1911 *January* The Sidney Street siege

*July* Agadir crisis. LG speaks at the Mansion House

*October* WSC appointed First Lord of the Admiralty

1912–13    *April* Home Rule Bill passed in House of Commons
Marconi scandal

1914    *January* 'Dreadnought' spending argument resolved

*3 August* WSC persuades LG to agree to declaration of war.
First World War begins

*September* LG's speech at the Queen's Hall in London

Failed attempt to defend Antwerp by WSC's Naval Division

1915    *March* LG becomes Minister of Munitions

*April* Gallipoli campaign.

*May* WSC forced to resign from the Admiralty. Coalition
Government formed under Asquith

*November* WSC goes to fight in France

1916    *April* Easter uprising in Dublin

WSC returns from the Front

*June* Kitchener drowned en route to Russia. Lloyd George
succeeds him as Secretary of State for War

*July* Battle of the Somme

*December* LG becomes Prime Minister; Arthur Henderson of
the Labour Party joins the Coalition Cabinet but WSC is still
excluded

1917    *April* The United States declares war on Germany

*May* General Nivelle's offensive fails

*July* WSC joins LG's Cabinet as Minister of Munitions

*September* Battles of Ypres and Passchendaele

*November* Publication of Balfour Declaration

Bolsheviks take power in Russia

1918    *March/April* Massive German offensive on the Western Front

*July* Tsar Nicholas and his family murdered by the
Bolsheviks

*September/October* Haig's successful advance against German
lines

*11 November* Armistice and surrender of German and
Austrian armies

*December* LG's Coalition (of Conservatives and Liberals)

elected by a large majority in Coupon Election. Liberal Party divided into Lloyd Georgian and Asquithian factions. WSC becomes Minister of War

1919     *January–June* Paris Peace Conference; Versailles Treaty signed

1921     *February* WSC appointed Secretary of State for the Colonies Cairo Conference. WSC carves out two kingdoms – Iraq and Jordan. Supports Jewish settlement in Palestine
*June* Death of WSC's mother, Lady Randolph
*August* Death of WSC's three-year-old daughter Marigold
*December* LG, WSC and Birkenhead play a major role in concluding the Anglo-Irish Peace Treaty

1922     *22 October* Chanak crisis. A meeting of Tories at the Carlton Club votes to dissolve the Coalition. LG resigns as PM, never to regain power
*November* Bonar Law becomes Prime Minister. WSC loses his seat in Dundee at general election

1923     LG embarks on three-month tour of the US and Canada
WSC spends six months in South of France writing *The World Crisis* and painting

1924     *January* Labour forms its first Government under Ramsay MacDonald
*November* Conservatives return to power with massive majority. The PM, Baldwin, appoints WSC Chancellor of the Exchequer

1925     *April* WSC restores the gold standard in the UK

1926     *May* General Strike

1929     Publication of *We Can Conquer Unemployment* by Maynard Keynes (Liberal party pamphlet, sponsored by LG)
*May* Ramsay MacDonald forms second Labour Government, pushing WSC out of office for the next ten years

1931     Economic crisis
*August* MacDonald resigns; National Government is formed, led by Baldwin and Chamberlain. WSC disagrees with Conservative leaders over the issue of independence for India

*September* Britain forced off the gold standard

*October* National Government remains in power, with largest election landslide in history

1933    *January* Hitler appointed Chancellor of Germany

WSC begins to warn Government of the urgent need for rearmament

1936    *January* LG and WSC on holiday together in Morocco

*March* Germany reoccupies the Rhineland

*June* Spanish Civil War begins; Mussolini invades Abyssinia

*September* LG attacks National Government on appeasement policy but accepts an invitation to visit Hitler

*December* LG and WSC take King Edward VIII's side in the Abdication crisis

1937    *May* Chamberlain succeeds Baldwin as PM; WSC is still excluded from new National Government

1938    *January* LG and WSC on holiday in Cannes (LG's Golden Wedding party)

*September* Chamberlain returns with Munich agreement

1939    *3 September* Second World War begins. 'Winston is back' at the Admiralty

1940    *April* Narvik expedition fails

*7–8 May* LG intervenes in Commons debate to secure Chamberlain's resignation

*10 May* WSC forms a coalition government

*13 May* WSC's first appearance in House of Commons as Prime Minister

*26 May–2 June* Over 300,000 British and French soldiers evacuated from Dunkirk

*29 May* WSC invites LG to join the War Cabinet but he refuses

*10 July–31 October* Battle of Britain

*November* Chamberlain dies. Roosevelt re-elected President for unprecedented third term

*December* LG turns down the post of British Ambassador in USA following the death of Lord Lothian. The eventual choice is Lord Halifax

1941        *January* Margaret Lloyd George dies
            *June* Hitler invades Russia
            *7 December* Japanese attack Pearl Harbor. US declares war on
            Germany
1942        *February* Fall of Singapore. Opposition to WSC strengthens,
            but he survives and the tide of war gradually turns
            *November–January 1943* Battle of Stalingrad
1943        *January* Casablanca Conference
            *May* Washington Conference
            Allies invade North Africa, then Sicily
            *December* Teheran Conference
            LG marries Frances Stevenson
1944        *6 June* D-Day
            *24 May* Last meeting of WSC and LG at the House of
            Commons
1945        *January* LG granted an earldom by WSC
            *28 March* Death of LG
            *29 March* WSC delivers tribute to LG in House of Commons
            *May* Victory in Europe
            *26 July* General election results in Labour landslide. WSC out
            of office
            *6 and 9 August* US drops atomic bombs on Hiroshima and
            Nagasaki, ending war in the Pacific
1951–5      WSC back in power. Gwilym LG joins his Cabinet as
            Minister for Food, then Home Secretary and Minister of
            Welsh affairs
1965        *24 January* Death of WSC

# Notes

## Chapter 1: 1863–1904

2     'Five years ago'. Herbert du Parcq, *Life of Lloyd George*, vol. 2, p. 67.

3     'I shall be speaking'. W. R. P. George, *Lloyd George: Backbencher*, p. 330.

4     'the Government have made'. Hansard, 18 February 1901, col. 397.

4     '. . . whatever the blunder'. Ibid., col. 399.

5     'It is difficult'. Hansard, 18 February 1901, col. 406.

5     'You might say'. WSC, *My Early Life*, p. 379.

6     'I do not believe'. Hansard, 18 February 1901, col. 407.

7     'I have often'. Ibid., col. 410.

7     'If . . . certain capitalists'. Ibid., col. 414.

8     'I cannot sit down'. Ibid., col. 415.

8     'After compliments'. Winston S. Churchill (hereafter WSC), *My Early Life*, p. 380.

11     'The day after we arrived'. Lucy Masterman, *C. F. G. Masterman*, p. 209.

12     'An early Easter'. Lord Beaverbrook, *Decline and Fall of Lloyd George*, pp. 48–9.

13     'Went to the Houses of Parliament'. LG, Diary, 12 November 1881, Lloyd George Papers, NLW.

14     'I would thrust'. *Lloyd George Family Letters*, ed. Kenneth O. Morgan.

18     'I am rather surprised'. R. S. Churchill, (hereafter RSC) *Winston S. Churchill*, vol. I, p. 196.

19    'All my dreams'. WSC, *My Early Life*, p. 76.

22    'Men of opposite parties'. Marvin Rintala, *Lloyd George and Churchill: How Friendship Changed Politics*, p. 6.

24    'I look more'. Magnus, *Kitchener*, p. 177.

24    'I hope the Conservative Party'. WSC to J. Moore Bayley, 19 December 1901, RSC, *Winston S. Churchill*, companion vol. II, part I, p. 103.

24    'Personally I think'. Ibid., p. 104.

26    'Never was the wealth'. Hansard, 28 May 1903, col. 194.

26    'You have to go back'. John Grigg, *Lloyd George: The People's Champion*, pp. 69–70.

27    'LG spoke to me'. RSC, *Winston S. Churchill*, companion vol. II, part 1, p. 284.

27    'I am an English Liberal'. Ibid., p. 243.

28    'Churchill soon fell under'. Grigg, *People's Champion*, p. 64.

28    'clutching at power'. Hansard, 29 March 1904, col. 1022.

28    'Mr Winston Churchill said'. Ibid.

29    'He entered the Chamber'. RSC, *Winston S. Churchill*, vol. II, p. 80.

29    'Naturally such a man'. WSC, *Thoughts and Adventures*, p. 60.

## Chapter 2: 1904–11

34    'The plain fact'. Frances Stevenson, Introduction to Malcolm Thomson, *David Lloyd George: The Official Biography*, p. 17.

35    'As for the junior member'. Hansard, 24 July 1905, col. 150.

37    'a quiet but certain revolution'. Grigg, *People's Champion*, p. 97.

39    'Fancy living in these streets'. RSC, *Winston S. Churchill*, vol. II, p. 113.

39    'the closest'. Violet Bonham Carter, *Winston Churchill As I Knew Him*, pp. 160–1.

39    'You've been talking'. Ibid., p. 163.

40    'By getting on the right side'. Grigg, *People's Champion*, p. 106.

40    'When the blow fell'. LG to WLG, 1913, Morgan (ed.), *Lloyd George Family Letters*.

43 'LG said he always remembered'. A. J. Sylvester, *Life with Lloyd George*, pp. 254–5.

43 'No one can have'. WSC, *Thoughts and Adventures*, pp. 58–9.

44 'new and untrodden field'. WSC, *Liberalism and the Social Problem*, p. 208.

45 'The new Liberalism'. Bentley Brinkerhoff Gilbert, *David Lloyd George: A Political Life: Architect of Change, 1863–1912*, pp. 355–6.

46 'Oh, that's detail'. *Masterman*, p. 154.

46 'Lloyd George has taken all the plums'. RSC, *Winston S. Churchill*, vol. 2, p. 296.

46 'seem to me to bear'. WSC on functions of Board of Trade, 1908, RSC, *Winston S. Churchill*, companion vol. II, part 3.

47 'Can nothing be done'. WSC to DLG, Churchill Papers (Churchill College, Cambridge).

48 'Winston is full'. *Masterman*, p. 296.

48 'I would give my life'. Wilfred Scawen Blunt, *My Diaries 1888–1914*, 27 September 1909, p. 690.

48 '[Lloyd George] . . . saw England'. C. P. Snow, *Variety of Men*, p. 101.

49 'Your luck'. DLG to WSC, September 1908, Churchill Papers (Churchill College).

49 'It will always'. WSC to DLG, 29 August 1908, Lloyd George Papers, HL.

51 'Tomorrow is the day of wrath'. 27 April 1909, RSC, *Winston S. Churchill*, companion vol. II, part 2, p. 887.

51 'to wage implacable warfare'. Du Parcq, *Lloyd George*, vol. IV, p. 677.

51 'There is plenty of wealth'. Karl de Schweinitz, *England's Road to Social Security* (NY: A. S. Barnes, 1975), p. 201.

51 'the end of all'. Grigg, *People's Champion*, p. 200.

53 'We shall send them up', *Masterman*, p. 114.

54 'upon the plain and simple issue'. RSC, *Winston S. Churchill*, companion vol. II, part 2, p. 900.

55 'It is rather hard'. Grigg, *People's Champion*, pp. 206–7.

55 'Have you been down'. Ibid.

56    'Who made ten thousand people'. Grigg, *People's Champion*, p. 225.

56    'The more I think about it'. WSC, *Liberalism and the Social Problem* (1909).

57    'I want things done'. Robert Boothby, *Recollections of a Rebel*, p. 151.

58    'Oh these dukes'. Grigg, *People's Champion*, p. 206.

58    'Winston . . . began'. Scawen Blunt, *My Diaries*, 2 October 1909, p. 689.

61    'did not think that Asquith'. Scawen Blunt, *My Diaries*, 13 February 1910, p. 703.

62    'My opinion on the Irish question'. WSC to H. H. Asquith, April 1908, Churchill Papers (Churchill College).

63    'I shall unswervingly oppose'. RSC, *Winston S. Churchill*, vol. 1, p. 337.

63    'I am not going to be *hen-pecked*'. (to Manchester constituents after joining Liberal Party 1906.) RSC and Gilbert, *Winston S. Churchill*, companion vol.

64    'We must observe courtesy'. RSC and Gilbert, *Winston S. Churchill*, companion vol.

64    'I might as well'. Scawen Blunt, *My Diaries*, 5 September 1909, p. 685.

65    'As we sat down'. *Masterman*, p. 170.

66    'Like her mother'. Ibid., p. 144.

67    'if they cut Diana's throat'. Morgan, *Churchill*, p. 317.

69    'Winston and Charlie'. *Masterman*, pp. 165–6.

70    'that woman'. Ted Morgan, *Churchill*, p. 187.

70    'It gives an entirely unfair'. WSC on Conciliation Bill, 1910, Hansard.

71    'He was very much disturbed'. *Masterman*, p. 211.

72    'The Liberal Party'. Grigg, *People's Champion*, p. 298.

## Chapter 3: 1910–14

75    'They are extremely funny'. *Masterman*, p. 152.

75    'L. George: Hello Lawrence'. RSC, *Winston S. Churchill*, companion vol. II, part 2, p. 1028.

77  'like chasing a quinine pill', 'a game whose aim', *Walton Health Golf Club Book*, 2003.

78  'I am delighted to find'. LG to WSC, 25 September 1910, RSC, *Winston S. Churchill*, companion vol. II, part 2, p. 1023.

79  'We enjoyed our visit'. Ibid., 6 October 1910, pp. 1024–5.

80  'What the hell'. *Masterman*, p. 184.

81  'On the morning of July 21'. WSC, *The World Crisis 1911–18*, pp. 44–5.

81  'I said that of course'. Ibid., p. 45.

82  '. . . if a situation'. Ibid.

82  'That's my speech'. WSC, *World Crisis 1911–18*, p. 45.

82  'For many years'. Snow, *Variety of Men*, p. 101.

82  'I have just received'. WSC, *World Crisis 1911–18*, p. 46.

83  'Although Keynes rightly described'. Boothby, *Recollections of a Rebel*, pp. 54–5.

83  'They sound so very cautious'. WSC, *World Crisis 1911–18*, p. 46.

84  'The German army'. RSC, *Winston S. Churchill*, vol. II, pp. 526–8.

86  'Will you come out'. Bonham Carter, *Churchill As I Knew Him*, pp. 236–7.

87  'The fading light'. WSC, *The World Crisis 1911–1914*, p. 68–9.

87  'You must tell no one'. Lord Riddell, *More Pages from My Diary*, p. 25.

89  'You have become a water creature'. Frances Stevenson, *Lloyd George: A Diary*.

90  'How perfect!'. Bonham Carter, *Churchill As I Knew Him*, p. 262.

90  'Those Greeks and Romans'. Ibid.

91  'Bankruptcy stares me in the face', 'Your only chance'. Lloyd George Papers, HL.

93  'it was probably that at this time'. RSC, *Winston S. Churchill*, vol. 2, p. 554.

94  'some of them were too stupid'. Ibid.

95  'Father was in'. Richard Lloyd George, *Lloyd George*, p. 180.

96  'It is clear'. Scawen Blunt, *My Diaries*, 11 October 1912, pp. 814–15.

97    'I have made a bargain'. Riddell Diaries, British Library, unpublished mss.

99    'I consider that you are going back'. WSC to LG, Lloyd George Papers, HL.

99    'I agreed to the figure'. LG to WSC, Lloyd George Papers, HL.

99    'No. You said'. WSC to LG, Lloyd George Papers, HL.

99    'Even though Churchill'. Riddell Diaries, British Library, unpublished mss.

100    'Yes, I know'. RSC, *Winston S. Churchill*, vol. II, p. 640.

101    'I have striven hard'. LG to WSC, RSC, *Winston S. Churchill*, companion vol. II, part 3, 17 January 1914, p. 1856.

102    'Only a line'. Ibid., 27 January 1914, p. 1855.

102    'The applause of the House'. David Cannadine, *In Churchill's Shadow* p. 101.

102    'in a rather maudlin mood'. HHA to Venetia Stanley, HHA, *Letters to Venetia Stanley*.

103    'For the next seven years'. WSC during Agadir Crisis, 1911, Morgan, *Churchill*.

104    'At one stroke of the wand'. Hansard, 30 April, 1912, col. 1721.


## Chapter 4: 1914–16

105    'the sky has never been'. Rintala, *Lloyd George and Churchill*, p. 111.

106    'The parishes of Fermanagh'. WSC, *World Crisis 1911–18*, p. 110.

107    'money was a frightened'. Frank Owen, *Tempestuous Journey*, p. 263.

107    'I am filled with horror', LG to MLG, 3 August 1914, *Lloyd George Family Letters 1885–1936*, ed. Kenneth O. Morgan, p. 167.

108    'a bloody peace'. HHA, *Letters to Venetia Stanley*, p. 129.

108    'geared-up and happy'. Mary Soames (ed.), *Speaking for Themselves*, 28 July 1914, p. 96.

108  Cabinet notes, 1–3 August 1914, Lloyd George Papers, HL.

110  'A major change'. Rintala, p. 117.

111  'The lamps are going out'. Edward Grey, *Twenty-Five Years*, vol. II, chapter 18.

111  'Upon this grave assembly'. Stevenson, *Lloyd George: A Diary*, p. 38.

112  'I know a valley'. Owen, *Tempestuous Journey*, pp. 275–6.

113  'Please look at this'. WSC to LG, Gilbert, *Winston S. Churchill* companion vol. III, part 1, 10 September 1914, p. 107.

114  'These military men'. WSC to CC, 30 May 1909, Soames (ed.), *Speaking for Themselves*, p. 23.

115  'nothing excuses'. Colin Clifford, *The Asquiths*, p. 238.

116  'Winston's trouble was personal ambition'. LG of WSC, Stevenson, *Lloyd George: A Diary*

116  'LG was often mistrustful'. Frances Stevenson, Introduction to Thomson, *Lloyd George*, pp. 16–17.

116  'I have not had a minute'. WSC to LG, 22 October 1914, Gilbert, *Winston S. Churchill*, companion vol. III, part 1, p. 213.

116  '[LG] . . . says'. Stevenson, *Lloyd George: A Diary*, 5 November 1914, pp. 10–11.

117  'one of those revolving lighthouses'. Magnus, *Kitchener*, p. 285.

117  'Winston told a wonderful story'. Robert Rhodes James, *Victor Cazalet*, diary, 3 November 1927, pp. 10–11.

118  'I feel deeply grateful'. LG to WSC, 28 October 1914, Gilbert, *Winston S. Churchill*, companion vol. III, part 1, p. 224.

118  'Certainly not his judgement', 'Winston: My God!' Margot Asquith, diary, 30 November 1914, 10 January 1915, Clifford, *The Asquiths*.

120  'I shall be the biggest man in Europe'. WSC to LG, January 1915, Stevenson, *Lloyd George: A Diary*.

120  'The Dardanelles campaign'. Stevenson, *Lloyd George: A Diary*, 8 April 1915, p. 41.

121  'It was *I* who'. WSC to LG, Gilbert, *Winston S. Churchill*, companion vol. III, part 1, p. 770, 5 April 1915.

122  'LG said that Winston'. *The Riddell Diaries*, p. 162.

122 'LG told me last night'. Stevenson, *Lloyd George: A Diary*, 19 May 1915, p. 52.

122 'At the end of last week'. Ibid., 24 May 1915, pp. 52–3.

124 'I lost all my practice'. Grigg, *Lloyd George: From Peace to War*, pp. 44–5.

124 'Churchill was thus, on the Tuesday night'. Beaverbrook, *Politicians and the War*, p. 118.

126 'Take Kitchener's maximum'. Owen, *Tempestuous Journey*, p. 295.

128 'I wonder whether'. Hansard, 20 December 1915, col. 121.

128 'We are out'. Owen, *Tempestuous Journey*, p. 320.

129 'There is neither clock'. Ibid., p. 327.

130 'I am so sorry'. LG to WSC, 16 November 1915, Gilbert, *Winston S. Churchill*, companion vol. III, part 2, p. 1271.

131 'Lloyd George and McKenna'. WSC to CC, 27 November 1915, ibid., p. 1290.

131 'I shall be glad'. WSC to LG, 27 December 1915, ibid., p. 1345.

131 'He expressed great distress'. CC to WSC, 29 December 1915, Soames (ed.), *Speaking for Themselves*, p. 141.

132 'The PM has not treated you'. CC to WSC, 30 December 1915, ibid., pp. 141–2.

132 'Lloyd George is no doubt'. WSC to CC, 2 January 1916, ibid., p. 145.

132 'It is developing'. CC to WSC, 27 January 1916, ibid., p. 163.

132 'I highly approve'. WSC to CC, 31 January 1916, ibid., p. 165.

133 'The group I want to work with'. WSC to CC, ?1 February 1916, ibid., p. 166.

133 'It seems to me'. WSC to LG, 10 April 1916, Lloyd George Family Papers, NLW.

134 'I know your feelings'. Lord Derby to WSC, 19 August 1916, Gilbert, *Winston S. Churchill*, companion vol. III, part 2, p. 1545.

135 'I got a letter from Olwen'. Dick Lloyd George to parents, MS in author's possession.

## Chapter 5: 1916–18

139    'Churchill's pugnacity'. Beaverbrook, *Politicians and the War*, pp. 234–5.

140    'a natural Lloyd Georgian'. Ibid., p. 489.

140    'The new Government'. Owen, *Tempestuous Journey*, pp. 345–6.

140    'Smith, this man knows'. WSC to F. E. Smith, ibid.

141    'Mrs A. . . . mentioned Megan'. Stevenson, *Lloyd George: A Diary*, p. 231.

142    'You could hardly imagine'. WSC, *Great Contemporaries*, p. 212.

143    'Don't let us make any mistakes'. Hansard, 7 December 1916, in Grigg, *Lloyd George* vol. IV.

143    'We accepted', Hansard, 19 December 1916, col. 1334.

144    'Winston made me a little speech'. *The Riddell Diaries*, p. 179.

144    'I am still a member'. WSC to Lord Riddell, Riddell Diaries, British Library, unpublished mss.

145    'I am sorry Asquith is not still PM'. Max Egremont, *Balfour*, p. 281.

145    'Father needed the Tory support'. Richard Lloyd George, *Lloyd George*, pp. 180–1.

147    'I am grieved'. WSC to Beaverbrook, 30 November 1926, Gilbert, *Winston S. Churchill*, companion vol. V, part 1, p. 890.

148    'Meanwhile D. is seriously contemplating'. Stevenson, *Lloyd George: A Diary*, 19 May 1917, p. 158.

149    'Some of them felt stronger', Richard Lloyd George, *Lloyd George*, p. 182.

149    'As the news swept through Parliament'. Ibid., p. 184.

149    'I have got back Winston'. Alan Clark (ed.), *'A Good Innings': The Private Papers of Viscount Lee of Fareham* (John Murray, 1974), p. 170.

150    'One of the most remarkable'. David Lloyd George, *War Memoirs*, vol. III, pp. 1067–72.

156    'It may be a blessing'. Mary Soames, *Clementine Churchill*, p. 386.

156    'Winston's brilliant Autobiography'. Egremont, *Balfour*, p. 321.

# Chapter 6: 1917–21

158    'On the night of the Armistice'. WSC, *World Crisis: The Aftermath*, pp. 20–1.

159    'I should deeply and sincerely'. LG to WSC, Gilbert, *Winston S. Churchill* companion vol. IV, part 1, 8 November 1918, p. 410.

159    '. . . am I unreasonable'. WSC to LG, 9 November 1918, ibid., p. 411.

159    'LG can *walk around Winston*'. Margot Asquith, diary, Countess of Oxford and Asquith Papers, Clifford, *The Asquiths*.

162    'It was a very warm-hearted'. WSC to LG, 4 May 1918, Gilbert, *Winston S. Churchill*, companion vol. IV, part 1, p. 310.

164    'I breakfast lunch & dine'. WSC to CC, 24 January 1919, ibid., p. 480.

165    'Russia had fallen'. WSC, *World Crisis: The Aftermath*, pp. 71, 75.

166    'I have worked with you now'. Owen, *Tempestuous Journey*, p. 521.

166    'The trouble with Winston'. Snow, *Variety of Men*, pp. 97–8.

167    'Since the Armistice'. Gilbert, *Winston S. Churchill*, companion vol. IV, part 2, pp. 1053–5.

168    'The most formidable and irrepressible protagonist'. David Lloyd George, *The Truth about the Peace Treaties*, vol. 1, pp. 324–5.

170    'If Winston, who is obsessed'. LG to Austen Chamberlain, 22 March 1922, Gilbert, *Winston S. Churchill* companion vol. IV, part 3, p. 1818.

170    '[Winston] got out his maps'. Snow, *Variety of Men*, p. 98.

170    'Winston, who has been fuming'. Stevenson, *Lloyd George: A Diary*, pp. 197–8.

172    'If you are going to include'. Stevenson, *Lloyd George: A Diary*, pp. 196–7.

174    'Winston in his most bellicose'. H. H. Asquith, diary.

175    'I require no honour'. Segev, *One Palestine, Complete*.

175    'Then comes the news'. LG to William Lloyd George, March 1917, William George, *My Brother and I* (London: Eyre & Spottiswoode, 1958), p. 258.

177    'The country for which I have worked'. Tom Segev, *One Palestine, Complete*, p. 240.

178    'Dr Weizmann, it's a boy!' Segev, *One Palestine*, p. 241.

178    'For Balfour, diplomatic opportunism'. Egremont, *Balfour*, p. 296.

179    'We made an equal pledge'. Lloyd George, *The Truth about the Peace Treaties*, vol. 4, p. 1193.

180    '. . . Palestine is complicated'. Ibid., pp. 1190–1.

181    'Winston still very vexed'. Stevenson, *Lloyd George: A Diary*, 26 April 1921, p. 210.

## Chapter 7: 1921–9

183    'I hope you may see your way'. Owen, *Tempestuous Journey*, p. 312.

186    'They only thought me worth £25'. Owen, *Tempestuous Journey*, p. 584.

186    'Tell Winston'. WSC, *World Crisis: The Aftermath*, p. 348.

186    'his own death-warrant'. Ibid., p. 588.

189    'the Goat'. H. Montgomery Hyde, *Baldwin: The Unexpected Prime Minister* (London: Hart-Davis, MacGibbon, 1973), p. 96.

190    'In the political confusion'. Rintala, *Lloyd George and Churchill*, p. 75.

190    'Winston has taken to gambling'. Rhodes James, *Victor Cazalet*, diary, 5 January 1923, p. 86.

191    'We are in for a big fight'. Rintala, *Lloyd George and Churchill*, p. 76.

192    'I have had a long talk'. LG to Balfour, 3 April 1924, Gilbert, *Winston S. Churchill*, companion vol. V, part 1, pp. 139–40.

193    'I had a long and very satisfactory talk'. WSC to CC, 19 August 1924, ibid., p. 178.

193 'I visited LG at Churt'. WSC to Lords Balfour and Carson, 1 September 1924, ibid., p. 190.

194 'so astonished by the offer'. Gilbert, *Winston S. Churchill.*

194 'Warm congratulations'. telegram from LG to WSC, 7 November 1924, Gilbert, *Winston S. Churchill*, companion vol. V, part 1, p. 238.

194 'When Churchill joined'. Boothby, *Recollections of a Rebel*, pp. 51–2.

195 'You cannot trust the battle'. LG at Albert Hall, 20 January 1925, Owen, *Tempestuous Journey.*

195 'Winston came to dine'. Beaverbrook to Lord Rothermere, 12 February, 1925, Gilbert, *Winston S. Churchill*, companion vol. V, part 1, p. 389.

196 'LG has returned'. WSC to CC, 25 March 1925, Soames (ed.), *Speaking for Themselves*, p. 293.

196 'tragically isolated'. WSC to CC, 5 February 1926, Gilbert, *Winston S. Churchill*, companion vol. V, part 1, p. 644.

199 'precipitate, unwarrantable and mischievous'. Owen, *Tempestuous Journey*, p. 705.

199 '[Asquith] is of course rather sad'. CC to WSC, 7 February 1927, Gilbert, *Winston S. Churchill*, companion vol. V, part 1, p. 935.

200 'Mr Lloyd George who used to be so sure of himself'. WSC to E. L. Spears, 27 May 1927, ibid., p. 1002.

200 'over two and a half hours of extraordinarily brilliant entertainment', Cannadine, *Churchill's Shadow*, p. 101.

200 'We are on opposite sides'. WSC, *Savrola*, p. 124.

201 'I particularly like your fairness'. Gilbert, *Winston S. Churchill*, companion volume V, part 1, pp. 1446–7.


## Chapter 8: 1929–38

202 'Churchill has no intention'. Beaverbrook to Sir Robert Borden, 26 March 1929, Gilbert, *Winston S. Churchill*, companion vol. V, part 1, p. 1451.

203 'was confronted with the ghost', Owen, *Tempestuous Journey*, p. 715.

204 'Your coming would crown', Ibid., p. 716.

204 'At this moment'. Ibid., pp. 718–19.

207 'Well, Gandhi may be a saint'. Frances Lloyd George, *The Years That Are Past*, p. 227.

208 'he had momentarily forgotten'. Sylvester, *Life with Lloyd George*, p. 65.

210 'Well, as a matter of fact'. Snow, *Variety of Men*, p. 93.

211 'There is no doubt'. Sylvester, *Life with Lloyd George*, pp. 139–40.

213 'You won't be satisfied'. H. Montgomery Hyde, *Baldwin*, p. 496.

214 'I believe the abdication'. Cannadine, *Churchill's Shadow*, p. 64.

214 'When Britain abandoned'. Frances Lloyd George, *The Years That Are Past*, pp. 255–6.

216 'Churchill was preoccupied'. Boothby, *Recollections of a Rebel*.

217 'You must not do'. Harold Nicolson, *Diaries and Letters, 1930–39*, 3 April 1939, p. 394.

# Chapter 9: 1939–45

219 'Lloyd George had none of Churchill's passion'. Snow, *Variety of Men*, p. 107.

219 'Winston was passionately fond'. Sylvester, *Life with Lloyd George*, p. 233.

220 'Look at his head'. Ibid., p. 235.

220 'sending a curate'. Ibid., p. 235.

222 'enormous increase', 'solely due to the fact', 'he was pressing', Gilbert, *Winston S. Churchill*, companion vol. VI: *1939–41*, p. 142.

222 'I can speak'. Ibid., 27 January 1940, p. 142.

223 'There is a theory'. Nicolson, *Diaries and Letters, 1939–45*, 1 May 1940, p. 75.

224 'You are probably right'. Boothby, *Recollections of a Rebel*, pp. 147–8.

224 'In the name of God'. Amery to Chamberlain, Hansard, 7 May 1940, col. 1150.

224 'But I say this'. Hansard, 8 May 1940, col. 1266.

224 'The Father of the House'. Rintala, *Lloyd George and Churchill*, p. 131.

224 'I feel that I ought'. Hansard, 8 May 1940, cols. 1277, 1279.

225 'Is there anyone'. Hansard, 8 May 1940, col. 1282.

225 'I do not think'. Ibid.

225 'I take complete responsibility'. Ibid., col. 1283.

225 'The Right Hon. Gentleman must not allow himself'. Ibid., col. 1283.

226 'He said, "I have got my friends".' Ibid.

227 'The political careers'. Rintala, *Lloyd George and Churchill*, pp. 72–3.

228 'I felt . . . that all my past'. WSC, *The Second World War*, vol. 1, pp. 526–7.

228 'Perhaps I may be permitted'. Hansard, 13 May 1940, cols. 1510–11.

229 'went to congratulate him'. Richard Lloyd George, *Lloyd George*, p. 240.

230 'Every one of us'. WSC in Cabinet, end May 1940, Lukacs, *Five Days in London*.

230 'We shall fight'. Hansard, 4 June 1940, col. 796.

230 'It took Armageddon'. Boothby, *Recollections of a Rebel*.

232 'Lloyd George would'. Gilbert, *Winston S. Churchill*, vol. VI, p. 474.

232 'He had lost his nerve.' Richard Lloyd George, *Lloyd George*, pp. 238–9.

232 'Winston lacks judgement'. Snow, *Variety of Men*, p. 124.

233 'LG's iron will'. Frances Lloyd George, *The Years That Are Past*, pp. 264–5.

234 'Lloyd George, whose affection'. *Chips: Diaries of Sir Henry Channon*, 24 July 1940, p. 262.

234 'He would like to try'. John Colville, *The Fringes of*

*Power: Downing Street Diaries 1939–1955*, 12 December 1940, p. 264.

235    'Rightly or wrongly'. Telegram to WSC, 15 December 1940, Colville, *Footprints in Time*.

235    'Might not a day come'. Owen, *Tempestuous Journey*, p. 751.

236    'good and great', WSC on MLG, January 1941.

236    'The Prime Minister must have a real War Council'. Hansard, 10 May 1941.

237    'Both men', Richard Lloyd George, *Lloyd George*, p. 178.

239    'The English people'. Colville, *Fringes of Power*, 22 December 1944.

239    'D. and I discussed today'. Stevenson, *Lloyd George: A Diary*, 27 May 1944, p. 328.

239    'Old Pethick-Lawrence'. Nicolson, *Diaries and Letters 1939–45*, 2 September 1943, p. 322.

240    'We respected each other'. LG on WSC in old age, family anecdote told to author.

240    'D. decided on Wednesday'. Stevenson, *Lloyd George: A Diary*, p. 328.

251    'LG: What beautiful scenery'. A. J. Sylvester, unpublished manuscript, National Library of Wales.

252    'We are all worms'. Bonham Carter, *Churchill As I Knew Him*, p. 16.

258    'The first time you meet Winston'. Edward Marsh, *A Number of People*.

261    'I believe that your people'. A. J. Sylvester, unpublished manuscript, National Library of Wales.

262    'a magnetism which made my heart leap'. Frances Lloyd George, *The Years That Are Past*, p. 42.

# Bibliography

H. H. Asquith, *Letters to Venetia Stanley*, ed. Michael and Eleanor Brock (Oxford: Oxford University Press, 1982)

Margot Asquith, *The Autobiography of Margot Asquith*, 2 vols. (London: Thornton Butterworth, 1920)

C. R. Attlee, *As It Happened* (London: Heinemann, 1954)

Lord Beaverbrook, *Decline and Fall of Lloyd George – and great was the fall thereof* (London: Collins, 1963)

*Politicians and the War 1914–16* (London: Oldbourne Book Co., 1960)

Geoffrey Best, *Churchill: A Study in Greatness* (London: Hambledon, 2001)

Frederick, Earl of Birkenhead, *Churchill 1874–1922* (London: Harrap, 1989)

Robert Blake, *The Unknown Prime Minister: The Life and Times of Andrew Bonar Law 1858–1923* (London: Eyre & Spottiswode, 1955)

Wilfred Scawen Blunt, *My Diaries: Being a Personal Narrative of Events, 1888–1914*, 2 vols. (London, Martin Secker, 1919, 1932)

Violet Bonham Carter, *Winston Churchill As I Knew Him* (1965; repr. London: Weidenfeld & Nicolson, 1995)

Robert Boothby, *Recollections of a Rebel* (London: Hutchinson, 1978)

David Cannadine, *In Churchill's Shadow* (London: Allen Lane, The Penguin Press)

Sir Henry Channon, *Chips: The Diaries of Sir Henry Channon* (London: Phoenix, 1996)

Randolph S. Churchill and Martin Gilbert, *Winston S. Churchill*, 8 vols. and 13 companion vols. (London: Heinemann, 1966–88)

Winston S. Churchill:

*The Story of the Malakand Field Force: An Episode in Frontier War* (1898; repr. London: Leo Cooper, 1989)

*Savrola: A Tale of the Revolution in Laurania* (London: Longman's Green, 1900)

*Lord Randolph Churchill*, 2 vols. (London: Macmillan, 1906)

*Liberalism and the Social Problem* (London: Hodder & Stoughton, 1909)

*The World Crisis* 6 vols. (London: Thornton Butterworth, 1923–31)

*Marlborough: His Life and Times*, 4 vols. (London: Harrap, 1947)

*My Early Life* (London: Thornton Butterworth, 1930)

*Thoughts and Adventures* (London: Thornton Butterworth, 1932)

*Great Contemporaries* (London: Thornton Butterworth, 1937)

*The War Speeches: Into Battle*, 7 vols. (London: Cassell, 1941–6)

*The Second World War*, 6 vols. (London: Cassell & Co., 1948–54)

*Painting as a Pastime* (London: Odhams Press, 1949)

*A History of the English Speaking Peoples*, 4 vols. (London, Cassell, 1956–8)

Colin Clifford, *The Asquiths* (London: John Murray, 2002)

John Colville, *Footprints in Time* (London: Collins, 1976)

*The Fringes of Power: Downing Street Diaries, 1939–55* (London: Weidenfeld & Nicolson, 2004)

Virginia Cowles, *Winston Churchill: the Era and the Man* (London: Hamish Hamilton, 1953)

George Dangerfield, *The Strange Death of Liberal England 1910–1914* (New York: Harrison Smith and Robert Haas, 1935)

Robin Denniston, *Churchill's Secret War: Diplomatic Decrypts, the Foreign Office and Turkey 1942–44* (London: Chancellor Press, 2000)

Frances Donaldson, *The Marconi Scandal* (London: Hart-Davis, 1962)

Charles Eade, *Churchill, By his Contemporaries* (London, Hutchinson, 1953)

Max Egremont, *Balfour: A Life of Arthur James Balfour* (London: Collins, 1980)

John Ehrman, *Lloyd George and Churchill as War Ministers – An Extract from the Transactions of the Royal Historical Society* (London: Octavo, 1961)

David Fromkin, *A Peace to End all Peace: The Fall of the Ottoman Empire and the Creation of the Modern Middle East* (London: André Deutsch, 1989)

W. R. P. George, *The Making of Lloyd George* (London: Faber, 1976)
*Lloyd George: Backbencher* (Ceredigion: Gomer, 1983)

Bentley Brinkerhoff Gilbert, *David Lloyd George: A Political Life*: vol. I: *The Architect of Change 1863–1912*; vol. II: *The Organizer of Victory 1912–1916* (London: Batsford, 1992)

Martin Gilbert, *Churchill, A Photographic Portrait* (London: Heinemann, 1974)
*In Search of Churchill* (London: HarperCollins, 1994)

David Gilmour, *Curzon* (London: John Murray, 1994)

John Grigg, *Lloyd George*:
*The Young Lloyd George 1863–1902* (London: Eyre Methuen, 1973)
*The People's Champion 1902–1911* (London: Eyre Methuen, 1978)
*From Peace to War 1912–16* (London: Methuen, 1985)
*War Leader 1916–18* (London: Penguin, 2002)

Roy Jenkins, *Asquith: A Portrait of a Man and an Era* (London: Collins, 1964)
*Churchill: A Biography* (London: Macmillan, 2001)

J. Graham Jones, 'Major Gwilym Lloyd George', *National Library of Wales Journal*, vol. 32, no. 2 (2001)

Thomas Jones, *Lloyd George* (Cambridge, MA: Harvard University Press, 1951)

John Keegan, *Churchill: A Life* (London, Weidenfeld & Nicolson, 2002)

T. E. Lawrence, *The Letters of T. E. Lawrence* (London: Jonathan Cape, 1938)

Anita Leslie, *The Fabulous Leonard Jerome* (London: Hutchinson, 1958)

Shane Leslie, *The Film of Memory* (London: Michael Joseph, 1938)

David Lloyd George, *War Memoirs of David Lloyd George*, 6 vols. (London: Ivor Nicholson & Watson, 1933–6)
*The Truth About the Peace Treaties*, 2 vols. (London: Victor Gollancz, 1938)

Owen Lloyd George, *A Tale of Two Grandfathers* (London: Bellew, 1999)

Richard Lloyd George, *Lloyd George* (London: Muller, 1960)
*Dame Margaret* (London: Allen & Unwin, 1947)

John Lukacs, *Five Days in London: May 1940* (New Haven, CT: Yale University Press, 2001)

*Churchill: Visionary, Statesman, Historian* (New Haven, CT: Yale University Press, 2002)

Philip Magnus, *Kitchener: Portrait of an Imperialist* (London: John Murray, 1958)

William Manchester, *The Last Lion: Winston Spencer Churchill* vol. I: *Visions of Glory: 1874–1932*; vol. II: *Alone: 1932–40* (New York: Dell Publishing, 1989, 1994)

Sir Edward Marsh, *A Number of People* (London: Heinemann, 1939)

Lucy Masterman, *C. F. G. Masterman* (London: Nicholson & Watson, 1939)

Jon Meacham, *Franklin and Winston: An Intimate Portrait of an Epic Friendship* (New York: Random House, 2003)

Peter de Mendelssohn, *The Age of Churchill: Heritage and Adventure 1874–1911* (London: Thames & Hudson, 1961)

Anthony Montague Brown, *Long Sunset: Memoirs of Winston Churchill's Last Private Secretary* (London: Cassell, 1995)

Alan Moorehead, *Gallipoli* (London: Hamish Hamilton, 1956)

Lord Moran, *Winston Churchill: The Struggle for Survival 1940–1965* (London: Sphere, 1968)

Kenneth O. Morgan, *Lloyd George: Family Letters 1885–1936* (Cardiff: University of Wales Press, London: OUP, 1973)

*Lloyd George* (Cardiff: University of Wales Press, 1981)

'J. Herbert Lewis', *Flintshire Historical Society*, vol. 36 (2003)

Ted Morgan, *Churchill: Young Man in a Hurry, 1874–1915* (New York: Simon & Schuster, 1982)

Jan Morris, *Fisher's Face: Or, Getting to Know the Admiral* (London: Random House, 1995)

Harold Nicolson, *Diaries and Letters 1930–38; 1939–45.* (London: Collins, 1966–8)

Frank Owen, *Tempestuous Journey: Lloyd George, His Life and Times* (London: Hutchinson, 1954)

Henry Pelling, *Winston Churchill*, 2 vols. (Norwalk, CT: Easton Press, 1991)

Robert Rhodes James, *Victor Cazalet* (London: Hamish Hamilton, 1976)

E. Royston Pike, *Human Documents of the Lloyd George Era* (London: Allen & Unwin, 1972)

Lord Riddell, *Intimate Diary of the Peace Conference and After, 1918–1923* (London: Victor Gollancz, 1933)
  *More Pages from My Diary 1908–14* (London, Country Life, 1934)
  *The Riddell Diaries*, ed. J. M. McEwen (London: Athlone Press, 1986)
Marvin Rintala, *Lloyd George and Churchill: How Friendship Changed Politics* (London: Madison Books, 1995)
Norman Rose, *Churchill: An Unruly Life* (London: Simon & Schuster, 1995)
Stephen Roskill (ed.), *Hankey: Man of Secrets*, 3 vols. (London: Collins, 1970–4)
Tom Segev, *One Palestine, Complete: Jews and Arabs under the British Mandate* (London: Little, Brown, 2000)
Geoffrey Shakespeare, *Let Candles Be Brought In* (London: Macdonald, 1949)
C. P. Snow, *Variety of Men* (London: Macmillan, 1967)
Mary Soames, *Clementine Churchill* (London: Cassell, 1979)
Mary Soames (ed.), *Speaking for Themselves: The Personal Letters of Winston and Clementine Churchill* (London: Black Swan, 1999)
Frances Stevenson, *The Years That Are Past* (London: Hutchinson, 1967)
  *Lloyd George: A Diary* (London: Hutchinson, 1971)
A. J. Sylvester, *Life with Lloyd George: The Diary of A. J. Sylvester 1931–45*, ed. Colin Cross, (London: Macmillan, 1975)
Malcolm Thomson, *David Lloyd George: The Official Biography* (London: Hutchinson, 1950)


*Unpublished Sources*

H. H. Asquith Papers (Bodleian Library, Oxford)
Cabinet Papers (Public Record Office, Kew)
Churchill Papers (Churchill College, Cambridge)
Lloyd George Papers (House of Lords Record Office) (National Library of Wales Archive)
Lothian Papers (Scottish National Archives, Edinburgh)
Countess of Oxford & Asquith Papers (Bodleian Library, Oxford)
Riddell Diaries (British Library)
Sir Henry Wilson Diaries (Imperial War Museum)

# Index

DLG = David Lloyd George; WSC = Winston Spencer Churchill